KINGS OF THE MOUNTAINS

Kings of the MOUNTAINS

HOW COLOMBIA'S CYCLING HEROES CHANGED THEIR NATION'S HISTORY

MATT RENDELL

AURUM PRESS

First published in Great Britain
2002 by Aurum Press Ltd
25 Bedford Avenue, London WC1B 3AT

Copyright © 2002 Matt Rendell

Text design by Roger Hammond
Maps by Reg Piggott

All rights reserved. No part of this book may be reproduced or utilized in any form or by any means, electronic or mechanical, including photocopying, recording or by any information storage and retrieval system, without permission in writing from Aurum Press Ltd.

A catalogue record for this book is available from the British Library.

Photo credits: 1–14, 16, 18, 20, 22, courtesy of El Colombiano; 15, 17, 19, 23–24 by Matt Rendell; 21, courtesy of Presse Sport.

ISBN 1 85410 837 9

10 9 8 7 6 5 4 3 2 1
2006 2005 2004 2003 2002

Printed in Great Britain by MPG Books Ltd, Bodmin

FIFE COUNCIL CENTRAL AREA LIBRARIES	
292166	
Cypher	06.07.02
796.62FEN	£16.99
KY	SPORT

To Gary

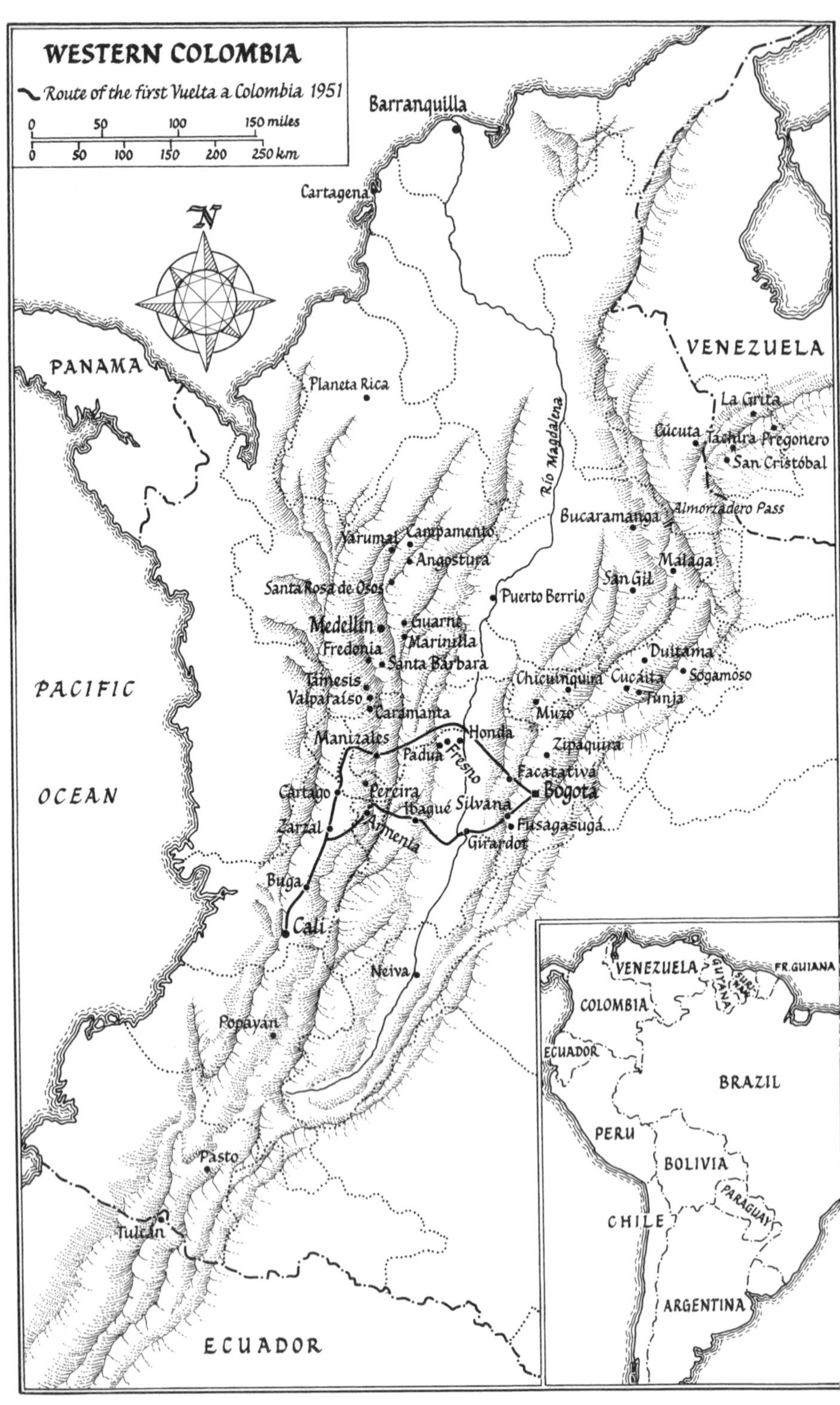

WESTERN COLOMBIA
Route of the first Vuelta a Colombia 1951
0
50
100
150 miles
0
50
100
150
200
250 km
N
PANAMA
PACIFIC
OCEAN
ECUADOR
VENEZUELA
Barranquilla
Cartagena
Planeta Rica
Río Magdalena
Yarumal
Campamento
Angostura
Santa Rosa de Osos
Puerto Berrio
Medellín
Guarne
Marinilla
Fredonia
Santa Bárbara
Támesis
Valparaíso
Caramanta
Manizales
Honda
Padua
Fresno
Cartago
Pereira
Ibagué
Silvana
Facatativá
Bogotá
Zarzal
Armenia
Girardot
Fusagasugá
Buga
Cali
Neiva
Popayán
Pasto
Tulcán
La Grita
Cúcuta
Táchira
Pregonero
San Cristóbal
Almorzadero Pass
Bucaramanga
Málaga
San Gil
Duitama
Sogamoso
Chiquinquirá
Cucaita
Tunja
Muzo
Zipaquirá
VENEZUELA
GUYANA
SURINAM
FR. GUIANA
COLOMBIA
ECUADOR
BRAZIL
PERU
BOLIVIA
PARAGUAY
CHILE
ARGENTINA

CONTENTS

1 The indomitable Zipa 1

2 A Colombian trinity 25

3 Olympus's faded hierarchy 34

4 On giants' shoulders 53

5 The independent republics 76

6 Pelé on a bike 97

7 The challenge of altitude 112

8 All the president's men 137

9 Snow White and the Renault fours 151

10 Café de Colombia 175

11 The sense of an ending 187

12 Blindspots 204

13 Unnecessary interference 218

14 Cathedrals in the sky 238

Acknowledgements 245

Longing on a large scale is what makes history. This is just a kid with a local yearning but he is part of an assembling crowd, anonymous thousands off the buses and trains, people in narrow columns tramping over the swing bridge above the river, and even if they are not a migration or a revolution, some vast shaking of the soul, they bring with them the body heat of a great city . . . going to a game.

Don DeLillo, *Underworld*

Je suis allé très loin dans la douleur.

Miguel Induráin, *Vélo* magazine

. . . Wir, Vergeuder der Schmerzen.
Wie wir sie absehn voraus, in die traurige Dauer,
ob sie nicht enden vielleicht. Sie aber sind ja
unser winterwähriges Laub, unser dunkeles Sinngrün,
eine der Zeiten des heimlichen Jahres–, nicht nur
Zeit–, sind Stelle, Siedelung, Lager, Boden, Wohnort.

(. . . How we squander our hours of pain.
How we gaze beyond them into the bitter duration
to see if they have an end. Though they are really
our winter-enduring foliage, our dark evergreen,
one season in our inner year–, not only a season
in time–, but are place and settlement, foundation and soil and home.)

Rainer Maria Rilke, 'The Tenth Elegy', *Duino Elegies*
(edited and translated by Stephen Mitchell)

1. The indomitable Zipa

A GROUP OF CYCLISTS, two abreast, glides past above the asphalt. From time to time laughter counterpoints their rhythm, measuring the miles. Imperceptibly, over hours, they withdraw into speed and silence, breathing the altitude like ghosts. The early sun above the Colombian department of Boyacá shines through the dust and smoke of the limekilns and glistens proud on club colours and racing bikes. Behind, the team manager's car shields his riders against the traffic. At some moment a squeaky counter-rhythm emerges from the mix, revealing a presence. A hat, poncho and felt galoshes appear among the close-fitting outfits: a peasant boy has stolen in on them. Roped onto the basket of his pig-iron butcher's bike, a milk churn.

The smirking riders increase the pace. Minutes pass, stretched out by speed. The boy remains. The sniggers have receded into lungs filling and emptying now to a level of discomfort. Presently the coach, irritated by the interloper's audacity, loses patience: 'Oi! You. Sod off.' The adolescent ignores him. There's a pause filled with concentration. Then: 'Go on. Take your bedstead and bugger off.'

This time, the boy answers. 'Eat shit! If you so fucking good, drop me.' He accelerates with such force that the team is strung out in breathless slipstream. The road turns skyward. Unrelenting, he begins to inch away, heartbeat by heartbeat, up to a brow. There, finally, the weight of his cargo of milk pulls him down into the valley on the other side.

RAPHAEL ACEVEDO STOLE three goats from his father to pay for his first bike sometime in the early 1970s. It was livestock well invested. Ten years after those juvenile milk deliveries, he joined the wave of Colombian riders that swept over Europe in the early 1980s.

Older now, all firmness and girth – you think this might be the athlete's dissolute uncle – Raphael opens photo albums on the dining room table. Two decades on, their instamatic colour is failing: one day soon, these will be so many off-white laminates. In one he wears a shirt decorated with big, red discs: the polka-dot jersey awarded to the best climber in the Tour de France, or its amateur equivalent, the Tour de l'Avenir (which translates as the Tour of, or for, the Future).

Like the points competition in the great three-week Tours – the Tour de France, the Tour of Spain and the Tour of Italy – victory in this mountains competition means a three-week fight to accumulate points. The contenders for the overall jersey can relax (the term is relative) for the first, normally flat week, enjoying the protection of team-mates and finishing with the group. As the mountain stages begin, they dose their energies for the stage finish. Unlike them, those competing for the points and mountains prizes must fight their way to the head of the race for each intermediate sprint or mountains prize, and make considerable exertions sprinting for the line each time. This may be two, three or more times during a single stage. It is a hard competition for hard men with absolute self-belief. Raphael Acevedo is one, and so are many of his countrymen.

In one photo Raphael stands beside Greg Lemond, twice World Champion and three times Tour de France winner. In another he leads five times Tour de France champion Bernard Hinault up a steep slope in the French Alps.

On their first expeditions to Europe, Raphael and the rest competed as amateurs. They took their first Tour de l'Avenir by storm, defeating the all-powerful Soviets. Unleashing frantic revolts against gravity and the prevailing logic of international bike-racing wherever the gradient steepened, Colombians monopolized the mountains prizes. Their *disinvoltura* soon attracted invitations from prestigious professional events.

Still amateurs, Colombians competed in the 1984 Dauphiné Libéré, a pre-Tour de France stage race through the northern Alps. It was their first opportunity, and ended in Colombian victory; Hinault and Lemond, indisputably the world's finest riders, filled only the minor podium places. Weeks later Luis Herrera, a slender god, rose towards Alpe d'Huez and won the most mythical stage of the Tour de France. His countrymen felt fated: a Colombian would surely win the Tour, cycling's greatest prize, before the decade was out. Herrera's tiny, extruded glass limbs had carried Colombia to the threshold.

Colombia's cyclists had been hungering for international recognition since the founding of their own national tour in 1951. Just two years later some did compete in Europe, travelling by sea to the Route de France, the old amateur version of the Tour. As rustic to the Europeans as Raphael Acevedo's adolescence had seemed to those club riders, most had been disqualified by the end of day one. By day four it was over. None could keep up with Europeans twice their size. None had ever ridden over such flat terrain.

They never made it to the mountains.

The 1980s, then, were a coming of age. In 1987 Lucho Herrera won the Spanish national tour; in 1988 Fabio Parra stood on the Tour de France podium. Their compatriots had won every major mountain competition. And then the bubble burst.

THREE CLASSES OF parasite have bled Colombia into economic anaemia: international capitalists, home-grown men of violence, and a corrupt political class. Today it presents the standard juxtapositions of the developing nation – mules co-existing with superbikes, horse-drawn carts competing with Landcruisers. The bicycle remains an essential work tool.

For ten years Colombia's finest athletes – footballers Valderrama, Asprilla and Ángel; cyclists Álvaro Mejía, Oliverio Rincón and Hernán Buenahora; the boxer Mauricio Pastrana – have performed in foreign lands for foreign paymasters, losing contact with younger athletes at home and their bond with a national audience. Yet throughout the 1950s, 1960s and 1970s, whatever the sportsmen thought, their achievements abroad were a secondary concern to the general Colombian public, whose attentions were consumed by a national obsession. Do what I did: ask any Bogotá taxi driver old enough to remember. 'Bogotá had a million inhabitants,' he'll tell you. 'And every one of them took to the streets to watch the Vuelta a Colombia, the Tour of Colombia. The pavements were like this!' He'll look over his shoulder at you waving clenched fingers, and his yellow cab will veer across the road to a chorus of klaxons. It's a story you hear with minor variations in Medellín, Ibagué, Cali and every other conurbation.

For the countryside speak to any agricultural daughter: 'We walked across the fields as far as those mountains to wave handkerchiefs as the riders passed.' Those mountains might be ten kilometres away or more.

Women as often as men, the aged and darting bands of kids, shopkeepers emerging at the door, columns of people with their chatter and concerns, merging into a common curiosity, the history of an enthusiasm. The ambitions and frustrations of a nation's demography, big questions and ones you only see side on, momentarily refracted in a rush of men trying to win a bike race.

And when the Vuelta's two-week test of courage was over and the competitors flew home, they were met with a hero's welcome by crowds of 10,000 or more, even those who had won nothing and never come close. Popular collections provided them with bikes, funds, parcels of land, homes to live in.

Cycling was, and remains, the national sport. Nothing Colombian can be alien to it. Today, of course, we tend to despise our ancestors. But we are dwarfs by comparison, and, as another saying goes, if we see further than they, it is only because we stand on the shoulders of giants.

I DISCOVERED CYCLING when I was eight. My mother counted out bank notes one by one into the three-fingered hand of a retired engineer in a leather overall. I couldn't take my eyes off the stump of his missing finger, and returned home bent like a question mark over the dented steel triangle that was my first bicycle. For the rest of my childhood my trousers were frayed and my knees skinned.

Perhaps I was already thinking of escape – from the battleground of British family life in the 1970s, from the boredom of life watching the traffic pass along a busy main road, from childhood itself. Perhaps that was what I was doing when I decided to read languages. One weekend when I was studying at a school for interpreters and translators in Trieste, Italy, a friend invited me to spend a weekend at his home. We travelled up into the Dolomites to watch the Tour of Italy pass. After weathering a blizzard for three hours, we watched as a huddled group of cyclists swept up the steepest part of the climb at a phenomenal speed. It wasn't just their athleticism, it was also their bloody-mindedness and their foreignness I identified with – their haunted look and driven discomfort.

Years later, sick of feuds and office politics, my academic career ended when I resigned from my post as a lecturer in Italian at a London university. I'd studied in Italy, France and Spain. Now I needed to distance myself from the past, somewhere away from here, but where I could still speak the language. After years working with my brain, I wanted to do something physical. A friend volunteered to cycle South America with me. To prepare for the journey we rented a North London flat together and rose in the small hours to ride deserted streets. Before the city awoke, Andean stillness reigned on Muswell Hill and East Heath Road.

We flew to the Tierra del Fuego and pedalled north. The length of the Andes I collected talking heads on video. An old people's home in a new economic area. Bolivians performing manual labour in the southernmost town on Earth. Patagonian sheep shearers and the Welsh pioneers of Trevelyn. Pinpoints in the Patagonian vastness, we melted into the landscape. In Santiago de Chile I spoke to Pablo Neruda's maid Rosita. In the Bolivian rainforest, Brazil nut workers. On the Peruvian Amazon, patients in a defunct leper colony who recalled an Argentine doctor who had treated them and then, many years later, resurfaced as Che Guevara. The brown river carried me, alone now, to Colombia and abandoned me in a town called Leticia, Latin for happiness. There, in Colombia's only outpost on the Amazon, I paid too much for an airless room and caught a flight to Bogotá in the morning.

Colombia is the only developing nation to have made an impression on the European heartland of international cycling. Yet there seemed to be no books on Colombian cycling in any language; the

European cycling press didn't cover Colombia, and the guide books – Footprint, Lonely Planet – although full of cultural and historical notes, didn't even mention the sport. We landed in Bogotá and I walked out into its thin air. Then, without knowing what I was looking for or why, but sensing somewhere speed and silence and athletes floating through the altitude, I began another journey.

IT STARTED WITH 'The Indomitable Zipa'. He never stood on a Tour de France podium or won world or Olympic titles, yet most Colombians, if tested, can recall the indomitable Zipa's real name, even at a distance of half a century.

Ephraim Forero Triviño's sobriquet was as hard-earned as his race titles. Before the conquistadors, his hometown of Zipaquirá, 48 kilometres north of Bogotá on a plateau half-way to the heavens, had been a Chibcha Indian settlement. Each Chibcha chieftain was a 'Zipa' – a warrior with a formidable reputation. But the Zipa's promised land was inspired less by God, or the gods, than by the French. He had a vision of clattering up to the mountains' shoulder and carrying right on until he'd strung a net over the nation. Rattled joints and lungs burning with the air's poverty. The irreducible steel taste of cranks and pinions. Splintered wooden rims in fingertips.

He also had an international pedigree. At the 1950 Panamerican Games in Guatemala the Indomitable Zipa had set a championship record for the 4000 metres and won gold with Colombia's pursuit team. When work commitments permitted – meaning permission from the soft drinks factory that employed him – he travelled to Bogotá to compete in regional events. Unbeatable at any distance, he held titles in the 1000-metre match sprint and the kilometre time trial.

The Zipa now resides in Bogotá, in a western suburb near El Dorado International Airport, squatting beneath the flight-paths. In his seventies, he is as vigorous as most men in their twenties. His sight runs ahead of him like a whippet, as quick as it must have done half a century ago. He talks easily and with absolute conviction. Fuelled by rich black coffee, he fixes you in the eye and gestures with parallel hands. 'When I began to cycle in 1949, I tried to read everything I could. Naturally I read about the Tour de France, and the mythology attached to the Alps and Pyrenees. I thought to myself, "With a landscape like ours, a Colombian national tour would be something extraordinary."'

His doubters declared it an impossible dream. Even if the roads had been anything but calamitous, the topography and extreme altitude would have been enough to make any such venture a physical impossibility. Common sense said so, and so did history. For instance, at the start of the century the first cyclist to attempt the route north from Bogotá along the Tunja highway, one Alberto Piedrahita Cordovez, bound for the capital of the department of Boyacá, had collapsed and expired as a result of his efforts. Shortly afterwards a German cyclist had set off from Bogotá. Dismounting in Tunja's central square, he too dropped dead on the spot.

The Tunja highway never drops below 2,440 metres along the easternmost of the three Andean knife-edges that diverge northwards across Colombia from their meeting point on the Ecuadorean border. In 1929, before the first Colombian cycling race for which complete records exist headed out of Bogotá along the Tunja highway, understandable objections had been voiced.

In a letter to the race director before the event, one of the twenty-five entrants, the national road-racing champion of Panama, J. Arturo Castillo, expressed concerns of a cardiological nature:

> As a means of measuring the cyclist's stamina I consider the route excessive, given the state of the road and the not unsubstantial climbs at an average altitude of nine thousand two hundred feet above sea level.
>
> The heart cannot operate efficiently in a cyclist who, at such altitudes,

> must also make the required efforts to complete (for example) the continuous five-mile ascent northwards from Boyacá Bridge.

But in spite of Panamanian scepticism, the race went ahead, and over the outward 130 kilometres of unmade road, an Italian named Carlo Pastore looked certain to win stage one. Before, that is, Pastore disappeared.

As the other competitors fought against the elements, the stewards organized a search. Presently Pastore's bike was found behind a hedge. Then the man himself: the Italian had exchanged his race leadership for a position he clearly preferred beneath a willing peasant girl. Although horizontal, he hadn't stopped pedalling.

And despite his extra exertions, Pastore rejoined the race and the following day managed to finish eighth overall. Colombia's cycling history was fathered by an Italian.

It's written history, at least. Three decades before, at 6.15 a.m. on 15 August 1899, the Cycling Circle of Bucaramanga, the administrative capital of Santander department, 160 kilometres north of Tunja, an earlier event had been scheduled to depart. The Bucaramanga Cycling Circle's newsletter that month expressed grand hopes: 'True, Colombia has few roads suitable for bicycling. But isn't this practice, which has proved of great utility elsewhere, an appropriate means of bringing about the construction of good roads for all – cyclists and non-cyclists alike?' Whether the race took place, and who the winner was, are questions unanswered by extant documents.

At the midpoint of the twentieth century the Indomitable Zipa's ambitions were less utilitarian. Between the looking-glass sky and the rutted highways, he dreamed of refining Colombia's cruelty into something compelling. 'Pablo Camacho Montoya, a journalist on the national daily *El Tiempo*, embraced the idea. He promised to approach his newspaper for backing if I could prove it was physically possible.

He had an ally: the chairman of the Colombian Cycling Association, Enrique Santos Castillo, was also *El Tiempo*'s editor. I chose the hardest stage of the proposed route, and early one morning in October 1950 I set off from Bogotá.' At an altitude of 2,590 metres on the eastern of the three cordilleras, Bogotá's chill can be bitter, even at this latitude, four degrees north of the equator.

We drove along that route days after our interview. I braved the cold to meet the Zipa early and, forsaking the relief of altitude, we descended into the cauldron, westwards and downwards towards the town of Honda, just 230 metres above sea level in the valley of the Río Magdalena. Fifty years ago the Indomitable Zipa rode these same lines over surfaces made of mud. Reaching Honda, his head throbbing with the sun, his eyes burning with sweat, the humidity smothering his lungs, he had found a Ministry of Public Works truck. 'The secretary of the Cycling Association, an Englishman named Donald Raskin, and its treasurer, Mario Martínez, were in the cabin waiting for me. I passed them, and they pulled onto the road to follow.'

We rose again into realms where geology is not abstract science but an everyday concern. The Andes' central cordillera, breached only by a freezing 3,660-metre col known as Letras, stands between the Magdalena valley and the town of Manizales, the capital of the Caldas department. For every 180 metres gained in height above sea level, the air temperature drops by an average of one degree centigrade. From Honda to the paramo at Letras, an increase in altitude of 3,444 metres, the temperature loss is twenty degrees. Wind-chill can easily double that.

The Zipa wrapped the land about him and tunnelled through the thinning air: 'They tried to stay with me on a steep climb through thick mud. At the village of Padua the driver didn't want to go on. I continued over Letras, where the rain and cold chilled me to the bone, then coasted down into Manizales. There I showered off the mud.

Two and a half hours later they arrived. The driver, a local man, told his friends I'd ridden up by bike. They didn't believe him at first. Then they picked me up on their shoulders and paraded me through the town.'

Today the road is beautifully asphalted. But it's still so steep you doubt it's possible to cycle up, even spinning the silliest mountain bike gear. The Zipa drives fast, accelerating through the corners. 'Now we knew it could be done.'

MILLIONS OF YEARS ago the gods of plate tectonics and the demons of erosion carved Colombia's cols. The resulting landscape, a natural paradise for most of the species that occupied their work, was ill-suited to the designs of a nation. Humanity's twin projects of nationhood and industrialization are little served by grandiose mountainscapes.

And what nature left undivided, men were happy to tear asunder. In the sixteenth to eighteenth centuries, huge areas of what is now Colombia were left unsettled by the Spanish Colony. The Catholic Church, the conquest's spiritual arm, often failed to convert the indigenous population, whose languages were unknown to the Franciscans. Spain's economic interests dictated the privileged treatment of some areas – especially those along an axis running northwards from the capital, Bogotá, through the fluvial and maritime ports that connected it to the European metropolis – and the abandonment of others.

In the nineteenth century, after independence, this geographical logic became even more acute. In 1850 an Italian military engineer and mercenary named Agostino Codazzi, who had fought for Colombia's independence and then became its greatest cartographer, calculated that the sweltering lowlands known as *tierra caliente* covered 75 per cent of the national territory. Life in these low-lying regions was mostly autonomous of central government.

The 1886 Constitution referred to these isolated regions as the 'National Territories' and authorized Congress to dispose of them at its convenience. It was a way of acknowledging that the State had failed to establish a monopoly of power in three-quarters of the national space. The *tierra caliente* and its communities lay outside the Constitution's normal jurisdiction.

Nearly six decades later the Great Depression uprooted numberless families and accelerated the processes of population shift into the lawless Territories. Bogotá was compelled to confront the challenge of incorporating them into the nation. Alfonso López Pumarejo, President of the Republic in the 1930s and 1940s, referred to this ongoing process as 'the rediscovery of Colombia'. The first Vuelta a Colombia was, implicitly, part of it.

But also encoded in the Vuelta were wanderings that had connected Colombia's communities for decades or more, and continue to bring them into occasional collision.

For decades populations of seasonal agricultural workers have chased the coffee and coca harvests, and exquisitely-skilled artisans working in wood, leather and the bamboo-like guadua have constantly travelled to find paying clients.

Periodic natural disasters caused by the volcanic landscape send entire communities into mourning marches. Peasants displaced by economic crisis or paramilitary violence converge on the cities. Some, turning to violence, formed guerrilla columns marching through the mountains and forests of the collective unconscious, serviced with firewood and food by secret mule trains in the Colombian night.

Light aircraft fly low over the forest to margins where desperadoes prospect for precious metals and gemstones. Smugglers pursue secret odysseys over inaccessible passes. And settlers, reproducing old feuds in new territories, are surrounded, in fantasy or reality, by those who inhabited the forest before them: invisible nomads treading noiselessly through the trees.

In 1951 the Indomitable Zipa's Vuelta, 1,154 exhausting kilometres along paths of sand, mud and stone, subdivided into ten punishing stages, joined Colombia's quest for identity, echoing and condensing the spirit of these various journeys into and across an undiscovered Colombia.

But there were other reasons why an event like a Colombian national tour ought to have been impossible – the Colombian countryside was no place to ride a bike.

Between 1946 and 1953 civil conflict displaced entire communities and left perhaps hundreds of thousands dead. Demarcation lines and no-go zones fragmented the national space. At the root of the violence was a division between Liberals and Conservatives that had riven the country in two, for Colombia was sustained, then as now, by political patronage.

Every Colombian homestead depended on the favour of family patrons holding political office. In the capital the manicured party chiefs were scrupulously parliamentary. Implicit in all their doings was the perpetuation of their privilege. However, when administrations changed in Bogotá, political appointees throughout the nation – administrators, secretaries, drivers, gardeners, their favoured suppliers and trading partners – could suddenly find themselves and their families out of favour and hungry.

The finer ideological distinctions dividing Conservatives and Liberals were lost in the vastness of the landscape, but poverty, insecurity and the Colombian's characteristic sense of ambition drove ordinary people to fight, and fight viciously, for their party.

The party lines were complicated by a question that cut across them: what was to be the common man's role in steering the fate of the nation? When, in March 1947, a lawyer named Jorge Eliécer Gaitán seized the leadership of the Liberal party, threatening the interests of an oligarchy through whose veins, he cried, flowed the petroleum extracted by their American paymasters, the country was polarized.

A moving orator and skilled manipulator of crowds, Gaitán's rhetoric inflamed passions across the country. The landowners, the established business community, and the traditional conservative and liberal hierarchies with their *entente cordiale* could never have allowed a populist adventurer like Gaitán into power.

Nations always sacrifice their Christs and Caesars, their Gandhis, Martin Luther Kings and Evitas. Jorge Eliécer Gaitán was no exception. In February 1948 he led a march by torchlight through the streets of Bogotá. A hundred thousand protesters against the anti-Liberal violence joined him. Gaitán was rapidly becoming an intolerable threat to the ruling elite. At 1.05 p.m. on 9 April, as he stepped into the street an introverted Rosicrucian named Juan Roa Sierra fired three shots into Gaitán's face. The assassin was captured and interrogated at a chemist's near the scene of the murder. He refused to name his masters, but before more persuasive questioning could begin, a mob burst in, dragged the assassin into the street and tore him limb from limb.

The violence rippled outwards, heightening and amplifying tendencies already alive in the countryside. For seven years Colombia ripped itself to shreds. But it was a rebellion without a cause. The scores settled were purely local; the territories liberated, no more than disconnected fiefdoms. Colombia's identity split into kaleidoscopic fragments. Its shattered mirror no longer reflected a recognizable image. In November 1949 a state of emergency was declared. Representative democracy was suspended. Congress remained closed for two years, and over the following eight, none of the three regimes that ruled Colombia was ratified by elections.

The first was presided over by a Jesuit-educated fanatic who had used his newspaper, *El Siglo*, to side with the axis powers during the war. Conservative leader Laureano Gómez had sought the safety of Franco's Spain in the aftermath of Gaitán's assassination, when city-centre rioters had torched both his Bogotá residence and the premises of *El Siglo*. On his return to Colombia he seized the presidency, and in August 1950 Gómez instituted a civilian dictatorship to defeat the unholy conspiracy of masons, Jews, Liberals and Communists that haunted his fascistic nightmares.

Deliberately intensifying the conflict, Gómez characterized the liberal party and its mass following as a deadly, disfigured organism preparing Colombia's demise: 'The basilisk was a monster with the head of one beast, the face of another, the arms of a third and the feet of some deformed creature. The whole was so horrific, so terrifying that its mere sight was fatal. Our basilisk moves on feet of confusion and stupidity, legs of brutality and violence that drag along its immense oligarchic belly; its breast is of anger, its arms Masonic and its tiny withered head, Communist.'

Mass executions took place, fomented by the institutional, if unconstitutional, leadership. With shots of severed heads, photographers immortalized the savagery. Colombia's national identity collapsed into cruelty and confusion.

In November 1950, in bed now with McCarthyist America, Gómez dispatched the frigate *Admiral Padilla* to patrol the seas around Korea. As Colombian troops also prepared to embark for someone else's war, Colombia's sense of self was in turmoil. Against this backdrop of blood and discontinuity, the first national bicycle race was surely not just logistically improbable, but also absurdly irrelevant?

The adventurers who assembled in central Bogotá on the morning of 5 January 1951, some in football shorts, some plus-fours, one in an old leather flying cap, preparing to trace their invisible lines over the nation, brought no solution to the internecine savagery. But they were expressing – now more urgently than ever – a related question: are we a nation at all?

IT WAS THEREFORE strange that an event so necessarily and peculiarly Colombian could never have taken place without the aid of an Englishman.

The son of a London textiles merchant with a warehouse in the Colombian capital, Donald Raskin's elegant grey suits are as impeccable as his English, painstakingly pronounced in the accents of a pre-war newscaster. Born in 1920, Raskin came to Colombia, aged twelve, with his father, mother and sister. They returned to London in 1938, but in September 1939, on the eve of World War II, came back to Colombia indefinitely. 'I worked for a while at the British Embassy. I started at the bottom and finished at the bottom: if you're not engaged by the Foreign Office in London, you're considered a local employee and you don't progress at all. So I was five years in the embassy's commercial section. Then I started to work for a company called Cassabel, a Belgian company. I used to deal with all their English correspondence. We imported whiskies and brandies. Gins. Good business in Colombia. The situation here was quite good.

'I used to be an athlete. I ran the 110-metres hurdles. I was local champion in Bogotá. I formed the local athletic federation and then friends introduced me to people involved in cycling and I started assisting them. Cycling was very rudimentary at the time because such roads as there were, were in a terrible condition.'

I wanted to understand what had drawn this manicured, understated Englishman from the drawing rooms of the brandy trade to the dirt and brutality of cycling. But perhaps he had lost the power to probe his soul in the old language, which he insisted on using with a compatriot. Or perhaps what seemed so mysterious to me was so obvious to him that he had no way of understanding my question.

'I owned a bicycle but didn't compete: I was a director. There were half a dozen good riders initially: the best were coming from Antioquia, Valle and Bogotá. The cycling association already existed, but it wasn't very important. There were probably about one or two national races a year before the Vuelta. I became secretary. I earned a living as an importer of bicycle parts from Dayton Cycles in London. I used the Vuelta to consolidate my position at the cycling association. To finance it I decided to sell each of the ten stages to sponsors.'

But, as Raskin soon found, the sponsorship options were restricted to a few major industries: 'Avianca, the Colombian national airline, sponsored stages one and nine. The newspaper *El Tiempo* stages four and six. *El Tiempo* didn't give us a penny, only publicity. The Bavaria brewery, part of the same group as Avianca, also sponsored two stages, and agreed to fund a rider.'

However, the majority of riders represented small businesses: cafés, electrical stores, sports shops. Argemiro Sánchez, a bike shop owner from Cali, sponsored himself. Carlos Orejuela, from Bogotá, rode in the colours of Dayton Bikes, London, courtesy of Raskin.

The race route defined the playground of Colombian cycling for the following fifty years. Cycling largely takes place on the eastern and central chains of the Andes, with occasional excursions onto the western line. It followed Forero's trial route downwards from the eastern cordillera into the valley of the Río Magdalena, then up the eastern face of the Andes' central cordillera. 'If we may be permitted the comparison,' *El Tiempo* editorialized, 'the roads of France and Colombia are as different as a billiard table and a big dipper. Its difficulty and demands will make the Tour of Colombia singular, if not unique, among the great trials of world cycling.'

At last the Vuelta was ready to depart. *El Tiempo*'s Pablo Camacho Montoya started the race in central Bogotá. Press reports paint the crowds in superlatives – extraordinary enthusiasm, a throng, an immense human sea, an avalanche of spectators, a multitude.

And from the outset it was as bloody as a bullfight. On stage one alone Adonías Ortega, from the department of Nariño on the Ecuadorean border, broke his collarbone in a collision with a truck. Jorge Ramírez of Cartago in the department of Valle struck another and destroyed the frame of his bike. Ortega's team-mate Guillermo Jurado buckled his rear wheel and ran the final few kilometres to the finish with his bike on his shoulder. And Pedro Nel Gil, from the department of Antioquia, fell, breaking bones in one hand and dislocating his collarbone – yet fought back to finish the stage in third place. Then, on stage three, as the lowland heat dissipated and the mountain chill reached two degrees, Forero and Nel Gil duelled shoulder to shoulder on the steepest part of the climb. The Zipa reached the brow yards ahead of his rival and flung himself down the suicidal descent. And suicidal it nearly proved: at high speed on the saturated stones, Forero lost adhesion and was catapulted across the road, landing spread-eagled on the verge, his left knee cut open. As he lay there, his rivals coasted past.

Forero's main assistant, his mother, found him. She swung out of the auxiliary vehicle and threw him back into the saddle. Almost consumed by her displaced ambition, she urged him up to insane speeds, and soon he was gaining on his rivals. Ahead of him, Nel Gil's tribulation continued when, with the violence of the descent, his front wheel collapsed. Bloodied but with an undimmed sense of urgency, he replaced the wheel himself and carried on in pursuit of the Zipa, again finishing the stage third.

The quality of the roads didn't help either. For the first four blocks on stage three, the riders ran, bikes in hand, up a slope too steep to pedal. Sixteen kilometres up the mountainside the torrential rain unleashed a mudslide, forcing the athletes to scramble over the loose terrain, bikes on their shoulders. Bitumen surfaces are first mentioned in the race summary for stage five: 'at 209 kilometres the longest of all, from Cartago to Cali, some stretches of which are asphalted'. Yet it, too, was marred by a series of appalling accidents. A spectator emptied a bucket of water onto the rear wheel of Nel Gil's team-mate Roberto Cano, throwing him to the ground. After minutes spent unconscious, he was revived, placed back in the saddle, and sped off to finish the stage. A motorcyclist swerved into the Zipa, forcing him off his bike and onto his injured left knee. Then the hapless Nel Gil went down again. And on the penultimate stage Cano once more hit the deck, this time within sight of the finish line, spending another four minutes unconscious. When he came to, he remounted again, crossing the line fifteen minutes behind the stage winner.

Even where no blood was spilt, the quality of the bikes and components available to the competitors left much to be desired. The immaculately prepared Zipa punctured six times on the first stage alone. With just two stages left, Cano and the Zipa duelled magnificently at the head of the race on Colombia's most feared climb, a forbidding 3,230-metre pass known as La Línea. Finally, on the steepest section towards the summit, the Zipa detected weakness in his adversary. He crossed the brow first and plummeted down, quickly gaining a commanding lead – before he punctured yet again. With no remaining tubulars, he had no choice but to keep pedalling. The tyre was soon flat. Then it began to shred, tearing free from the rim. By the time he reached the line, after long looks over his shoulder, the rim was bare. Cano arrived barely three minutes later.

Yet despite – or perhaps because of – the horrific injuries and repeated equipment failures, the race was compelling. From shops and warehouses throughout Bogotá, loudspeakers broadcast radio commentaries into the street. 'There was radio coverage,' Raskin recalls, 'but not as it's done today. Because of the mountains, the radio journalists couldn't transmit. They had to arrive at the town and then telephone Bogotá to give information.'

The most popular commentator was Carlos Arturo Rueda. Originally from Costa Rica, he had worked in Venezuela before coming to Colombia. Rueda's word-paintings of each stage, improvised from copious notes taken at the roadside, are legendary. His arrival in each tour town was greeted by hysteria, and his eloquence, the most celebrated in Colombian history – even outshining Gaitán's – rooted cycling in the national consciousness. Yet I could find no transcripts or recordings of his commentaries, and no one could quote him, however briefly, or even describe his style. Rueda – the word means 'wheel' – has disappeared into nothingness, leaving only his name, and a vague, enchanted memory.

From the outset the Zipa proved indomitable. On day one, in the 35°C heat of Honda, it was he who arrived first at the stage finish. After five hours thirty-four minutes in the saddle, and out of it to wade across the Rioseco River close to the finish, he was acclaimed in scenes of 'indescribable enthusiasm' by 'crowds that had congregated the length of Honda'. He had, continued *El Tiempo*, 'a heart the size of a cathedral', adorned now in the race leader's white jersey with red, white and blue bands. Twenty-two and a half minutes after the Zipa, the second-placed rider crossed the line. Others were still arriving an hour and a half later, after the newspaper journalists had filed their copy. The media, and the public at the roadside, were in ecstasies.

The Zipa consolidated his lead by winning the following day's 41-kilometre climb up to Fresno, on the lower slopes of the climb to Letras. After the stage, a journalist noted, 'We watched him attentively all day, and swear that the demands of the race have left no signs of effort in his face.'

And so they arrived at Manizales for the first rest day. The Zipa's overall lead after three stages was an hour and sixteen minutes.

Benefactors infected by the general enthusiasm sent new bicycles, spare parts, even support vehicles for the duration of the race. Impromptu collections arrived from all over the country. Then the race route descended westwards from the central cordillera into the valley of the Río Cauca, for two long, hot, flat days. Roberto Cano arrived first at Cartago, with the Zipa thirty-three seconds behind him.

Leaving Cali the next day, the Zipa had once more been unseated when a car drove into him, fortunately without lasting consequences. Indeed, returning north and gaining height in the central cordillera on the way to the town of Sevilla, he was irresistible. He won the stage by nearly six minutes from Cano, with Gil in third place. Shadowing the mountains, stage seven continued northwards to the town of Armenia, where the Zipa triumphed yet again. With two stages left, Forero's overall race lead had stretched to two hours, one minute and five seconds over Cano, with Gil third at nearly two and a half hours. The Zipa's lead seemed unassailable.

But the following day mechanical problems dogged him once more. The penultimate stage of the Vuelta descended again, dropping from Ibagué into the heat of the Magdalena valley and the town of Girardot. Twenty minutes after the stage start, Forero was at the roadside, squinting through the dust thrown up by the passing vehicles as he re-linked his broken chain. Six minutes later the chain parted again. And a third time, an hour and fifty minutes later. The mechanics provided by the race organization were inexpert. After each pause to repair his own machine, the Zipa chased down the pack alone, to finish the stage in second place.

During the rest day that followed the penultimate stage, Girardot witnessed scenes of collective celebration which, residents said, were unprecedented in the town's history. Once again spare parts and gifts reached the riders. The Zipa rebuilt his three bicycles. When a fourth arrived, donated by a wealthy well-wisher, Forero presented one of his machines to a team-mate, saying, 'It's used to winning, so stay with it tomorrow.'

Then the final day.

From Girardot the riders began the long climb out of the Magdalena valley. Early punctures left the Zipa behind the field. But as the race entered the eastern cordillera and began the long approach to Bogotá, he raced through the peloton and joined Orejuela, the Dayton Bikes rider, at the head. Sucking energy out of the air as the altitude increased, Forero disappeared into the mountains. Alone he passed the crowds that lined the roads into the capital. The roar of hundreds of thousands urged him on after five hours on the road. He crossed the finish line eight minutes ahead of Roberto Cano. Nel Gil arrived four minutes later. The city was in raptures.

Shortly after this first Vuelta had finished, the national cycling association issued a press release. Though many private businesses and individuals had donated prizes during the Vuelta, Colombia's cyclists, it emphasized, were amateurs: there could be no cash prizes. 'The Association will arrange for such monies to be collected. They will be used to buy spare parts and accessories, and the remaining sums will buy trophies which will be awarded to the different winners.'

'The riders were generally from poor families,' Raskin remembers today. 'Their main object in life was to escape poverty – to overcome their own limits by winning prizes to support their families. It was a means of surviving. By winning the Tour of Colombia or one of the stages, they could gain access to patronage and find employment. But it was an indirect route.'

Like most settler countries, Colombia is a land where every town and community commemorates its founding fathers. In January 1951 Ephraim Forero Triviño, the Indomitable Zipa, entered his nation's mythology. His hometown of Zipaquirá declared 20 January a day of celebration, and the town took to the streets to greet its champion. Like the Chibcha people who had settled there centuries before, attracted by its salt mines, the Zipa had excavated crystals of pain from the thin air to become Colombia's first great cyclist.

Lesser riders were also greeted by massive festivals, irrespective of their positions in the General Classification. José Alfaro, fifth overall, was welcomed like a hero in his hometown of Facatativá, south of Bogotá. In Bucaramanga, Alonso Navas, sixteenth overall, nearly ten hours adrift of Forero, was accompanied from the airport by a procession led by twenty motorcyclists in Indian file, 300 cyclists and numerous cars fêting the champion with their horns. Such scenes were repeated wherever riders were returning home. At the midpoint of the twentieth century Forero had tapped a nation's resources of hope. Through cycling, perhaps, Colombia might achieve some unexplained absolution.

YET AFTER FIFTY years it remains an exotic location for occasional excursions, never a heartland of international cycling. Over time, some of cycling's greatest names did visit Colombia: Fausto Coppi and Hugo Koblet in the 1950s, at the end of their careers. In the 1970s, Felice Gimondi. Hinault, Fignon and Lemond, the greats of the 1980s. And at the World Championships in 1995, Indurain, Rominger and Pantani. Some remarkable careers even began in Colombia, with amateur European teams that rode the Vuelta a Colombia almost since its inception. In the 1960s the Spaniard Julio Jiménez, three times mountains king at the Tour de France. A decade later the Dutchman Johan de Muynck, a Giro d'Italia champion. And in the 1980s a youthful Andrei Tchmil, one of the great one-day riders of the 1990s. In no other Latin American country has cycling been so central to the popular culture.

But the odds have always been stacked against it. Colombia's distance from Europe, and its relative poverty, are almost insuperable obstacles. Even the first Vuelta, despite its huge popularity, was a flawed enterprise – its thirty-five starters represented no more than seven of Colombia's thirty-two departments. The race route went through just five: a meagre catch for an event that purported to be national. But a beginning.

2. A Colombian trinity

There is nothing strange in a nation seeing itself reflected in one sport or other, as America does in baseball or Ethiopia in long-distance running. Or that smaller communities should do the same: black and Hispanic pockets throughout the Americas in boxing, or neighbourhoods of Newcastle and Glasgow in soccer, or the people of Cuenca, Ecuador – home of 1996 Olympic 20km Walk champion Jefferson Pérez – in race-walking. Nothing strange at all, despite modern sport being metaphorically and literally utopian. Metaphorically, in that it posits individuals competing equally under one set of all-encompassing laws. Literally, because modern sport has no sense of place. It standardizes space and time, fixes and polices uniform rules, clones and distributes playing surfaces. Major global championships bring together each discipline's elite. National, even continental, competitions are made to seem peripheral to a fabulously wealthy core.

Modern sport formalizes movement and channels it into the pursuit of records and victories. To compete, athletes must transcend local wisdom and reinvent themselves through laboratory regimes. Scientists mould bodies over the racks and tools of each sport. Dress dispels heat and drag. Recipes are designed to deliver energy and oxygen to sculpted muscles. Modern sports programmes devour budgets beyond most poorer countries. Yet sport replicates itself wherever human culture has colonized the earth. Not even the most radical Kenyan nationalist rails against the cultural colonialism of global track and field, while the Taliban used their football stadiums for executions as well as, not instead of, soccer.

Cycling, however, like fell running and mountaineering, breaches some of these tenets. It glories in the landscape's uniqueness and makes no pretence of equality in competitive conditions. If the contest is man against mountain, the inequality is obvious. If man against man, it is equally obvious that the inherent difficulties vary: on the same face of the same mountain the conditions can change by the minute. Comparison and repeatability are of little interest: timings exist for Alpe d'Huez, the Tour de France's notorious mountain challenge, for example, but they are irrelevant. Nonetheless, with a global governing body – the *Union cycliste internationale*, or UCI – and a rulebook that applies everywhere, cycling too has universalizing tendencies. The transformation occurred in the 1980s, thirty years after the Zipa won Colombia's first national tour. In 1984 the French cycling magazine *Vélo* created a points table inspired by the APT system used in tennis. It identified a World Number One cyclist and allowed every professional in the world to be classified. The system was adapted and adopted by the UCI. In 1985 the international cycling calendar was reformed, with only partial success, to incorporate the newly professional nations, including the USA, Sweden, Denmark, Ireland, Australia and Colombia.

At the hub of the system is the greatest bike race, the Tour de France. Like the Olympics or Homer Simpson, it is part of global culture, secreting shared memories that, some would argue, counter other 'world experiences' like war and economic exploitation. Certainly the medals, laurels and trophies that symbolize victory, derivations of classical antiquity, are now awarded in places unheard of by the Greeks and Romans – places such as, for instance, Colombia. Gold, silver and bronze are lexical items in a language that is almost universal.

Colombia's syncretic culture gives that universal tongue a local accent, for long before the conquistadors, millennia before the advent of global sport, Colombia's indigenous craftsmen were experts in gold, silver and bronze, employing all known founding and moulding methods, plus other, forgotten techniques. The art of their masterpieces is remarkable. And of the surviving pieces the greatest is the Poporo Quimbaya – the gourd of the Quimbaya.

The Quimbaya were a small people who inhabited the western folds of the central cordillera during the sixteenth century. The enormous range of artefacts to which their name was later attached was mostly produced by cultures that preceded them by centuries, and deposited in tombs. Of the people who put them there, little is certain. The *poporo*, made out of gold strengthened with copper, is a bulbous vessel with an ornate base, a narrow neck and, in place of a mouth for pouring, four spheres set symmetrically around a narrow opening. Its proportions are exquisite; its execution could scarcely be bettered by computer-assisted manufacture in any material. In these materials it could not be produced today. Manuel Uribe Ángel's *General Geography and Historical Compendium of the State of Antioquia in Colombia* (1886) includes an etching of the Poporo Quimbaya, and notes: 'Golden bottle found during excavations of a tomb in the place named Pajarito, between Yarumal, Campamento and Angostura . . .

After studying it, some say that Benvenuto Cellini would have gladly passed it off as the work of his own hands.'

A proud and extraordinary symbol of Colombia, the *poporo* founded the Bank of the Republic's Gold Museum in central Bogotá, and is reproduced on the old 20-peso coin and, in a modified form, in the trophy presented to the winner of the Vuelta a Colombia. But the geographer was wrong: the *poporo* is no bottle or drinking vessel. It was the gourd of a tribal elder, similar to gourds still in use today – mostly in marrow-skin – and used by the indigenous peoples of the Andes to store the lime they chew with coca leaves. Therefore the Vuelta a Colombia is no mere instalment in the classical Olympian odyssey of global sport, rewarded with a Graeco-Roman urn. Questing backwards through time towards the age of coca, ritual and tribal enchantment, the Colombian national tour designates young men to undergo a gruelling rite of passage on the nation's behalf.

I first saw the winner's trophy of the Vuelta a Colombia – *two* winner's trophies – in the Bogotá apartment of José Jaime González Pico, otherwise known as Chepe González. It was my first trip to Colombia and Chepe was the brightest star in Colombian cycling. In 1996, his first European season, he had won a stage at the Tour de France. Over the previous two seasons he had won the Vuelta a Colombia twice.

When he was a child, Chepe's mother had sprinkled holy water on his bike before each race; he even carried a bottle of it with him on his bike, despite the extra weight. And he just couldn't stopped winning. By the time we met, he had been supporting his mother and five sisters with his race wins for fifteen years. Twice a stage winner in the Tour of Italy, and twice King of the Mountains there, Chepe González literally climbed out of poverty. And he can hardly finish a sentence without offering thanks to God.

But at the age of fifteen, the sport that later saved Chepe nearly cost him his life when a fall left him nursing terrible head injuries, the scars of which he bears today. His mother forbade him from riding, and only the intercession of Henry Cárdenas, a brilliant climber who later rode alongside Ireland's Tour de France winner Stephen Roche and the two great Italian riders Claudio Chiappucci and Marco Pantani, convinced her to relent.

Today, Chepe's high-rise apartment in the capital looks out over the city towards the hills to the east. There a statue of the Virgin of Guadalupe keeps watch over Bogotá, like her more celebrated son Christ the Redeemer over Rio de Janeiro. In the 1950s the Indomitable Zipa and his rivals had raced up to her vantage point over the city. Colombia is a nation of mountaintop Madonnas, in sanctuaries that preserve an earlier spiritual geography. For long before the conquistadors, the indigenous inhabitants had erected shrines on Colombia's hilltops. The motif of the mother and child was typical in indigenous iconography, and when the Catholic Church arrived, it was a simple task to substitute its symbols for those already in place. Catholic spirituality was simply grafted onto pre-existing traditions. The cyclists paid homage to both strands in their spiritual heritage by placing their finishing lines beside them and sprinting up the mountainside with religion in their hearts. The line dividing bike racing from pilgrimage was never clearly defined.

Beside the Virgin of Guadalupe, the basilica of Monserrate calls pilgrims to severe heights. One Sunday I joined them, dodging heavily laden mule trains on the steep steps. Inside the church a tortured image of the Fallen Lord gazes from above the altar, his contorted face mirroring a cyclist's pain on the steepest stretch of the climb. In a landscape like this, any belief system intending to take root has to make a virtue of the uphill struggle. The Catholic Church, the first global institution of the modern age, always has, and Christ's agonies on the way to Calvary provide a model for Colombia's athletes.

Indeed, in the 1950s a Colombian priest and national broadcaster claimed that the Son of God had revealed to him a plan to create Christilandia, a region governed according to God's law, and that Colombia was his chosen land. The Christilandia myth still hangs over Colombia, and with it the bloody fate that seems to attend nations shaped in the image of their respective gods, for example the Iran of the Ayatollahs, Guatemala under the fundamentalist Protestant General Ríos Montt, or Israel.

But today's community of Catholic saints fights a rearguard action in Colombia against energetic young sects with modern marketing departments. Overworked even in the afterlife, they struggle like rural priests to maintain their constituencies. We breathed the pilgrims' air above Bogotá, while far below us a nation's spirituality subdivided before our eyes into multiple belief systems.

The soul of Bogotá city centre belonged to the Franciscans. The Mormons had moved into the wealthy north side, where their magnificent tabernacle graced the skyline. Between them the shrines of the Lutherans and the Baptists shared the chaotic thoroughfares with the Sanctuary of the Queen of Grace and the Temple of the Amazonian Indian. When demand for spiritual succour overflows its permanent fonts, Charismatic Evangelism takes short leases on the theatres. Far from losing their religions, the people of Colombia have been acquiring more and more of them. And when times are hard, the dividing line between spirituality and desperation sometimes blurs; installed between the places of worship were the betting shops – the only institutions as ubiquitous.

The Catholic God remains dominant among Colombia's supreme beings, and beside the Catholic churches stand stalls and walk-in stores trading in trinkets: scapulars, religious posters reproduced in picture frames, clock faces, barometers and cigarette-card saints.

Near the cathedral of the Franciscans I went into one. The staff eyed me suspiciously, perhaps detecting in my features their mongrel mixture of Danish and Saxon warlords and wenches, united violently a thousand years ago on my violent island of mestizos. The blue-eyed Caucasian Christs that stood before me in a range of scales were as aberrant. Beneath each garden gnome beard, an open wound divided every chest. Christ's left hand held His disembodied heart, palpitating with plastic realism to the fake pulse of an intermittent bulb. A tumescence painted on it was supposed to evoke a holy flame. At its centre a ring of bent arrows dripped with moulded blood. Worse than graven images, they struck me as monuments to bad taste. But proximity to poverty's degree zero must draw us closer to the realm of miracles – the Sacred Heart of Christ has offered Colombia's poor their only protection for nearly two centuries.

In November 1898 the Colombian government welcomed a papal proposal to recognize the 'social sovereignty' of Jesus Christ. Four years later the State pledged funds to build a temple in honour of the Sacred Heart in Bogotá, and State representation at a solemn religious service there 'to pacify the Republic'. In June 1970 a former president reflected in his speech on the Day of the Sacred Heart: 'Since the origins of our nationality, the God of Colombia has been the light of our history, the lamp of our homesteads, the key to our culture, the guide of our statesmen, the inspiration of our ideals and the firm sustainer of the institutions that govern us.' A quarter of a century on, in 1994, when the Constitutional Court declared the 1952 laws incompatible with the freedom of worship enshrined in the 1991 Constitution, Colombia's *El Tiempo* newspaper was outraged: 'Tradition demonstrates that with this judgement or without it, with the Constitution or without it, with the magistrates or without them, with the Constituent Assembly or without it, this was, is and shall continue to be the country of the Sacred Heart of Jesus.'

The iconography of the Sacred Heart, like the Fallen Lord of

Monserrate, seemed to me to contain more ingredients that explain Colombia's fascination with cycling. The national affection for agonizing Christs and bleeding hearts predisposes the Colombians to detect hints of salvation in the labours of their cyclists. On cigarette cards I discovered the Miraculous Christ of Buga. The town of Buga, between Bogotá and Cali, is a regular Tour of Colombia town. It is a place of national pilgrimage, for *el milagroso* works many miracles. He too drips with blood – like fallen cyclists grimacing from a thousand race photographs, constant in their devotion – and promises that reward shall come only after the cruellest abstinence.

But not all the trinket shop's treasures included cyclists in their constituency. Opposite the Sacred Hearts, huddled like penguins, communed the Virgins of Carmen. Commending themselves to the Virgin of Carmen before their gunfights, Carmen hears the supplications of transport workers, railwaymen and emerald miners, but she is also the patron saint of the paramilitary death squads and Medellín's teenage gangs. When, on the 1952 to 1955 Tours of Colombia, the Virgin of Carmen adorned a huge scapular hung around the neck of a rider named José Alfaro, however, she proved powerless to help. (Though in one respect, so the story goes, she did assist Alfaro: throughout the course of the Tour he would dine in the finest restaurants and, presented with the bill, would announce, 'The Virgin will provide.')

Most important of all, the Virgin of Chiquinquirá, Colombia's patron saint, stared out from plastic picture frames. In December each year, tens of thousands of Colombians make the pilgrimage to her home town, north of Bogotá, to behold, in a priceless emerald crown, the inaccessibility of their nation's wealth. The emerald bosses donated its jewels in 1986 to commemorate Pope John Paul II's visit – as their henchmen lined the road to the mines with corpses. The following year one of Colombia's finest ever cyclists, Lucho Herrera, took the trophy of the Vuelta a Colombia to receive the blessing of the Virgin, in a gesture of profound significance for his country. And at Morcá, near the town of Sogamoso – home of hosts of fine cyclists, including Raphael Acevedo, Chepe González, Henry Cárdenas, and others I only met later – a tiny shrine marks the place where the Virgin Mary appeared on a hillside 300 years ago. 'At the Tour de France,' Raphael told me, 'we all used to receive her blessing and commend ourselves to her.' Henry added, 'Here in Colombia there were nine or ten cyclists, and all of us were devoted to the Virgin of Morcá. I think She helped us, because since we left the scene, no Colombian cyclists have achieved what we did in Europe. That's because of the Virgin's blessings.' Some see in sport the embryo of a new and universal religion for an age in which the traditional ones, bound to time and place, have lost their meaning. Colombia's cyclists suggest that cycling, and perhaps all sport, lies squarely in a tradition of spiritual discipline and self-denial as old as humanity itself. Far from founding a new religion, sport in Colombia – sport everywhere? – is merely a modern form of devotion. Cycling, Colombia and Catholicism are an ineffable, indivisible trinity.

3. Olympus's faded hierarchy

LONDON, 1948: THE peloton was still together even after five and a quarter hours. Then, half a mile from the finish, a twenty-two-year-old shoemaker from Lens surprised the group. Pre-empting the pure sprinters, the French rider José Beyaert crossed the finish line eight lengths ahead of the field. France had won a third consecutive Olympic road-racing title. The sequence ended there. For the remainder of the century French success in the event was a distant memory. Almost as distant as José Beyaert.

For the course of Beyaert's life was altered in London, not by Olympic victory, but by friendship. Roberto Serafín Guerrero had ridden the 4000-metre team pursuit for Argentina at the Games. In post-Olympic exhibitions across Europe, Beyaert and Guerrero became firm friends before the Argentine crossed the Atlantic and returned home to far off Buenos Aires. Years later a letter arrived at Beyaert's home in Lens, postmarked Medellín, Colombia. It was from Guerrero. The Colombians, he said, were mad about cycling. There was work; Guerrero was coaching there.

'I realized,' Donald Raskin explained, 'that if Colombian cycling wanted to make a name for itself, it needed coaches. Here, there were none. So we decided to look abroad.' In March 1951, weeks after the first Vuelta, a Colombian team competed in the Panamerican Games at the Argentine capital. The Colombian delegate spoke to Guerrero and another Argentine rider, his close friend Julio Arrastía. An international meeting was being planned for the opening of Bogotá's new velodrome. The two Argentines were cordially invited, and in September that year Roberto Guerrero and Julio Arrastía travelled to Colombia by steamer. Raskin had sent them tickets, paid for by the Colombian Cycling Association. They crossed Argentina by train and took the Pacific Steam Navigation Company's *Reina del Mar* from the Chilean port of Valparaíso. Raskin flew out to Cartagena on Colombia's Caribbean coast to meet them. Arrastía and Guerrero settled in Medellín, where they began to build a formidable squad of riders. With their help Roberto Cano and Pedro Nel Gil, second and third in the 1951 Vuelta, were preparing to offer the Zipa greater resistance next time.

But as things turned out, their main rival in the second Vuelta was not from Zipaquirá but Pas de Calais. Beyaert had responded to Guerrero's letter by making the long journey by land and sea. Recognizing the publicity coup, a regional frame manufacturer, Automoto of Cali, offered the Frenchman good money to ride the 1952 Vuelta a Colombia. Beyaert accepted. The previous year only a farrago of regional riders had stood between the Indomitable Zipa and his first title. Now the reigning Olympic road-racing champion was muscling in.

But conditions in Colombia, Beyaert found, could not be compared with Europe. 'Only pride stopped me abandoning on stage one,' he recalled. 'I was, after all, Olympic champion. I didn't want to be beaten by riders no one had ever heard of, who didn't have a decent bike between them. In Colombia I learnt the meaning of courage.'

Hardened by the ordeal, Beyaert shell-shocked Colombia by destroying the autochthonous opposition on the way to victory in the second Vuelta in 1952. Forero, the strongest Colombian, suffered mixed fortunes. On stage six his fork snapped. He was lucky to escape alive: with the handlebars still in his hands, his face took the full impact. If the blood streaming from his swollen brow caused his ambitious mother to blanche stoically, when he was forced to retire from the race she wept disconsolately.

Five stages fell to the Frenchman. Three went to an Argentine named Humberto Varisco, second on the overall podium. Behind 1952's victorious foreigners, Antioquia's Pedro Nel Gil stood on the lowest rung.

It was admiration, not xenophobia, which greeted Beyaert's victory. On behalf of the right-wing President Laureano Gómez, incapacitated by illness, Colombia's acting premier Roberto Urdaneta Arbeláez offered Beyaert the post of national cycling coach. 'I accepted,' he said, 'because I knew I could teach these riders something.'

BUT BY 1953 Beyaert was no longer the reigning Olympic champion. Colombia, too, had moved on. The successes of Nel Gil and Cano in the first Vuelta had vindicated the faith of a town – Medellín – and an industry – the textiles manufacturers – that would soon occupy centre stage in Colombian cycling.

Stretched along the Urabá valley, a corridor set deep in the central Andean cordillera, Medellín is approached from all sides by mountainous passes that cut across the department of Antioquia, north-east of Bogotá. Its hills bathe in the gentle warmth of an eternal spring. A thriving modern city of glinting steel and glass office blocks, Medellín has at its heart a chisel-shaped skyscraper: the headquarters of the Colombian Textiles Company, or Coltejer. And Coltejer occupies a special place in the story of Colombia's cyclists. By the early 1950s Medellín was the centre of Latin America's greatest textiles industry, and Coltejer the town's greatest producer. Its owners now staked their company's future on the sport. The transport needs of the industrialists ensured early asphalting of the road network, while the textiles manufacturers sought a publicity vehicle that would be economical and effective. Medellín was synonymous with cycling long before the years of cocaine. Coltejer had sponsored Cano and Nel Gil. But the future would belong to neither of them. An unknown office boy at Coltejer inherited the remains of the decade.

One day Ramón Hoyos Vallejo, from the village of Marinilla in Medellín's hills, would humble the finest cyclists in the world. His experiences on stage one of the 1952 Vuelta – recounted in a subsequent biography written by a future Nobel Prize winner for literature, Gabriel García Márquez – give an early sense of the calibre of the man. He recalls that, cold, shaking with nerves and emotion, he began 'pedalling like an idiot. I would have preferred an uphill stage because I felt more secure when I was climbing. But at the same time I wanted to descend as quickly as possible, to make it down into the heat of the lowlands, because the altitude and cold of the capital were asphyxiating. When the peloton began to break up, I realized that I was helpless. One by one, all the cyclists were leaving me behind. I felt ill, blinded and an irresistible urge to cry. One consideration kept me going: I didn't want to let my sponsor down. I remember that for an hour at least I was completely alone on the road. The people who had gone out to applaud the cyclists had disappeared. I was the last one. Even the riders in the remains of the peloton were gaining time on me, but I kept pedalling all the same.

'I don't know how it happened. I remember feeling I was losing control of the bike, and then flying head first towards the rocks. A fraction of a second, no more. I felt a tremendous blow to my forehead. Then I lost consciousness.'

Hoyos awoke to the voices of race auxiliaries: '"Put him in the truck. He's seriously injured. He can't go on." When I finally managed to open my eyes, I saw two men trying to lift me. The first thing I did was to see if my bicycle was still there. It was, and in working order, next to a truck that wasn't ours. That was all that mattered to me. My head was throbbing, my heart was beating hard, but I didn't care. All that mattered was that my bike was still intact.'

Ignoring the protests of his helpers, Hoyos remounted and pedalled pathetically to the finish line. 'I was expecting crowds and a huge reception, but there was nobody. "Where's the stage finish?" I asked. "It was here," they told me, "but everyone's gone now."' Passers-by, shocked at the two-inch wound above his left eye, walked him to Honda's hospital. That evening, tended by nuns, he learnt he had been expelled from the race.

The following morning he wandered slowly towards the race departure. There he watched with envy as the other riders prepared to depart: 'I was at one side of the park with my suitcase and bicycle when I noticed something going on: a group of soldiers was arguing hammer and tongs with one of the race directors.' The reason? One of their cyclists, First Sergeant Manuel Ramírez, had also been disqualified. A group of officers was insisting that he be reinstated. 'I knew who was going to win the argument and I wasn't wrong. When Sergeant Ramírez was allowed back in the race, the other eight of us who had been disqualified began to argue, "If Sergeant Ramírez is riding, so are we." And we all set off. My sponsor, Don Ramiro Mejía, quickly asked me, "Can you ride with one eye?" Without thinking twice, I said, "For all there is to see, one eye's enough."'

That day, race leader José Beyaert won his second stage. Three minutes behind him, Hoyos crossed the line in second place.

I met Ramón Hoyos at his hillside home above the Medellín–Bogotá highway. His elder brother, José, had driven me out from central Medellín. Ramón spent the afternoon humiliating his brother for his lack of athletic talent. His prepotence revealed an inner cruelty. This, I reflected, was the arrogance that had made him great: an inability to believe he could be beaten. He told me much the same story García Márquez must have heard nearly fifty years before.

On stage four of the 1952 Vuelta, Hoyos had duelled with the Zipa. Between the two men began an enmity that would continue until the end of the century. Hoyos was desperate to win. 'The stage was special because it finished at Medellín, where my mother and my friends were waiting for me. And it was a hard stage, which I felt strong enough to win despite my injuries.' Of the fifty riders who had started the Vuelta, twenty-eight had already abandoned it when stage four began. 'On the climbs the aching in my head subsided, so I rode hard towards La Pintada. I arrived at the village in fourth place, only twenty minutes behind the Zipa. Over the following 20 kilometres I made up that time. When I caught him, I decided to try to drop him as soon as possible.

'We rode side by side in the mud, beneath a torrential cloudburst which was followed by a hailstorm. Two kilometres above Santa Barbara I tried to lose him, but he stuck to my wheel. I knew I had to gain as much time as possible, because on the descent the pain would come back. The Zipa was still stuck to my wheel. At the decisive moment I sprinted. The Zipa went at exactly the same time, and we arrived together, as if the wheels of both bicycles formed part of the same machine. We were together at the mountain prize.'

The two men descended together. On the more even roads leading into Medellín, the Zipa's greater time trial speeds gradually began to wear down his rival, and the man from Zipaquirá won this stage by four minutes. But though the Zipa was as physically strong as any Colombian rider of the decade, Hoyos was younger, a climbing specialist and from a town boasting unrivalled resources of finance and expertise. Four days later he won the first of thirty-eight Tour of Colombia stages in a career that would dominate Colombian cycling in the 1950s.

His win attracted the attention of Julio Arrastía. When the Antioquian League made the Argentine their regional cycling coach, Hoyos's athletic career really began.

Cycling on loose stones is an art; Ramón Hoyos did it well – lightness of touch, even pressure on the pedals, controlled accelerations. The best Colombian cyclists of the 1950s supplemented the skills of the European *routier* with a supernatural ability to avoid punctures. In this, Hoyos and Forero were equals. But Arrastía, in charge of Antioquia's road-racing teams, was prepared to sacrifice many promising careers to ensure Hoyos's ascendancy. The Argentine ensured that there was always a team-mate on hand to lend him a wheel and a team car never more than seconds away. The following year Arrastía's methods revolutionized Colombian cycling.

The Zipa won the first stage of the 1953 Vuelta out of Bogotá. Beyaert took the gruelling climb from Fresno to Manizales on stage three. Then it was Hoyos, day after day after day. As the race reached Antioquia, he powered out of the peloton and danced between the coffee plantations through the heartlands of Colombian cycling, dominating four consecutive stages, heading first northwards from Manizales to Aguadas, thence to Medellín, south to Riosucio, and finally from Riosucio to Pereira.

When the Vuelta reached for the first time into the Colombian south-west, embracing Popayán, the capital of the impoverished department of Cauca, Hoyos extended his lead with three more stage wins. The final stage ending in Bogotá, his eighth win of the race consecrated his dominance. He had won the overall individual prize by one hour, six minutes and seventeen seconds from Beyaert. The Antioquians, under Arrastía's direction, easily took the team prize.

But the danger of those early Vueltas on coarse, stony roads was underlined by the fate of one of Hoyos's team-mates. Conrado 'Tito' Gallo, an Antioquian, was admired as the most fearless descender, spiralling lustily downwards on stony paths. His sponsor was the National Road Surfacing Company. When stage five of the 1953 Vuelta had left Aguadas for Medellín, with Hoyos attacking on the Alto de Minas and crossing first, followed by Beyaert, Gallo, in third place, had hurled himself over the lip of the col in pursuit of the Frenchman.

A journalist named Oscar Salazar Montoya was following Tito Gallo in a Company truck. Montoya is now retired and living on Colombia's luscious Caribbean coast, but his memories of the tragedy are fresh. 'The Company director looked over at me and said, "The boy's going to kill himself before he reaches the Frenchman." He told the driver to catch him and tell him to slow down, but it was impossible. Anyway, the descent was nearly over. Then a long way below us we saw something fly into the air and crash down into the road. It looked like a bird, or a clutch of banana leaves, like the ones waved by the crowds at each stage finish. When we reached it, we found Tito Gallo, foetal and still, blood all over his face. His bicycle was yards away. The fork had sheared.'

In the no man's land of his delirium, perhaps Tito Gallo caught and passed the Frenchman. Three times during the Vuelta his death was announced. The other riders wept on their handlebars. Yet forty-nine days later what remained of Tito Gallo emerged from the wilderness of coma. His faculty of memory had been destroyed, his speech shattered into incoherence, his right side intermittently paralysed.

The 1953 race had silenced another rider. Ephraim Forero, the Indomitable Zipa, was fourth, nearly three hours behind the winner. Yet echoes of his glory days continued to resonate over the mountains. After the first Vuelta he had received a letter from the Ambassador of France inviting the first Colombian champion to lead a national team to the greatest race on Earth: the Tour de France.

The expedition had taken time to organize. Beyaert, the natural team manager, was dispatched with his feuding leaders, Forero and Hoyos, and five other riders on a slow boat to France. In Paris the Colombians competed in amateur events. Forero, Hoyos and Fabio León Calle, another Medellín native, had some success. But the ambassador's letter cut no ice with the Tour de France. With no accommodation, vehicles, auxiliaries or budget, the Colombians got short shrift from the organizers. Beyaert's Olympic prestige managed to secure them a compensatory place on the Tour's poor relation, the Route de France, an amateur event later replaced by the Tour de l'Avenir. It soon awoke Colombia from that early dream of European glory.

On the first, fast stage of the Route de France, on the flat, all but Forero and Hoyos arrived outside the time limit and were disqualified *en bloc*. Beyaert's pleas for leniency were in vain. By the end of stage four constant mechanical problems with their substandard machines had forced the remaining riders out. Cash-strapped and discouraged, the Colombians never made it to the mountains of France. Perhaps the Europeans would have humiliated them even there: Forero and Hoyos were, after all, part-timers who trained only in order to beat each other. Either way, France wouldn't wait to find out.

All the riders wanted was to return home. But at the Colombian Embassy, instead of their return tickets, bad news awaited. While they had been riding in France, a military coup had taken place at home.

The presidential elections of March 1953 had been a shambles. From exile the Liberal leadership had boycotted the vote. The moderate Conservatives who opposed Laureano Gómez's demagoguery advised its followers to abstain. The ruling rightists threatened bloody retribution, even against abstaining Conservatives, and the political violence plumbed new depths of depravity. So on 13 June 1953 the commander-in-chief of the Colombian armed forces, General Gustavo Rojas Pinilla, seized power.

'On his way out,' Hoyos recalls, 'the minister responsible for our return trip stole the money for our tickets. We had to sell what we could. Beyaert guaranteed a loan and we bought the cheapest boat ride home. On the long journey from Paris to Cannes we had no money for food.' Hoyos and the younger riders sailed for Colombia.

But if the Indomitable Zipa was to succeed outside Colombia, it had to be now. He had sold everything he owned for this opportunity. He remained in Europe, trying to become the first Colombian to succeed in the Old Continent. Trying months lay ahead of him. A few meaningless one-day races – amateur, of course – inscribed his name in their honours list. Some provincial French archive perhaps preserves the details. But with little French and no one to recommend him, Forero soon spent what money he had. At the end of August, with the permission of the Colombian Cycling Association, he travelled to Lugano in Switzerland for the World Championships.

In the amateur road race he was in the decisive breakaway with success in sight. But a lap-and-a-half from the line, disaster: a puncture forced him out of the race. 'We had all been issued with gas-fired pumps, but when I tried to use mine, I found it was cracked through.

It took five whole minutes for the mechanic's vehicle to arrive. By then there was no way back. I was going to abandon but I couldn't bear to watch other riders pass me, so I joined a group of stragglers and led them to the finish. I didn't even want to know my time or position.'

The race was won by an Italian named Riccardo Filippi, the pupil of Fausto Coppi, the greatest rider in the world, whom he partnered in the two-man time trials of the 1950s. Second was Gastone Nencini, King of the Mountains in the 1957 Tour de France. Third was Rik Van Looy, later world professional champion twice.

The Zipa, meanwhile, went home to Colombia penniless and downcast.

General Rojas Pinilla had inherited a country partly ruled by terror, sometimes actively insurgent and everywhere on the brink of social and political crisis. By placing the nation before sectarian interests and brandishing the slogan 'Peace, Justice and Freedom', the dictator's benevolence caught the public mood. His support crossed political boundaries. Where Gómez had treated the guerrillas as delinquents, Rojas Pinilla recognized them as a political force and opened negotiations. Pamphlets distributed from the air offered generous terms to insurgents prepared to lay down their arms. Preaching reconciliation, the General associated himself with Colombia's most persuasive symbol of unity: the Vuelta. Reinforcing the popular hegemony of the military ruler, Ramón Hoyos, performing his national service, was riding in the colours of the Armed Forces.

Reflecting the state of the nation, the 1954 Vuelta route was more extreme than ever. The dictator's daughter, María Eugenia, waved the riders off in Bogotá, and for three stages they journeyed northwards, first to the Boyacá town of Duitama, then rising into the troposphere over the 3,960-metre Guantiva pass. Passing through the Santander township of Málaga, it drove onwards into North Santander, then towards Venezuela and the border town of Cúcuta. On stage four the Almorzadero pass between Pamplona and Bucaramanga again took the Vuelta above 3,960 metres.

The Antioquian dominance was remorseless. Hoyos won the three terrible mountain stages, leaving the rest like crumbs for his regional colleagues.

The riders then faced a long transfer from Socorro through the forested Casare valley in eastern Santander to the oil town of Puerto Berrío on the Antioquian bank of the Magdalena River. The Vuelta, still largely conducted between departmental capitals, was attempting to embrace new territories. Most riders slept at Socorro before confronting a twenty-hour odyssey through the suffocating forest. Shortly after the Rojas Pinilla coup, the liberal guerrillas who roamed the Casare had surrendered their arms. Now the dense forest echoed to the cacophony of chattering monkeys. Suspicions of jaguars and the hissing of snakes ensured shallow sleep for the majority of riders driving tortuously through the wilderness. But the wealthy Antioquians, with the Armed Forces team and the Valle delegation, flew direct to Medellín. There, a sound night's sleep was followed by two rest days training on the excellent roads around Medellín.

Beyaert was incensed. In part he was angry at the preferential treatment the Antioquians were enjoying. But he must also have felt an almost infantile frustration at the Antioquian omnipotence. Mobilizing eleven other riders, he headed the protests. Tempers flared. By refusing to ride stage six from Santiago to Medellín, Beyaert and the strikers irked the Vuelta organizers. New Colombian Cycling Association president General (Ret.) Arámbula Durán – coincidentally from Antioquia – had the Frenchman arrested. In a nearby barracks the former General threatened to expel the Olympic champion, not just from the race, but from the country.

That evening in Medellín the rebellion was eventually defused.

The protesters were attributed the time of the slowest finisher of the day and penalized a further ten minutes. The Antioquians completed a sequence of six stage wins out of six by the Santiago–Medellín stage. With irresistible vitality, the Medellín-based riders powered towards victory. Five stages went to Hoyos, bringing him a second Vuelta title.

But even as María Eugenia Rojas was waving off the riders in Bogotá, the seeds of her father's downfall were sown. Rojas Pinilla had appointed his daughter Director of the Rehabilitation and Aid Office, a new institution. Accusations of nepotism were the first signs that the regime's popular mandate was conditional. Later it emerged that the hardline Conservatives still controlling the State intelligence services were using the official records of insurgents who had laid down their arms to identify and murder them. Assassinations in the departments of Valle, Quindío and Tolima damaged the Rojas regime's credibility in the eyes of the peasant-guerrillas. Any remaining trust was destroyed by events in the mountain province of Sumapaz, to Bogotá's south-west.

SINCE 1949 A PEASANT army had been fighting to defend the land claims of small farmers against the demands of powerful landlords. The regime's routine policy was negotiation sweetened by financial help for reintegrated insurgents. In Sumapaz it took sides. The army was put in at the behest of the *latifundistas* (the owners of large landed estates), and in spring 1955 surrounded the area. On 4 April it moved in. The operation was envisioned to last a matter of days. Days became weeks, and weeks, months. Eventually a third of all army personnel saw active service in Sumapaz. A torture centre known as the Cunday concentration camp was built to support the campaign.

In May 1955, as that year's Vuelta began, the killing continued. Hoyos, no longer with the forces, was back in Antioquian colours, and rode the perfect race. His win in the first stage decided the race on day one. The riders snaked out of Bogotá and through the coffee axis. When stage five entered Medellín with the implacable Hoyos at its head, the celebrations paralysed the town. It was his fifth stage win. Again the Vuelta was expanding its coverage. As it stretched down to Pasto, the capital of the border department of Nariño, and then across the Ecuadorean border to the town of Tulcán, Hoyos marked his territory with stage wins.

The penultimate stage ended at Melgar, where Rojas Pinilla greeted the riders from his residence. The following day Hoyos, victorious in twelve of the Vuelta's eighteen stages, rode triumphantly into the capital.

In the General Classification seven Antioquian riders occupied the first seven places. Only Beyaert, with three stage wins, and Mexico's finest rider, Rafael Vacca, could break the Antioquian monopoly. Day after day, orchestrated and conducted by Julio Arrastía, the Antioquians called the race's tune, dictating when to attack and when to mark tempo. When they co-ordinated their work rate, any rider who defied their dominance was simply destroyed.

And this was how they tamed the Indomitable Zipa. One after another the Antioquians whipped away from the group, wearing down his solitary resistance. Through the commentaries of Carlos Arturo Rueda, this human machine – unrelenting, merciless – acquired a humorous, chilling title: Hoyos and his team-mates were collectively immortalized as 'the Antioquian liquidizer'.

During the race the national daily *El Espectador* had obtained exclusive permission to publish the champion Hoyos's biography. It was a journalistic coup that guaranteed increased sales. So while the annual Colombian Tour was establishing itself as a huge festival of national passion, another national institution was dispatched to conduct five intense days of interviews.

Between weekly cinema reviews, occasional commentaries on

everyday affairs under the rubric 'Day by Day', and two works of fiction – a collection of critically-acclaimed short stories entitled 'La Hojarasca' (published in English as 'Leaf Storm') and the novel 'One Hundred Years of Solitude' – a man called Gabriel García Márquez was the newspaper's main producer of investigative reportage.

From 5 to 22 April 1955 García Márquez had produced a twelve-part account of the ordeal of Luis Alejandro Velasco, shipwrecked on a raft in the Caribbean with neither food nor water for eleven days. The story had already been exhaustively covered, but in García Márquez' hands became a *cause célèbre*. His series of articles nearly doubled the paper's circulation and consolidated García Márquez's national literary reputation. It was with the same intent that he was asked to write the life of Colombia's greatest athlete.

His ghosted autobiography of Ramón Hoyos in twelve parts, published between 27 June and 12 July 1955, repeated the Velasco coup. García Márquez turned Hoyos's victories into a swashbuckling tale mixing tragedy and triumph, for Hoyos's stature in the country was immense. As García Márquez wrote, 'Cycling has no specific patron saint. Each rider prays to the saint of his own devotion. In Antioquia's humble homes, many go further, exposing and illuminating, beside a holy image, a photograph of Ramón Hoyos, cut from the newspapers.'

IN JUNE 1956 the Vuelta started outside Bogotá for the first time. When the riders departed in June from Bucaramanga, the capital of the department of Santander, the public response was enormous.

Stage one departed at 8.00 a.m., undulating south over the sweating lowlands to the town of San Gil and then to the communities of Duitama and Tunja on the high-altitude Boyacá plateau. It was on the altiplano that Hoyos began to impose his relentless resources of strength. Allowing his Antioquian team-mates occasional glories,

Hoyos dominated eight stages. The pretenders knew who to watch and hung on his rear wheel until eventually – inevitably – it became impossible to stay with him. The Indomitable Zipa was third. His individualism had cost him dear: if he had been supported by a team with an Arrastía at the helm, Hoyos might have been vulnerable. Instead, the Zipa feuded with his team-mates and rode himself out of contention.

By the late 1950s Colombian cycling had begun to evolve. True, the race organization remained amateurish: the race marshals were sometimes ignorant of the regulations, and the timekeepers still used the race as an annual holiday. Intermediate sprints and mountains prizes often depended on local knowledge. Frequently they weren't even marked. And the Vuelta was still full of treachery. Some recall the team car of Bogotá-based Roberto Buitrago, a powerful Ford 350, which, positioned squarely behind Buitrago, a fine climber, with its exhaust pipe directed downwards towards the dirt of the road surface, raised a smokescreen of dust and fumes on the ascents to prevent attacks from the rear.

But many of the contours of modern sport were appearing. The peloton was becoming structured and hierarchical. The time gaps between riders were no longer measured in hours, but in minutes and seconds. And every team brought coaches and auxiliaries in a registered vehicle. The Antioquian cycling machine, in turn, was becoming enormous. So enormous, in fact, that its coach was presented with an uncomfortable conflict of interests.

In June that year Julio Arrastía was race director for three teams sent by the Antioquian Cycling League. Antioquia 'A' included Hoyos and Honorio Rúa. Both cyclists, and their companions Octavio Olarte and Ernesto Zapata, rode for Coltejer, who reportedly subsidized the Argentine's income.

Antioquia 'B' and 'C', for which Arrastía was also responsible, were assembled more for bureaucratic convenience than for group cohesion. Each team comprised of four individually sponsored riders. Coltejer's commitment, however, demanded results, and created a glaring contradiction in Arrastía's duties, which determined the outcome of the 1957 Vuelta.

The race was expanding its theatre of operations to new parts of the national territory. On 19 June the Vuelta left Barranquilla (in the department of Atlántico), the port through which football and cycling first entered Colombia. It traced its way to the great colonial fortress town of Cartagena on the Bolívar department's Caribbean coast, and thence to Sincelejo in Sucre. From Sucre and then the junction of Planeta Rica in the department of Córdoba, the riders raced to Antioquia. For three stages Hoyos had been conspicuously absent from the podium. But in Hoyos's home territory, Cundinamarca's Jorge Luque had the effrontery to win two stages.

Hoyos had started the Vuelta as the natural favourite, but ended stage one in precarious health. Three days later, after Luque had won the fourth stage into the Antioquian town of Yarumal, Hoyos was taken to a clinic to be treated for diarrhoea and vomiting caused by micro-organisms in his drinking water. The following evening, as Luque won again into Medellín, Hoyos was hospitalized. The rest day in Medellín gave him hope, but the following day was the gruelling stage from Medellín to Riosucio.

It was Hoyos's favourite stage. He had won it in the 1953 Vuelta. Over the same roads two years later he had triumphed from Medellín to the town of Caramanta. And in a new, yearly event from Medellín to La Pintada and back – the '*El Colombiano* Classic', organized by a Medellín-based national daily in 1956 and 1957 – Hoyos had had no rivals. The route covered every terrain and included a terrifying 30-kilometre descent from the 2,446-metre Alto de Minas.

Hoyos was in no condition to compete: health problems had

hampered his preparation. And for the first time in his career he faced a rider capable, on his day, of defeating him. Hernán Medina Calderón was a chemistry student at the University of Antioquia. The Union Brewery funded his studies and sponsored his ride in Antioquia 'C'. An explosive climber with a tremendous desire to win, Medina's elegant economy of style and predilection for study earned him a nickname purloined from the Richard Thorpe Cinemascope production distributed in Colombia in 1955, *The Student Prince*. The day belonged to Medina, who entered Riosucio with a lead of fourteen minutes. In second place was a Spanish rider, José Gómez del Moral. Honorio Rúa was fifth, thirty minutes behind, and Ramón Hoyos twelfth at three-quarters of an hour. The Zipa, in fourteenth place, was fifty-two minutes off Medina's merciless pace.

Now scandal broke. That evening, after the stage, the commissaires published a press release. On one of the smaller ascents, it announced, two Antioquia 'A' riders, Hoyos and Rúa, had been pushed. Each was given a five-minute penalty. Antioquian pride, already bruised by the stage wins of Bogotá's Luque, was outraged. Arrastía, faced with a crushing victory by the Union Brewery rider, was provided with an unmissable opportunity to save face with his Coltejer paymasters.

The commissaires' allegations, the Antioquian team therefore declared, were false 'in concept and substance'. The retraction they demanded from the race director did not materialize. So in the name of team solidarity and regional pride, Arrastía withdrew his team. With the race slipping out of Coltejer's clutches, it was preferable for a foreigner to win than an Antioquian sponsored by someone other than his employer, Coltejer.

With Medina out of the race, the Spaniard José Gómez del Moral headed the General Classification, a lead he defended to Bogotá. The

Zipa was second, his Cundinamarca team-mate Jorge Luque third. Their rivalry prevented them uniting to threaten the Spaniard.

For the second time – after Beyaert's victory in 1952 – and the last of the century, a foreign rider had won the Vuelta a Colombia. And José Gómez del Moral was not even the most celebrated foreign cyclist to ride in Colombia in 1957.

4. On giant's shoulders

EVEN NOW FROM faded yellow photographs, solitude shines in his messianic eyes, marvelling at some absent thing beyond the visible. Perhaps it was the gaze, perhaps the impossible fragility of his physique. Wherever its root, charisma had descended on Fausto Coppi, inspiring followers around the world and introducing cycling to a new public.

Fausto Coppi had steered cycling into the nuclear age. In 1942 his Italian compatriot Enrico Fermi installed the first nuclear reactor in a Chicago squash court. In the same year, Coppi took to the curved space of Milan's Vigorelli velodrome, accelerating to a world hour record of 45.871 kilometres. As the Cold War began, gravity collapsed before him in the highlands of Italy and France, where the enormous margins of his mountain stage wins made him victorious in five Italian tours and two Tours de France.

Coppi was the most complete cyclist who had ever lived. And although the world he inhabited could hardly have been further from Colombia, he was one of the catalysts that conjured Colombian cycling from the chaos. 'When I first cycled, I began to read what I could about the great Europeans,' remembers Ephraim Forero, the Indomitable Zipa. 'It was then that I discovered Fausto Coppi. Something in him impressed me deeply. I thought of him in the same way I thought of Superman.' The Zipa had seen him in the flesh for the first time at Lugano, Switzerland, in 1953, where he was the first rider to represent Colombia at the World Championships – Coppi had become world professional champion by over six minutes. Seven seasons began and ended with Coppi. He won the first classic of the year, the Primavera from Milan to San Remo, three times. And he won the last, the Tour of the Falling Leaves around Lombardy, five times. Twice, the most prestigious time trial event, the Grand Prix des Nations, was his. And with his protégé Riccardo Filippi he won the two-man time trial Baracchi Trophy three times.

In 1940 the twenty-year-old Coppi had exploded into world sport by winning the three-week Giro d'Italia. Then the war devoured five years of his athletic prime, long months of which he spent sick with malaria in a British POW camp at Megez el Bab in North Africa. Amputate five years of competition from Merckx or Hinault, and the remains of their careers can't compare with Coppi. This was the colossus on cycling's horizon. A distant figure for the Colombians, who had prospered against Latin American competition but knew that cycling's centre of gravity lay elsewhere.

So in 1957 all Colombia was dumbstruck to read a press release announcing Coppi's imminent arrival. An Antioquian entrepreneur named Oscar Hernández claimed to have spoken with him. An agreement had been reached, he said. Before the year was out, Coppi would be in Bogotá. Colombia's cyclists had longed to learn at the feet of a master – to dance out of the saddle on a learning curve to infinity. Now they would have their chance.

Hernández was the director of the South American Entertainments Co., which brought singers and showmen to the *belle époque* of 1950s Medellín. The press portrayed him as well-meaning, if occasionally unreliable. The cycling authorities were less generous. He should stick to his cabaret artists, they thought; the profit motive had no place in the temple of Colombian cycling. Hernández was met with envious suspicion, but, reluctantly, his schemes were tolerated. In the streets, however, among the general public, Hernández was a hero. For the moment, at least.

The Colombian media made much of Coppi's record but little of his age. By 1957 Coppi was thirty-seven. The 70-kilometre solo breakaway with which he won the Italian national championship in September 1955 had been the swan song of his career. The greatest of his victories were at least five years behind him. True, his last professional road race win was in 1957, but it was in the Baracchi Trophy, and he had won the two-man time trial on the flat thanks to the herculean efforts of an extraordinary twenty-four-year-old: in 1956 Ercole Baldini had become world 4000-metre pursuit champion, set a world amateur hour record of 46.394 kilometres, and won the Olympic road race by a full mile. Within a year of his Baracchi Trophy win with Coppi, he had won the Giro d'Italia and the professional World Championship.

No longer the formidable road racer of his prime, Coppi agreed to participate in a series of exhibition races on the track in Colombia. His Swiss friend and rival Hugo Koblet agreed to join him later in the trip. In 1950 Koblet had been the first non-Italian to win the Tour of Italy. The following year he won five Tour de France stages, including both time trials, and the overall title without the support of a full Swiss team. But Koblet, too, was at the end of a career that had shone brilliantly but briefly. In 1952 kidney problems had shortened his season. A broken collarbone sustained on the descent from the Aubisque during the Tour de France ruined his 1953 season. Thereafter, Koblet never competed to the same standard again. Both riders came with thoughts of future business activities after retirement from competition: Coppi was promoting his bicycle frame business in Argentina, the birthplace of his son Faustino. There was talk of motor industry franchises.

Venezuelan Postal Service Flight 266 carried Coppi overnight to Curação and on to the Colombian capital. At 3.00 p.m. on 18 December 1957 an immense crowd gathered to greet him at Bogotá's Techo Airport. 'Coppi was met by a sea of enthusiasm,' says the Indomitable Zipa, who was there to greet him. 'Then a tide of vehicles full of athletes and fans swept him to his hotel.'

It was the first time Colombia had lived such emotions since the early days of professional football in Colombia, when its wealthy clubs had ignored national wage caps to attract some of the world's finest footballers, like the Argentines Alfredo Di Stefano and Adolfo Pedernera, the outstanding former Manchester United left-winger Charlie Mitten, and later, the stars of Uruguay's 1950 World Cup winning side, among many others. But this era, known as El Dorado, had ended in 1954 to leave a vacuum in Colombian sport. Now, single handedly, Oscar Hernández had launched cycling's own El Dorado. Indeed, in Donald Raskin's opinion, Coppi had an even greater impact on Colombia than Di Stefano. 'Cycling was far more important than football. And anyway, Di Stefano had only come from Argentina. Coppi came from Italy, where the Vatican is. It was as if he had come from another, holier world.'

The following day Coppi went out to train with a few local riders. José Duarte, to whom Coppi's reception at the airport had seemed 'as if the Pope had just arrived', was one of the Colombians who rode with him. 'We headed north out of Bogotá. Coppi was in the autumn of his career, but he pedalled with ease and power and it was hard for us to stay on his wheel.' The man who had finished second and third in the previous two Tours of Colombia, Jorge Luque, was amazed: 'On the flat we couldn't stay with him. He was phenomenal; his style spellbinding.'

'But Luque was an extremely temperamental sort,' Duarte recalls, 'and as we turned to head home, he vented his anger: "He's putting us through hell. Listen, José, when we get to Patios" – a climb on the outskirts of Bogotá, seven kilometres of unmade road with a sharp gradient – "I'll give a signal and we'll show him what we're made of." And that day we beat them. I hadn't even ridden the Vuelta a Colombia, and Luque said to me, "You've just beaten the greatest rider on Earth."'

The following day, after training on the long Las Rosas climb south of Bogotá, Coppi commented, 'Colombia must have brilliant climbers.' He began to talk about inviting Colombian cyclists to compete in Europe. After three short days in Bogotá, he left for a series of business meetings in Argentina, promising to train hard between engagements to provide the paying public with value for money on his return on 2 January.

In his absence, Colombia plotted deicide. Teams were selected, led by Ramón Hoyos and Ephraim Forero. Training camps were organized. And in the meantime, Colombia's prestige in Latin American cycling grew exponentially. Venezuela and Panama arranged to dispatch their national teams directly after the Tour of Puerto Rico to learn from Coppi and Koblet. From all over Latin America requests arrived for the champions' presence. Endless unauthorized versions of Coppi's commitments began to circulate, fed by those seeking to associate themselves with the great man. Luigi Casola, one of Coppi's former *domestiques* temporarily resident in Colombia, even claimed to the press that Coppi had agreed to ride the 1958 Vuelta a Colombia.

On 2 January he was back. On the day of his second coming his promoter Hernández intervened. Coppi's presence at the Vuelta would cost 120,000 pesos, he claimed, and no less than three major business interests – all Antioquian – had independently agreed to shoulder the costs. Fostered by Casola, the rumours acquired intriguing details. Coppi would be returning for the Vuelta with two special team-mates: Riccardo Filippi, Forero's vanquisher at the world amateur championship in 1953, and Coppi's Bianchi team-mate Michele Gismondi, fourth in the 1953 and 1954 World Championships

It was true that in Italy, Coppi had already begun to organize his own cycling teams. Talking privately to Ramón Hoyos, he elaborated his plan to select eight Colombians, led by the Antioquian, to compete in the 1958 Tour of Italy from 18 May to 8 June. The Colombians would ride machines bearing the Coppi marque. Every idea, every thought, every utterance that passed the great man's lips was carved in stone, and tributes of hope placed before it. The fixed intensity of his slow, brown eyes and the gestures of his enormous hands were fascinating. Those who met him left convinced that the future of their nation's most important sport was safe with Fausto Coppi, the adopted archangel of Colombian cycling.

By the morning of Sunday 5 January, when 8000 spectators squeezed into the First of May Velodrome in Bogotá, Coppi's most longstanding *domestique*, Ettore Milano, had flown in from Italy to join him. A roar met their appearance on the track. Spellbound silence followed as the first race began, over twenty laps with intermediate sprint bonuses. Coppi didn't compete in the first sprint, allowing local rider Guillermo Campos to take the points. But Campos abandoned soon afterwards. The following three sprints all went to the Italian. With three laps to go, Coppi increased the pace. No Colombian had ever ridden so fast, and none attempted to stay with him. The Italian accelerated away to win alone.

A series of side-shows occupied the public as the riders towelled off. Then Coppi's second event began, an elimination race in which the last rider was excluded at the end of every other lap. And once again, it ended in a solo Coppi breakaway. He was in a class of his own.

Finally, in an eighty-lap race, Colombia triumphed. With two team-mates taking turns on the track, exchanging places by a hand-sling, Ramón Hoyos and Aureliano Gallón beat Ephraim Forero and Guillermo Campos. A poor performance from Luigi Casola relegated Coppi to third place. For the first time Colombians had prevailed over top-class European competition.

Very early the following morning, Coppi rode north out of Bogotá. 'To stay in form,' he said, 'you need to train everyday.' Casola and Milano rode with him. Their discipline amazed the Colombians, whose training regimes were comically lax by comparison. But Coppi recognized the quality of Colombia's human material. At the Hotel Continental in Bogotá he penned a note for *El Tiempo*: 'My first impressions of the Colombian cyclists have been excellent. I think they need greater contact with European cyclists, and also some good coaches to improve their training techniques, and above all their tactical awareness. Fausto Coppi, 6 Jan. 1958.' The newspaper published a facsimile of his note, as though by contemplating the loops and minims of Coppi's handwriting, the Colombians might somehow uncover the secret of his genius.

With the press, Coppi was circumspect about the possibility of competing in the Vuelta a Colombia. He was still a long way from reaching a decision. And on the subject of Colombians at the Giro d'Italia, he warned, both the riders and their fans would have to learn patience. 'It's an extremely difficult race, and they could risk deep disappointment with their results. But the journey is certainly feasible, and the riders need this experience with top class opposition. This, and working with excellent coaches, is the only way they will progress and develop their talent in this beautiful sport.'

Meanwhile, in a fifty-lap race with sprints every ten, the Antioquian rider Honorio Rúa Betancur beat Coppi into second place. It was a war of attrition: Coppi eventually fell while Rúa crossed the line with no front tyre. In Bogotá's El Campín velodrome the drama held 18,000 spectators rapt.

Rúa's victorious scrap with Coppi was tribute to his rare ability. Potentially the most complete rider of his generation in Colombia, Rúa's talent went to waste. Although an excellent climber, he had a tall, elegant physique suited to the track at a time when there were simply no specialized coaches in the country. Neglected by the Antioquian coaching staff who championed Ramón Hoyos, for whom he was an eternal *domestique*, Rúa's best Vuelta result was second overall in 1955. But two years later Rúa had set Colombia's first hour record. After New Year trials at Medellín velodrome, he travelled to Bogotá in February 1957 with his Argentine coach, Roberto Serafín Guerrero. There he spun silently through the thin air for sixty minutes, completing 44.198 kilometres.

A quiet man whose gentle demeanour belies the ferocious athleticism of his prime, Honorio Rúa's memories illustrate just how isolated the Colombia of the 1950s was from cycling's European homelands. 'Much later, Guerrero read in an old magazine that I had come close to a world record distance. If we'd known, I would have made a second attempt the following day.' As every European rider knew, an Italian named Carizzoni had ridden 44.026 kilometres at Milan in October 1954; later the same day, and on the same track, Ercole Baldini had surpassed him by 844 metres. It was a record that lay within Rúa's enormous reach, astonishingly for a man who had never trained systematically, in an age when the effects of altitude on endurance athletes were little understood.

Coppi suffered a slight fever after his accident in the fifty-lap race. The following morning he didn't train. Hernández held his breath – he was in financial difficulty, exacerbated by the Antioquian Cycling League's exorbitant fees for the use of its facilities.

Soon Hugo Koblet had flown in to join the circus. He had arrived in Bogotá the evening before the first meeting and watched from the stand. On 11 January he finally appeared at the First of May Velodrome with Coppi. Before he could stamp his authority on an eighty-lap race, a cloudburst washed out the meet. Earlier, Coppi had led the four-man Italian team to victory over Hoyos, Rúa, Herrón and Campos in a nine-lap pursuit race. The Italians were forcing their hosts to ever greater speeds. Had the race been held over 4000 metres, the Colombians would have set a national record of 4 minutes 39 seconds. When rain stopped play, Coppi was leading the eighty-lap event with just two sprints remaining.

Sunday 12 January, the last of the Bogotá exhibitions, saw Koblet compete for the first time. With his partner Sivilotti he won a tactical victory in the 100-lap race, lapping the field after thirty circuits. Later Coppi's partner, the Argentine Jorge Batiz, twice world silver medallist as a sprinter, won a one-lap flying start time trial. On the way he spurred the Colombians to record-breaking results. Rúa went first and equalled the track record of 26 seconds. Another local rider, Mario Vanegas, went one better by setting a Colombian national record of 25 seconds. Then the Argentine rode 24.8 seconds. The meetings, dubbed the International Cycling Series, had been a great success. Colombia's riders had gained invaluable experience and Antioquian cycling had demonstrated its primacy over the rest of the country.

On 13 January, Coppi, Koblet and their entourage flew to Medellín. There, at the Atanasio Girardot Velodrome, the tour continued on 18 January. Yet although the Colombian athletes were profiting greatly from the quality of the competition, the public was largely staying away, baulking at high ticket prices. Hernández was feeling the pinch.

The series finally ended on Saturday 25 January with a road race: two 80-kilometre semi-stages to the village of La Pintada, south from Medellín, and back. Sponsored by a Medellín-based national daily, the third '*El Colombiano* Classic' was to become legendary in Colombian cycling history.

The race left Medellín at 10.45 a.m., and the field stayed together as far as the village of Caldas. At this point Forero punctured, and a breakaway formed, including Koblet, Hoyos, Coppi, Casola and the eighteen-year-old Hernán Medina. When Luigi Casola felt his rear wheel soften, gaps began to appear between the leading riders. Hoyos and Coppi climbed the Alto de Minas in parallel. Six seconds behind them, Koblet prepared his pact with gravity, and on the way down towards La Pintada provided the Colombians with a master class in descending. He arrived at La Pintada forty-five seconds ahead of Hoyos, with Coppi third in the same time.

After an hour's rest at La Pintada, the participants departed in the order in which they had arrived. Looking to capitalize on his lead, Koblet attacked immediately, reaching the foot of the Alto de Minas climb a minute ahead of Hoyos and Coppi. But as he soon discovered, the gradient and extreme temperature, unknown in European races, gave the Colombians an insuperable advantage.

'On the stage from Medellín to La Pintada they'd toyed with us,' José Duarte remembers. 'But on the return leg all that changed. Because of its location, La Pintada is 40 degrees in the shade – unbearable. The ascent begins at La Pintada, and it's relentless. There are some forgiving metres where you can catch your breath, but very few. Early on the terrain varies, with steep sections that take you higher and higher and higher to a place called La Quiebra. From there the gradient is much more severe. You dig deep and dance out of the saddle from La Quiebra up to Santa Barbara, then Valparaíso and finally Minas.'

As Hoyos began to devour Koblet's lead, Ettore Milano, Coppi's great *domestique*, was forced to abandon with terrible sunstroke. Four decades later, from comfortable retirement in Italy, he told me, 'I decided not even to attempt the climb. I followed them in the broom wagon with a glass of cold Coke. Hoyos was incredible. He climbed like a man possessed.' The youngster Medina, seeing the Europeans begin to flag, passed them and joined the race leader.

Forero was also catching Coppi and Koblet. 'I had punctured twice on the outward leg and lost a lot of time. So I started quickly and soon had the Europeans in my sights. Amazingly, I was gaining on them fast. I increased my pace to try to reach them, but Koblet pulled over and stepped down.'

There are no newspaper accounts of what happened next, but a Medellín family witnessed the end of Coppi's race. I heard the story in the Museum of Antioquia in central Medellín – I was talking about the event with one of the curators when a visitor butted in. 'I was there,' she said, 'I'll tell you exactly what happened.'

Carmenza Angulo had been thirteen at the time. 'We always went to Minas to see the Vuelta a Colombia go past. The climb from La Pintada was incredibly steep and gave you plenty of time to get a good look at the riders. The stage from La Pintada to Medellín was normally halfway through the race, and the climb told you who would win the Vuelta. So it was our favourite vantage point.

'We'd left home at 5.30 that morning because they were closing the road at 6.00. We watched the riders descend, then ate our picnic. In the afternoon I saw Hoyos come past. But it was Coppi we'd all come to see.

'Finally he appeared, not dancing out of the saddle like Hoyos, but slumped back in the saddle, his face pale and bloodless. He was pedalling unbelievably slowly. As he drew closer, he wobbled violently, then right at my feet – he collapsed. I looked away, and when I looked back, I saw his face was green and his lips yellow. His eyes were rolling, mostly white. He was soon surrounded by medics and soigneurs trying to bring him round. It was tragic to see this great athlete reduced to such pathetic straits.'

Hoyos carried on, unaware of the drama behind him. He won the second mountain prize of the day at Minas, and on the descent dropped Medina. With only Colombians left in the race, Hoyos extended his lead, despite Medina's efforts, and won by three minutes forty-five seconds. At the Atanasio Girardot Stadium in Medellín, the crowd cheered their own. Coppi, Koblet and the other Europeans arrived at the finishing line by car. Europe suddenly seemed small.

THE RESULT WAS a brilliant vindication of Antioquian sport. But Ephraim Forero, the Indomitable Zipa, considered the event a cynical ploy to score regionalist points at the expense of venerable masters. 'The heat was intense that day. Coppi had come to ride in exhibitions, and they organized that cruel race. In my view it wasn't right. The event was held in order to see him defeated. On a varied, more undulating route the Europeans would have given us a tremendous show. You have to remember they weren't at their peak. The heat certainly affected them. But that day the Antioquians wanted to beat them at any price, so they planned a merciless race route to force him into submission. It was shameful, and we missed the chance to see Coppi really perform.'

Nonetheless, the following morning's news of Hoyos's victory covered the front page of *El Colombiano*. The strapline on the inside pages alluded to the truth: 'Beneath the tropical sky, the speed of Hoyos melted Koblet and Coppi.'

The international news agency Agence Presse France spread news of Coppi's defeat by Ramón Hoyos throughout the world. In Italy, Giro director Vincenzo Torriana was said to be examining the feasibility of an international team participating in the 1958 race. Australian riders had expressed an interest, led by sprinter Russell Mockridge. It was mooted that they join the South American athletes in a combined team, mirroring a proposed German–Swiss team including four riders from each nation.

Coppi, meanwhile, showed a champion's generosity in defeat. The Colombians had talent, he said, and with more experience their domestic successes could be confirmed abroad. 'He was very affectionate and open with everyone, despite his formidable record. Friendly and warm,' remembers the Zipa. 'Despite the fame and wealth, Coppi had the gift of simplicity, a greatness of spirit.' Speaking to the organizer of the '*El Colombiano* Classic', Coppi also outlined detailed plans for taking a Colombian team to Italy. His bicycle manufacturer would provide equipment, and the daily sports paper *La Gazzetta dello Sport*, the race owner, would contribute the team's travel expenses. Coppi also enthused about his future participation in the Vuelta a Colombia. He spoke of bringing a team, including Hugo Koblet, to avenge his defeat at Medellín, for which he offered no excuses.

THE VISIT OF Coppi and Koblet created a wave of enthusiasm. Plans to build velodromes were drawn up in towns all over Colombia. In Cali, the final destination of the European tourists, 1959 was designated 'The Year of the Velodrome'. And thanks to the enterprise of Oscar Hernández, Colombia's cyclists were already preparing for a triumphant return to Europe.

But the Zipa has more ambivalent memories. 'At that moment a huge public turned out to follow the Europeans. Everyone wanted to see them, to meet them. And for a while everyone wanted to get on a bike. But those of us who competed did so for love, nothing more. In the long term we cyclists were left with a few happy memories and little more.' And despite the general euphoria, within days the entire edifice of Colombian cycling seemed about to collapse.

Oscar Hernández accompanied his riders from Colombia to Mexico, where the Europeans didn't have the necessary licences to compete. Hernández evidently hadn't cleared the tour with the Mexican Cycling Federation. Oscar Salazar Montoya, the cycling correspondent of *El Colombiano*, witnessed the confusion: 'After several nights in the hotel, the manager asked Coppi to settle the accounts. Coppi was livid. He exchanged views with Hernández, and then Coppi and Koblet demanded immediate payment of their outstanding fees. Hernández wrote out a $5000 cheque for US made out to Koblet, who refused to accept it. He snatched Hernández' passport from his shirt pocket and using it as security demanded cash.

'Hernández was forced to go straight to the bank. He made a big show of taking me with him as a witness to prove his good faith. When we reached the bank he told me to wait outside. He closed the door behind him . . . and that was the last anyone ever saw of him, either in Mexico City or in Medellín. With the connivance of the bank tellers – and who knows what story he concocted? – he obviously left by another entrance and disappeared forever.'

Salazar, distraught, returned to the hotel. The bank officials had looked at the cheque made out to Koblet and told Salazar it was a worthless fake. 'Coppi and Koblet were deeply offended. But they were wealthy men and well known, and their embassies instantly provided them with travel passes and cash. Coppi returned to Italy with Batiz. Koblet decided to remain in Mexico to discuss several invitations to coach there. Casolla, Milano and Sivilotti had to sell their bikes and personal items in order to cover their hotel bills before returning to Colombia. I was left penniless and with no way of getting home.

Only the generosity of the Mexico Cycling Federation and local journalists helped me and Ramón Hoyos fly back to Colombia.'

In Colombia the facts became known only when Coppi's *domestique* Luigi Casola reached Bogotá on 18 February, raising fears that any appeal by Coppi or Koblet to one or other of the world governing bodies, the International Cycling Union or International Olympic Committee, could lead to censure and the collapse of whatever dreams of international competition Colombia was clinging to. In the event, Koblet contacted the Swiss Cycling Federation, which wrote in cordial terms to its Colombian equivalent. The Colombians promised to take up Koblet's case with Oscar Hernández, but in October 1958, when the case last surfaces in the press archives, it still hadn't been settled.

Meanwhile, recognizing Colombia's appetite for European competition, and stung by the propaganda coup of the Conservative and Antioquian *El Colombiano*, the Liberal Bogotá-based paper *El Tiempo* announced in block headlines on 28 February 1958, 'El Tiempo and Avianca will send a team to the Vuelta a España.' It would, according to *El Tiempo*, mark 'a transcendental and important turning point in the development of Colombian cycling's presence in international competition'.

It was desperate stuff, and on 15 March the surge of enthusiasm suddenly dispersed. According to its regulations, the Vuelta a España could admit only full teams of ten riders, a technical director, two mechanics, two soigneurs, three cars (two of which had to be Renaults) and four DKW vans. 'Spain imposes impossible conditions,' *El Tiempo* announced. The Colombian dream of competing with Europe's best riders was once more frustrated.

Later in 1958 a solitary Colombian did travel to compete in Europe. Ramón Hoyos Vallejo, who had won his fifth Vuelta a Colombia in May, was contracted by the Swedish bicycle manufacturer

Monark, which had a factory in Medellín, to ride a number of amateur events in Europe, culminating in a six-day track race in Stockholm starting on 29 August. In Milan, Hoyos encountered Coppi. The 1958 World Championship course in Reims, insisted the Italian, might have been designed with Hoyos in mind. The race was taking place on 31 August, during the Stockholm event. His ambitions whetted, Hoyos immediately contacted the Colombian Cycling Association asking for permission to ride in the competition. The reply was negative: the Association did not want to risk upsetting Monark, a major presence in Colombian industry. By the time a second letter arrived on 27 August, reversing the Association's earlier decision and authorizing Hoyos to ride in France, he had fixed his travel plans. Hoyos dutifully flew to Stockholm the following day, only to learn that the six-day competition had been postponed until 11 September. But it was too late: there was no way of reaching Reims in time.

Time and time again, Colombia stood on the brink of international recognition. Each time some chaotic factor sent her lurching towards frustration. Colombia's moment would come – but not just yet. Furthermore, the Colombia Cycling Association's avowed amateur status prevented Hoyos from making money as a professional athlete in Europe. 'I could have turned professional,' he reflects. 'Coppi was prepared to give me an excellent reference. I only had to say the word. I could have earned enough money cycling to pay my way, because I received little financial help from Monark. But each time the opportunity arose, I thought of my country. I wanted to represent Colombia for as long as possible. That is why I didn't take that final step.' Hoyos returned to Colombia dejected.

For virtually all of Coppi's *domestiques* the Colombian trip marked a turning point. In Mexico, Casola fell in love and later married. There he coached and joined the Vuelta a Mexico organization, supervising nine national tours and bringing men like Stan Ockers, 1955

World Champion, and Rik Van Steenbergen, World Champion in 1949, 1956 and 1957, to compete in Latin America. Batiz, the Argentine, travelled to Italy, where Coppi arranged for him to compete on road and track. Milano travelled to Caracas where he raced for the last time before returning home to Novi Ligure, near Alessandria in north-west Italy, to take up coaching.

Strangely, for all the biographies of Coppi and Koblet in Italian and French – and Coppi, especially, is the subject of a mountain of publications – none mentions their Colombian adventure. And both men returned home cursed by destiny.

Colombia's call to Coppi had coincided with a wanderlust that gripped him in his late thirties, which in December 1959 saw him accept an invitation from the government of Upper Volta (now Burkina Faso) to celebrate Independence Day with an exhibition criterium around the capital Ouagadougou. A subsequent day's hunting on the savannah with the cream of French cycling – Henri Anglade, Jacques Anquetil, Raphael Geminiani, Roger Hassenforder and Roger Rivière – proved mosquito-infested, and when the party returned home, Coppi and Geminiani complained of flu symptoms. The Frenchman was diagnosed with *plasmodium falciparum*, a lethal strain of malaria. Coppi's doctors rejected the diagnosis and treated their patient for double haemorrhagic viral pneumonia. According to the accepted version, Coppi lost his life to a diagnostic error, although some now claim that he was poisoned by local witch doctors. Whatever the truth, he could not be saved, and died on 2 January 1960, aged forty. The day of his death was also, coincidentally, the day of Ramón Hoyos's marriage. The Colombian was leaving the church, surrounded by well-wishers and photographers, when he heard the news of his friend's death.

Koblet meanwhile returned home early in the 1960s to be beset by financial problems and a broken marriage. On 2 November 1964 he crashed his own white Alfa Romeo at high speed and died four days later, aged thirty-nine. The only witness believed the crash had been deliberate.

HOYOS'S 1958 VUELTA a Colombia win was fuelled by anger: 'I wanted to prove I didn't need help to win the Vuelta.' He took just two stage wins to triumph by eighteen full minutes over Hernán Medina. It was his final Vuelta win. His appetite for suffering was sated; he could finish just fourth in 1959 and again in 1960, when his single stage win lifted his career total to thirty-eight. In 1964 he attempted a comeback. But by then a new generation of Antioquian riders had appeared whose young years would not redeem the passage of his age. Hoyos made the team, but only to carry water and protect from the wind more youthful, stronger riders as, in cycling parlance, a *domestique*.

Cycling had made Hoyos one of the most famous men in Colombia. Already portrayed in the press by Gabriel García Márquez, Hoyos was depicted by the Colombian Postal Service on two 1957 postage stamps marked 'Extra Rápido'. The stamps were issued, ironically, to celebrate the seventh Vuelta a Colombia – the race from which Hoyos and his team-mates had retired.

A year later Colombia's most celebrated artist, Fernando Botero, painted *The Apotheosis of Ramón Hoyos* for exhibition at the 1959 Colombian Salon. And whereas García Márquez's first impression of Hoyos – one he soon revised – was 'of a boy with a sickly body and a crude spirit', Botero depicts him as a massive brute with disfigured shoulders and huge, shapeless fingers, his face dark with the mud of competition. He towers over a heap of ten serene-faced corpses, some decaying, all bloated, hands raised as if death had caught them at prayer. Tiny cycling caps cling to their scalps. Four sunflowers dot the pile of bodies, recalling the winner's bouquet. His grotesque figure rests its right hand on the handlebars of a rudimentary bicycle the colour of wood. His left arm is extended sideways: he resembles a matador taking the crowd's applause or a leading man inviting it for his cast. Beneath the huge limb another massive figure leans slumped into his armpit. The composition is flooded with shades of red, from fresh pink to the left of the champion, above the more recently deceased, to a dark, congealed purple to his right, over blue and yellow heads now putrid with decay. Below his outstretched hand is what appears to be the handle of a knife whose blade penetrates the chest of Hoyos's most recent victim. Behind him, a garish, unidentifiable flag; on the lower edge of the composition, a tiny Colombian flag disappears from the canvas.

By bloating his figures until they fill the canvas, Botero suppressed the background contexts, which fail to contain the figures he depicts. Colombian art critic Marta Traba described the canvas as 'an x-ray of the country, its misery, and the profound vitality that prevents it from sinking entirely – even when relentless forces seem to propel it into the depths'. 'What is left,' Traba goes on to ask, 'to a country so drastically marginalized from the normal processes of economic and political development?' She supplies her own response: 'Its great personalities and the possibility of reportage.'

While Hoyos received the attentions of writers and artists, Hernán Medina was paid the most precious of homages by a rival of flawless credentials. Robbed of the 1957 Vuelta by the politics of sponsorship, Medina had the satisfaction of presiding over Hoyos's decline. Medina was victorious just once, in the 1960 Vuelta, but finished second in 1958, 1959 and 1961. Competing in the 1961 race with the Spanish amateur team was twenty-four-year-old Julio Jiménez, who finished fourth overall. The following year Jiménez was King of the Mountains in the Vuelta a España. Second in the 1967 Tour de France, he won five Tour stages in his career and was three times King of the Mountains. When asked who was the finest climber in the world, Jiménez replied that it was a young amateur rider in distant Colombia: his name was Hernán Medina Calderón.

But when Medina retired from competitive cycling in 1962, the great Antioquians of the 1950s disappeared.

THE RELATIONSHIP BETWEEN industry and cycling in Colombia was symbiotic. Sponsorship from Medellín's huge textiles mills secured the cycling's future; and by winning five Tours of Colombia, Hoyos's success secured Coltejer's primacy in Colombian industry. But the reason for the success of the Antioquian teams of the 1950s perhaps ran deeper into the region's popular culture.

One local conviction, firmly held even today when cable television and syndicated magazines bombard the Medellín male with images of the most celebrated female flesh, is that the womenfolk of Antioquia are the most beautiful in the world. Cycling answered the Antioquian male's need to impress the objects of his desire with shows of strength and stamina.

And then there was the region's traditional cuisine, which provided small farmers, and now the riders, who came from the same peasant stock, with the carbohydrate fuel they required. The *arepa*, a grilled pancake of sweetcorn pulp, butter and salt, provided the ideal pre-race breakfast. The Antioquian appetite for *mazamorra*, a maize broth with milk and sugar, and *natilla*, a maize starch blancmange, earned Medellín's riders the epithet of 'maizeros' or maize-men. The term proudly echoes the nickname 'mazamorreros' or mazamorra-eaters, applied to the independent miners who had founded Antioquia's regional identity 150 years before.

The regional cuisine was celebrated in a medley of popular songs dedicated to the triumphant Antioquian teams of the 1950s. 'Viva la Arepa' ('Long Live the Arepa') depicts cycling as a show of virility powered by the miracle-foods of the local culture:

Que viva la arepa y viva la natilla
Que producen fuerza en la pantorilla;
Que viva la arepa y la mazamorra
Que producen fuerza en la cachiporra.

Long live the arepa and natilla
Which strengthen the calves;
Long live the arepa and mazamorra
Which strengthen the loins.

Another popular song, 'No pueden ya con el equipo antioqueño' ('They Can't Compete with the Antioquian Team') attributes their invincibility to the food and the landscape:

La arepa siempre se impone
Donde quiera que la llamen.
Que coge todo el maíz
Aunque algunos le reclamen.

Ramón Hoyos el valiente
En esta tierra nació.
Que vivan los antioqueños
Orgullo de esta región.

The arepa always wins
Wherever it goes.
Let the maize win all the prizes
Whether the others like it or not.

Ramón Hoyos the Brave
Was born in this land.

Long live the Antioquians,
The pride of the region.

By defeating amateur national teams from Argentina, Mexico and Spain, the Antioquians could feel more than a mere region, a cycling superpower on the international stage. In 'Los valientes del pedal' ('The valiant champions of the pedal'), written during the 1958 Tour when Hoyos returned to winning ways, the Antioquians become Colombia's *de facto* national team. The names of the key riders are enshrined in mnemonic verse:

En esta Vuelta a Colombia
Los paisas vuelven a ganar
Porque ni los extranjeros
Les igualan para esperar.

Que vivan los antioqueños
Orgullo de esta nación.

Con Hoyos, Zapata y Mesa
Otálvaro, y Gallón,
Con Honorio Rúa y Medina
Han sido la sensación.

Que vivan…

Sevillano el argentino
A Ramón Hoyos lo quiso ganar
Pero llegó a la meta fundido
Y ya se iba a desmayar.

Que vivan . . .

The Paisas have won
The Tour of Colombia again
Not even the overseas riders
Had a hope of equalling them.

Long live the Antioquians
The pride of Colombia.

With Hoyos, Zapata and Mesa,
Otálvaro and Gallón,
With Honorio Rúa and Medina
They were the sensation of the race.

Long live . . .

The Argentine Sevillano
Wanted to defeat Ramón Hoyos
But he arrived at the finish exhausted
And on the point of collapse.

Long live . . .

Long after the age of the great Antioquians had passed, the melodies echoed down the years from scratchy seventy-eights.

5. The independent republics

It's very early. The wind chill picks through your clothing. Bogotá's buses loom out of the night's depths and dive into the bitter morning. Sunrise reveals the brilliant plumage and chromium bumpers of the coachwork, grumbling like obese birds of paradise. The night quietly diffuses behind their huge windscreens, which thrust dim lists of place-names into the sky.

The names of these Bogotá neighbourhoods speak of all human history: bus routes lead to Palestine and Egypt, Jericho, Jerusalem, Bethlehem, even Babylon. There are pilgrimages to the suburb of Lourdes, grand tours to the residencies of Rome, Florence and Venice. Buses go to the housing projects at Casablanca and Meissen, Armenia and Potosí, the Divino Rostro – the Divine Face – and to Paradise itself. The communities with the most other-worldly aspirations are also the humblest.

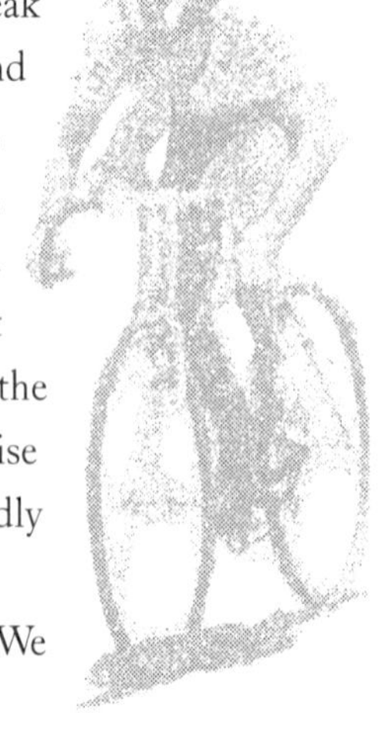

I boarded a service heading north out of Bogotá. We

reached cruising speed on the dips and bends leading down into the heat. I sank into my seat, and the early start and the drone of the engine wooed me into sleepy meditations on mountains. Natural obstacles will always frustrate what we call development, but bike racing, I mused, turns the topography to its advantage. It even imbues these mountainous obstructions with pride. Anything but indifferent rock, they are Minas, Letras and La Línea – the great passes of the Vuelta a Colombia. But a national bike race also depends on roads and bridges, fuel stations and accommodation, food and water, power for television and radio, and telephones for the print journalists. In other words, if the national tour is running, the inhabitants know that the country is in at least passable health.

The Tour of Colombia will never incorporate the forested expanse of Colombia's Oriente – departments like Vichada, Guainia, Vaupés, Putumayo – forested areas where State weakness and sometime ineffectual vigilance have allowed guerrilla activity and coca production to flourish. But the Vuelta a Colombia, it seemed to me, remained a structure with which to imagine the nation. Where Colombia's history appears locked in circular time, its tragedies endlessly repeated, cycling converts that circular motion into linear progress. And in this intensely Catholic culture, where the mountains point to heaven like cathedral spires, a nation acts out the struggle for paradise in the heroic ascents of its cyclists. The superimposed memories of countless bike races form a network of lines connecting distant realities.

With repeated jolts out of narcosis, my disorientation deepened. Other people's curiosity began to unsettle me. The rising temperature, the tropical foliage, the knowledge that guerrillas fished for hostages along these roads; all this was now helping to give my contemplation a fevered edge. It occurred to me that the discipline of Colombia's cyclists honours humanity's immemorial techniques of spiritual quest. They pursue self-emaciation, pay almost tantric attention to breathing and heart rate, and expose body and mind to gruelling pain. But why? Because to do so, it seemed to me, is to suspend their nation's travails and tend it with spiritual relief. The Vuelta a Colombia, I concluded, heals wounds in the national psyche. We were drawing near my journey's end now. Medellín, and the greatest Colombian rider of the modern era.

BY THE END of the 1950s the personnel of Colombian cycling were changing. After his long tyranny, during which not even his most trusted team-mates were allowed token wins, Hoyos was waning. His natural heir was the brilliant Hernán Medina. But then a tiny man from the coffee town of Pereira, Ruben Darío Gómez, temporarily became the custodian of the tradition. Another magnificent climber, he won the Vuelta a Colombia in 1959 and 1961, was second twice, and won the Tour of Guatemala in 1964. He also won the first edition of an event that years later would supplant the Vuelta as Colombia's most glamorous bike race, the 'RCN Classic', sponsored by the TV and radio network Radio Cadena Nacional under the aegis of its subsidiary, the Voice of Medellín radio station. Yet although Ruben Darío Gómez had won that first RCN Classic by a massive margin, he was soon replaced at the helm of Colombian cycling by the teenager who finished second, thirty-two minutes and fifty-seven seconds adrift.

'Cochise' Rodríguez took his nickname from a 1951 Western. When Jeff Chandler played the Apache chief Cochise in the movie *Broken Arrow*, Martín Emilio Rodríguez Gutiérrez was a child. But the nickname stuck all his life, and half a century later, every Colombian knows Cochise, Medellín's greatest citizen.

As the riders of Arrastía's great Antioquian teams had begun to retire, the task of producing their heirs had fallen to two private citizens of Medellín: a medical doctor named Vinicius Echeverry and his partner, Isabel Ángel, whose firm Caribu represented Wrangler jeans in Colombia. Together they ran the Club Mediofondo, an

The La Linea mountain climb
100 km from Armenia to Ibagué
CALDAS
TOLIMA
Calarcá
Armenia
La Línea
Cajamarca
Ibagué
Barcelona
Boquerón
Santa Marta
Barranquilla
ATLÁNTICO
Cartagena
GUAJIRA
MAGDALENA
CESAR
Sincelejo
SUCRE
Montería
PANAMA
VENEZUELA
BOLÍVAR
NORTE DE SANTANDER
CÓRDOBA
Caucasia
TÁCHIRA
N
Yarumal
SANTANDER
ANTIOQUIA
Medellín
Alto de Minas
Santa Bárbara
La Pintada
BOYACÁ
CHOCÓ
Ríosucio
① RISARALDA
② CALDAS
③ QUINDÍO
Manizales
CUNDINAMARCA
CASANARE
Pereira
Bogotá
Armenia
Ibagué
Girardot
ALTO SUMAPAZ
Tulua
EL DUDA
VALLE DEL CAUCA
Buga
TOLIMA
META
ALTO ARIARI
Cali
MARQUETALIA
Neiva
RIO CHIQUITO
GUAYABERO
CAUCA
HUILA
EL PATO
GUAVIARE
NARIÑO
CAQUETÁ
PUTUMAYO
ECUADOR
The Independent Republics
Route of 1964 Vuelta a Colombia
0 100 200 miles
0 100 200 300 km
Medellín to La Pintada and back
Altitude (m)
4500
4000
3500
3000
2500
2000
1500
1000
500
0
Depart Medellín 1542m
Caldas 1750m
Alto de Minas 2244m
Versalles 2200m
Santa Bárbara 1750m
Bella Vista 1040m
La Pintada 550m
La Bucana 550m
La Pintada 550m
Bella Vista 1040m
Santa Bárbara 1750
Versalles 2200m
Alto de Minas 2244m
Caldas 1750m
Estadio Atanasio Girardot Medellín 1476m
km 0 10 20 30 40 50 60 70 80 90 100 110 120 130 140 150
22.0km
69.0km
116.1km
152.0km

impromptu cycling club for teenagers that produced the major talents of the 1960s: Javier Suárez, a brilliant climber recognizable by his magnificent proboscis and ironically dubbed Pugnose; Gabriel Halaixt Buitrago, the winner of the 1964 RCN Classic; Mario 'Papaya' Vanegas, a kilometre sprinter on the track, who had a great international career; and Roberto Escobar, known as the Bear, who represented his country in the team time trial to great success, but is now chiefly associated with his younger brother Pablo, who years later became the archetypal cocaine lord.

Eighty-four and still competing on his bike, Dr Vinicius is a strange mixture of old age and physical strength. Given the opportunity, he'll seize your hand and thrust it into his tensed abdominals – 'Feel that!' – and insist you contact the Guinness Book of Records to check whether he's the world's oldest competitive cyclist. 'Martín came to us when he was eighteen,' he remembers. 'His legs were skinny but his thoracic expansion was seven inches. I remember it even today. What incredible lungs! I gave him a bike, and trained him on road and track. I put together teams of four to compete against him over 4000 metres. The quartets he trained against were made up of riders who later rode internationally. He beat them time after time.'

Cochise is not a youngster any more, of course, and when he invites you into his home, you feel he's the one that's out of place. Or out of time. You can still make out the physique, the enormous lung capacity, which would have characterized the athlete in his prime, in the jolly man with the grey moustache approaching sixty. He's playful and quick to laugh and, with his almost incomprehensible Medellín dialect, makes no concessions to the foreigner. No one could be more Antioquian; no one embodies Medellín so completely. But he seems a stranger to his own clothes. The athlete has gone now. Only the man remains.

Two weeks after Cochise was born, his father, a peasant-farmer, died. As a teenager, Cochise found work as a cycle courier for a pharmacy. A year later he met Pugnose Suárez. On Dr Vinicius's advice, they pooled their earnings and bought milk and bananas. 'Ninety-nine per cent of Colombia's cyclists began like us, earning a living by making deliveries. We were all the sons of peasant farmers who had moved to the towns. It was the same for Hoyos and his generation, and for those who came after us.'

His first Vuelta was in 1961. He was eighteen. From Pereira to Cali, a flat stage along the Cauca River, he attacked. Another rider joined him but refused to share the workload. Cochise led for nearly five hours. Fifteen minutes from the stage finish at Cali he was caught. The stage was won by the Spaniard, Julio Jiménez. 'I was angry. If my breakaway companion had worked with me, I'd have given him the stage win and taken the leader's jersey myself. But in those days team directors were tactically very naïve.'

Julio Jiménez was soon a legend in European road racing. Three times King of the Mountains in the Tour de France and second overall in 1967, Jiménez rode against giants like Eddy Merckx, Jacques Anquetil and Felice Gimondi. But when I spoke to him thirty years later, his memory of Cochise had not been appeased. 'Cochise was still a teenager, but he was already a complete cyclist. Not the classic Colombian climber, but an enormously powerful physique. Today you'd say he had the constitution of Miguel Induráin. He won a stage and finished a couple of places behind me in the General Classification. Anyone could see that he was going to become a monster.'

After the event, the Spanish team had to wait weeks for a flight home. While they were waiting, they were offered money to take on their Colombian rivals in a series of exhibitions. Assuming they meant track racing, the Spaniards agreed. It transpired that the challenge was to fight bulls. 'They assumed that since we were Spanish, we must be toreadors. But we had no idea about bull fighting. We trained at the Plaza de Toros in Bogotá with young animals, then flew down to Cali.

We took on Hernán Medina, Roberto Buitrago and the Zipa Forero. When our turn came, two of my team-mates, Martín Piñera and Juan Escolá, refused to fight. Ángel Guardiola went out to perform and survived. Then it was my turn. I wasn't doing badly, but then the bull caught me and threw me in the air. Thankfully I wasn't hurt, but it was the end of my career as a matador.'

The Zipa told me, 'The only way a Colombian cyclist could survive was to perform stunts like that. We were risking life and limb for paltry sums, but we had no choice.'

AS JIMÉNEZ RECOVERED from his venture into bull-fighting, Colombia's ruling class awoke to their nation's disintegration. In November 1961 a Conservative senator told Congress, 'It has not been recognized that there are in this country a series of independent republics which do not recognize the sovereignty of the State, where the army may not tread. The national sovereignty is shrinking like a handkerchief. The president will go down in history as the founder of five independent republics.' The speech augured a new era of violence and a new era in the relations between city and country.

Today the boutiques, bookshops and conspicuous consumption of Colombia's cities suggest an urban identity far removed from the daily struggle to scratch survival from the earth. But the nation's systems analysts and economists are sons and daughters of the peasantry, and over even the most sophisticated suburbs, the countryside is reflected in the polished surface of the sky.

The independent republics grew out of conditions that already existed at the end of World War II. Seventy per cent of the population lived in the countryside, 50 per cent was illiterate and just 3 per cent controlled half of all titled land. In 1944 the landed oligarchy had passed laws to prevent settlers seeking title to the parcels they had hacked from the virgin landscape.

Colombia was expanding inwards. Yet, as the borders were forced back, the institutions of State were nowhere to be seen. Communities fleeing the violence were forming an internal diaspora. Mule trains crossed the valleys of the south and the eastern plains. Peasant farmers settled on hillsides and prepared to defend them. And while the disputed terrains were opened, there were prior occupiers to be absorbed or expelled, and livestock to rustle for hungry children.

Some of the rebels, who had started by questioning the land laws, ended up rejecting the concept of property altogether. In 1949 Conservative henchmen began a campaign of terror against one such group of peasant proto-Communists in Tolima. Uprooted families fled south into the shadow of the 5,750-metre Nevado del Huila, where they merged with the Liberal guerrillas. One of the peasant leaders, known by his alias, Manuel Marulanda Vélez, or the nickname 'Tirofijo' ('Sureshot'), later recalled, 'The march lasted three months: we set off, doubled back in the face of police attacks, and zigzagged through two townships.' He settled on an inaccessible mountainside known as El Támaro, and renamed the colony's 5000 square kilometres Marquetalia, after a Caldas village.

In December 1952 another column left the hills above Melgar in northern Tolima for the cruel mountains of Sumapaz, south of Bogotá. The march lasted four months.

Violence flared between Liberals and Communists. Their differing responses to the Rojas Pinilla coup in June 1953 had hardened the differences: the Liberal freedom fighters had laid down their arms, while the Communists had merely looked on in suspicion.

Colombia, in short, was storing up misery for the future, and the names of Marquetalia and Sumapaz were to resonate down its history for the following half-century. But they were just two of half a dozen new territories opened by the peasant-guerrillas in the mid-1950s. Alto Sumapaz and its neighbour El Duda were spread over 1,010 square kilometres high in the eastern cordillera where Cundinamarca meets Meta and Huila. Another, Ariari, sat on Colombia's eastern plains in the department of Meta, where the extraordinary rock formation of Serranía de La Macarena rises abruptly to 975 metres. Ariari extended over 3,885 square kilometres. Midway between the Paramo of Sumapaz and La Macarena lay Guayabero, covering more than 2,070 square kilometres. On the western slopes of the central cordillera, to the south of the Nevado del Huila, Riochiquito covered 777 square kilometres. And El Pato, the last of the settlements, took its name from the El Pato River, draining south-westwards from the eastern chain of the Andes through the north-eastern extent of Cáqueta. The collective surface area of the independent republics was lost in Colombia's immensity. Between them, colonist-guerrillas circulated constantly, moving by night, learning to leave no trace.

Colombia's cyclists moved in parallel with the diaspora. Their ordeals mirrored the rigours of the route march: they, too, wandered the landscape and became homeless. They may have done so temporarily, and through choice, but they expressed something about their nation in a language that was neither violent nor despairing.

Meanwhile, in May 1957 far away in Bogotá, allegations of corruption brought down Rojas Pinilla. A cosy pact between Liberals and Conservatives replaced him, and a military junta supervised the transition to civilian government. In May 1958 the new government's first act was to enshrine alternating Liberal and Conservative administrations for the following sixteen years in the Constitution. The arrangement was patriotically named the National Front. Yet it effectively disenfranchised the nation, and having done so, the president then appealed to it to dedicate itself to the supreme task of suppressing the violence. An absurd show trial followed, at which the disgraced Rojas Pinilla was stripped of his civil and political rights – only for the Supreme Court to restore them just as quickly. The principal victim was democracy itself.

The National Front guaranteed Liberal and Conservative privileges but did nothing to restore property lost during the violence, or resurrect the dead. As traditional battle lines dissolved, the conflict between expansionist landlords and an armed peasantry became fragmented and bloody. There was timid talk of an amnesty for perpetrators of political violence, with conditions attached. But the proposed rehabilitation schemes were soon snuffed out: the political battle between those favouring conciliation and the hawks who took the line of confrontation paralysed the coalition, and the proposed far-reaching programme of social inclusion achieved no more than a police checkpoint at every crossroads. The roads themselves became a symbol of exclusion. The only traffic excluded from the conflict was the cyclists. 'In the valleys you'd shake hands with the generals,' the Zipa told me, 'and in the mountains you'd see the guerrillas at the roadside.'

And as the National Front proved its inability to incorporate the new territories into Colombia's social fabric, ripples from the Caribbean north flowed over Latin America. In Cuba in 1959 rebels led by Fidel Castro and Che Guevara defeated the incompetent generals of the despot Batista. In Colombia, as the economy slumped and even the parliamentary left-wing threatened to take up arms, the peasant self-defence movements – inspired by the successes of the Cubans – began to transform themselves into a revolutionary army. The autonomous settlements became the revolution's feed stations. Their peasant-farmers trained as resistance fighters. They studied Marxism and Mao's Long March.

In May 1959 central Bogotá was crowded with 200,000 people or more to see the President and his ministers wave off the ninth Vuelta a Colombia. Restlessness and aggression gripped the country; roaming the landscapes of the national unconscious was a death squad for every colour on the political spectrum. Yet Colombia gathered at its roadsides and radios to follow the cyclists. Cycling alone could reflect the nation back to itself in a form it could recognize. 'It brought the country together,' Donald Raskin remembers. 'It was a national cult. The country's radios were tuned into it continuously. Every big radio station broadcast race commentaries, and at times there were nine transmitting vehicles following the race; the logistics were very interesting. The Vuelta outweighed the violence in the nation's mind.'

Cuba, however, changed the international framework of Latin America's rebels. By the start of the 1960s the Conservative president, Guillermo León Valencia, could choose to view them as a Cold War threat, and appointed a war minister who had commanded Colombia's troops in Korea. Superpower interference aggravated the situation. In 1962 US President John F. Kennedy dispatched a military mission to Colombia to train the security forces in paramilitary, sabotage and terrorist tactics. It was part of the US strategy of converting the Latin American military from 'hemispheric defence' to 'internal security' – in other words, turning them against the domestic population. In 1961 the military raided the colony of Marquetalia and in 1962 Guayabero. The inhabitants of the autonomous peasant settlements addressed a series of appeals to the government to lift the state of siege and suspend hostilities. Bogotá's response was to arm irregular squads of mercenaries financed by local *latifundistas*. It explained away the measure as 'maintaining the existing equilibrium between armed bands'.

IT WAS AGAINST this escalating crisis that Cochise's early career developed. The departure of stage three of the 1962 Vuelta was held up for three hours after Tirofijo's troops were spotted on the slopes of La Línea. The caravan eventually departed, with misgivings. Javier Suárez dominated the climb, but descended slowly on the slippery road for fear of a fall and lost the stage. Cochise, with three stage wins, lost the Vuelta by eight seconds. The following year he returned to fulfil his promise, by winning six stages and the General Classification.

Since his Club Mediofondo apprenticeship, Cochise had been sponsored by Isabel Ángel, whose Wrangler franchise now grew and grew, nourished by the publicity of its cycling team. Her Caribu company had no more than fifteen employees, yet in the 1960s Isabelita's Wrangler-Caribu cycling team became the phenomenon of Colombian sport. By 1964 Cochise was a national figure.

Marquetalia, meanwhile, had been targeted by the government as the first independent republic to be restored to the nation because, as one of the officers entrusted with the campaign explained subsequently, it was the closest to economic, geographical and political centres. But it was well protected by the surrounding terrain and commanded by the most established and capable guerrilla leader. Colonel José Joaquín Matallana wrote, '*Tirofijo* had the best strategic mind, the greatest determination, the most combat experience and the deepest political conviction.' When several troops were shot dead in 1963, on the slopes beneath Marquetalia, the army blamed Tirofijo. The State called on the military to destroy the insurgents and return the Nevado to the rule of law.

Government preparations during April and May 1964 included a much-publicized pledge to invest in infrastructure. Given the terrain and the consent of many of the extremely poor locals to the rebels' cause, civilian casualties would be the inevitable consequence of any assault on Marquetalia. Hostilities were to begin in June, the month of the fourteenth Vuelta a Colombia. Colombia was already bating its breath in anticipation of Cochise's shows of strength, and now the Vuelta provided the armed forces with the perfect smokescreen. With popular feeling focussed on the race, the generals were free to wage total war.

Operation Marquetalia met the modest demands of the peasants – a school, a road, freedom from fear – with disproportionate and overwhelming violence, backed by Washington. Although Tirofijo was talked up as an evil genius, the reality was that US helicopters and fighter-bombers, supported by an army of 14,000, stood before a ragamuffin peasant force of less than a hundred. It was Vietnam in a teacup. The campaign began on 14 May but there was no fighting until 27 May, well below Marquetalia. It was the first of a series of skirmishes that continued for ten days. On 6 June helicopters buzzed the area. On 7 June two reconnaissance aircraft flew overhead, taking stills and moving images. And on 8 June, as US-sponsored bombers prepared to strafe the peasant communities, the Vuelta began. In the calm before the serious hostilities, Cochise's team-mate Halaixt Buitrago won stage one and donned the yellow jersey in Barranquilla. As stage two rolled into Cartagena, the press reported the deaths of three guerrillas. Stage three belonged to Cochise, who took over the leader's jersey by three seconds.

As Cochise found his rhythm on the early, flat stages, *El Tiempo*'s coverage fell into a pattern. The front page was headlined with Marquetalia, flanked each day with a cover photograph from the Vuelta. The press collaborated with the government by understating the terror and factoring down the casualties. On Tuesday 10 June the story describing 'Three of Tirofijo's Insurgents Killed' ran beside a photograph captioned 'Prize for Effort: a beautiful Cartagena girl rewards stage winner Julio Roberto Caro.' Two days later, 'Two More Bandits die in Marquetalia' was juxtaposed with another picture captioned 'Contrasts in the Vuelta: yesterday's stage winner Hernán Herrón signs autographs (left), and (right) a mule blocks the peloton during the race.'

On Saturday 14 June the race reached the hills and the real Vuelta began. Fighter-bombers unleashed 500kg bombs on the enemy – two guerrilla bands of forty men each – and local homesteads. On the road to Yarumal, Cochise finished third behind another team-mate, Pugnose Suárez, and extended his overall lead to three minutes. Under cover of the aerial bombardment, the 14,000 troops moved in.

Initially, splitting into small platoons and blending into a landscape they knew intimately, Tirofijo's guerrillas inflicted grave damage on the army. But as Cochise's Antioquia 'A' – Cochise, Suárez, Halaixt Buitrago and Hoyos – took stage after stage, the army reversed its fortunes, and Tirofijo lost many of his most valued lieutenants. Faced with insuperable odds, the guerrillas were being overwhelmed.

Suddenly, the massive government forces found themselves alone. The rebels had melted into the forest. On Monday 15 June 1964 *El Tiempo* trumpeted a decisive victory: 'End of the Independent Republics: "Marquetalia" pacified. Army takes total control of the region.' A front-page still beside the war coverage showed Cochise in solitary sacrifice racing towards his home town of Medellín, his second stage win of the race and a huge advantage in the General Classification. In the sports section on page nineteen the banner was 'Total Antioquian Domination'. Cochise was building a commanding lead in the Vuelta. By winning the Medellín stage by nine minutes, he tightened his grip on the leader's jersey.

The Antioquians were in ecstasy: they knew the Vuelta was won. Behind Cochise, soigneur Darío Herrera Buitrago accompanied his faithful *domestique* Halaixt Buitrago towards second place in the stage. Speeding through the crowds, stretched out of the car window with a wide grin on his face, he didn't see the horse tied at the roadside. The impact killed him before the awareness of death could cool his happiness. His lifeless corpse still bore a wide smile. It was stage seven.

Day after day Cochise rode in first: to Pereira, Manizales and Tulúa. To Buga, Ibagué and Guamo. On stages seventeen, from Guamo to Neiva, and eighteen, Neiva to Girardot, the race threaded its way between the seven independent republics. On 27 June 300,000 people lined the streets of Bogotá to welcome the Vuelta home and celebrate Cochise's victory. Squeezed along the streets of the capital and into the velodrome, they screamed a nation's admiration and relief.

Cochise had accumulated nine stage wins, overall victory by an hour and four minutes, and all the category titles.

The events of June 1964 left a permanent impression on the Colombian consciousness. The Marquetalia débâcle transfigured Cochise. In a fractured nation where no political leader was capable of rising above the chaos, he was now more than an athlete: he had taken on the aura of a messenger, passing freely between the visible and invisible realms, writing Colombia's unifying myth in the language of cycling.

Reports of Tirofijo's defeat, however, were premature. The search for him continued. Rumours had him on a mysterious flight bound for Cuba or lost in the infinity of the eastern plains. In fact, using secret routes, he and his men had retreated undetected through the porous blockade to reach supplies stored high in the mountains, then through the central cordillera to the Independent Republic of Riochiquito. There he held the first Conference of the Southern Bloc Guerrilla. In 1965 the military attacked the independent republics of Riochiquito and El Pato, and at a second Conference from April to May 1966 the loose militia of the peasant settlers were transformed into a co-ordinated national guerrilla army, the Revolutionary Armed Forces of Colombia, or FARC.* By confronting Colombia's dislocations with arms, the ruling regime had created the nemesis it most feared. The march of Manuel Marulanda Vélez, Tirofijo, has lasted over half a century. Today, thirty-five years on, the FARC remain in the

* The mid-1960s saw a proliferation of left-wing subversive groups in Colombia. Besides FARC, Colombia's second largest guerrilla army, the National Liberation Army, or ELN, had been founded the previous year, on 4 July 1964, by activists educated in Cuba. The People's Liberation Army, or EPL, was created on 17 December 1967 with the aim of 'destroying the enemy forces in armed combat and constructing the People's Republic of Colombia'. The EPL was disbanded in 1990; its members rejoined civilian life in Colombia. The FARC and EPL survive, and are more active today than ever before.

Colombian hills and lowlands, guaranteeing the nation's divisions. Tirofijo is still in command.

THROUGH THE 1960S more and more of the national territory embraced Colombia's Vuelta. The 1960 and 1963 races had started in the terrible humidity of Cúcuta, the Colombian border town pressed up against Venezuela. Then in 1965 the Vuelta began abroad for the first time, in San Cristóbal, the capital of the Táchira, Venezuela's frontier department named after the navigable river separating it from Cúcuta and the department of North Santander.

Except that for all practical purposes the Táchira's capital was Cucutá. It was the first conduit for the Táchira's exports to the Old World, the major supplies centre, and a point of pilgrimage for Táchiran sports fans. During the El Dorado years, many of Uruguay's World Cup winning footballers played there. An enormous following crossed the border for every home match.

Bogotá had always been closer to the Táchira than Caracas. Even its newspapers arrived first. Colombia and Venezuela had been squabbling over the border like crotchety sisters since 1830, when Venezuela had seceded from Simón Bolivar's dreamed-of Nueva Granada. Polite Caracas opinion referred to the Táchirans as *andinos*, Andeans, a crude mountain people lacking metropolitan sophistication. For administrators the region was a provincial backland: since colonial times, to be named proconsul of the Táchira had been regarded as banishment. The legal status of the border hung on a verb ending. Gowned against the mildew, generations of jurists, palaeographers and grammarians had pored over Spanish colonial documents. If they could have agreed that the verb stem *qued-* in a 1768 royal cedula ended with an imperative 'e' – 'may it remain' – the boundary line would have been fixed in perpetuity. But there was reasonable doubt: the word-final curl could have been an 'a' – 'it remains' – which left the question open.

Neither country could resist involving itself in the internal conflicts of the other, and by 1965 the hope of finding off-shore petroleum reserves had refuelled the border controversy. As the Vuelta crossed the border, a new round of talks about marine and submarine sovereignty was beginning.

These issues divided the politicians of Bogotá and Caracas. However, in the Táchira the populations merged. By racing over the frontier heedless of the formalities, the 1965 Tour made a significant gesture. And in San Cristóbal, hosting their extraordinary Colombian cousins from their own Andean hillsides, the people of Táchira suddenly found in the sport of cycling the ideal synthesis of their geographic and cultural identities.

In return the Táchira provided the Colombians with a firm foundation on which to establish their hemispheric supremacy. For in the aftermath of the 1965 Vuelta – won by Cochise's only rival, Javier Suárez – a group of volunteer firemen planned a bike race around the Táchira. After several false starts, it was decided that the race would form the centrepiece of the local agricultural show in January. Accommodation was organized through fire-service contacts throughout the state; a collection of pillows, sheets and blankets was launched, which fire-service vehicles transported ahead of each stage to the church halls and private homes of those who hosted the competitors. In spite of the homespun facilities, the forty-three riders who started stage one of the first Vuelta al Táchira – seventeen circuits around San Cristóbal on 29 January 1966 – included the cream of Colombian cycling. Martín Emilio Rodríguez led the Antioquian team; teams from Cundinamarca, the Federal District of Bogotá and North Santander also travelled to compete against riders from six Venezuelan regions. Lacking local experts in cycling coverage, the San Cristóbal station 'Echoes of Torbes' invited Colombia's best commentators from RCN and Caracol. An inattentive listener might have believed the transmissions originated from a pirate station over the border in Colombia. Cochise was soon as well known in the Táchira as he was at home in Antioquia

As the Colombians seduced local listeners with their eloquent commentaries, Cochise lit up the roads with his genius. To speak of clean sweeps by the Colombians over the event's first decade would be to understate their domination. The first Venezuelan home in the inaugural Vuelta al Táchira finished tenth overall. In the second year the first Venezuelan was eighth, and in 1968 twelfth. Yet the passions of the Táchiran spectators were undiminished by the absence of local success. In the first Vuelta al Táchira no Venezuelan won a stage or even crossed the line among the first six finishers. But faced with the Colombian onslaught, the Venezuelans were forced to mature rapidly. On 11 January 1967 during the second race Guillermo Cárdenas was the first Venezuelan to win a stage. They won two stages of the third Vuelta, four in the fourth, two in the fifth, and six in the sixth.

Cochise, by contrast, won the first Vuelta al Táchira by thirty-one minutes, and fell in love with the race. He rode three Táchiras in all, in 1966, 1968 and 1971, and won them all. Of the twenty-four stages he rode, he won nine and finished second in three, never arriving outside the first ten finishers. 'The differences between us were enormous,' he recalled subsequently. 'We didn't know the route, so we waited for the race organizers to pass us in their cars. We used to disappear in the cloud of fine dust they raised and arrive black.'

Cochise's association with the Vuelta al Táchira had a curious spin-off. In 1972 Ramsés Díaz León, sports editor of *The Nation*, a San Cristóbal daily, travelled to Europe to cover the Munich Olympic Games. In a courtesy car escorting journalists around the road-race route, Díaz found himself next to Jacques Marchand, cycling correspondent of the French sports daily *L'Équipe*. Through the bilingual Canadian crammed between them, Díaz asked

Marchand whether a town like San Cristóbal, with a population of just 300,000, could hope to host the World Cycling Championships. 'Marchand guffawed,' Diaz told me. 'I wasn't sure if it was generous or scornful laughter. It wasn't the size, he said, but the cycling that mattered. He'd never heard of San Cristóbal. I mentioned the Vuelta al Táchira. Without waiting for the translator, Marchand repeated the word, "Táchira? Táchira? Cochise!" "Yes, yes," I said. "Cochise." Five years later, with the help of Marchand and *L'Équipe*, the World Championships came to San Cristóbal.'

Despite its long cycling tradition, Colombia only hosted the world cycling championships nineteen years later.

UNLIKE THE TOUR of the Táchira, Mexico's national tour had consistently punctured Colombia's pride. In 1956 Hoyos had finished fifth. Four years later Rubén Darío Gómez had come second, although he would have won convincingly if he hadn't been given a two-minute penalty for changing bikes. In 1963 Cochise had been third, and two years later, sleight of stopwatch had been suspected when eleven seconds separated him from victory. It wouldn't have mattered had the conquest of Mexico not represented the next step in an instinctive internationalization that led to Europe and the Tour de France.

When the International Olympic Committee decided to take the 1968 Games to Mexico City, the Tour of Mexico suddenly took on a special significance. The challenge of altitude suddenly began to preoccupy world sport, and the year before the Olympics a distinguished cast of European cyclists took part in the Mexican national tour to experiment with the conditions. In October 1967 the irresistible force of aspiring Olympians – Soviet, Hungarian, East and West German, Italian, Polish and Dutch – met the immovable object of Colombian ambition.

Cochise was the obvious spearhead. Second on stage one, he commented, 'I don't like winning the first stage.' Colombia immediately headed the team table, and took the lead in the mountains category through a fine rider named Álvaro Pachón. It took three days for Cochise to take the leader's jersey. On stage three, a 40-kilometre time trial, he was second to Holland's René Pynen. In the afternoon he won the stage and took over the race lead. By evening Colombia led every category. Then, between Iguala and Toluca, Pachón unleashed a 160-kilometre attack, giving him a massive lead in the mountains competition. It also gave him a two-minute advantage over his teammate Cochise.

Today, Álvaro Pachón owns a bicycle shop in Bogotá's Calle 13, where burly whores jaywalk through the fumes even by day, and street hawkers squat at exhaust-pipe height, surveying trinkets on felt sheets through the fumes. Meticulous and ambassadorial – almost English in manner – Álvaro Pachón recalls the Mexican adventure with special pride. 'Once I had taken the lead, Cochise agreed to support me. All that mattered was a Colombian victory. I wore the leader's jersey for the remaining eleven stages, and led the mountain competition from start to finish.'

Far behind him in the classification was a young Dutch rider named Joop Zoetemelk. By the time Zoetemelk won the Tour de France in 1980, he had finished the world's wealthiest bike race in second place five times and fourth twice, and had become World Champion in 1985. With every brilliant Zoetemelk performance, Pachón's legend in Colombia grew. In some respects he was Colombia's Zoetemelk, more bridesmaid than bride. Between 1965 and 1980 he finished fourteen Vueltas a Colombia in the top ten. By 1970 he had won two Vueltas al Táchira, and in 1972 won a second Tour of Mexico.

Before the 1967 Tour of Mexico, Colombian victories abroad had been scarce. Ramón Hoyos had won the 1954 Tour of Puerto Rico. In the Tour of Brasil, Honorio Rúa had finished fifth in 1954, and Pachón second and King of the Mountains in 1966. Javier Suárez was ninth in the 1965 Vuelta a Cantabria in Spain. But the 1967 Mexican win led to a dam-burst of foreign victories, and unparalleled regional supremacy. In 1970 Colombians took the Vuelta a Barinas – another Venezuelan race – and the Tour of Costa Rica. In 1972 it was the Tour of Guadalupe. By the mid-1970s Colombian riders were travelling to, and winning, every international event in the region: the Panamanian Tour of Colón, the Tour of Guatemala, the Jalisco Grand Prix in Mexico, the Andes Crossing between Chile and Argentina, the Tour of Chile and the Battle of Carabobo Classic (also Venezuelan). Cochise and Pachón had opened the door to undisputed Colombian hegemony over South and Central American cycling. What had started at the mid-point of the twentieth century as a means of self-knowledge had, by the end of the 1960s, become an instrument of international self-assertion.

Then Cochise prepared his bid for Colombia's first world title in any sport.

6. Pelé on a bike

THE 1963 AND 1964 Tours of Colombia were playthings to Cochise. He was barely in his twenties, and his winning margins were thirty minutes and an hour respectively. In 1962, when he lost the event by eight seconds, he had still been a teenager. Road-racing champion of Colombia in 1965 and Central America in 1966, champion of the Vuelta al Táchira in 1966 and 1968, second in the Tour of Mexico twice (1964, by eleven seconds, and 1967, to his team-mate Álvaro Pachón), Cochise was the greatest Latin American road-racer of his time. In the 4000-metre pursuit he had no hemispheric rival. He had won gold at the Central American Games in 1962, the Bolivarian Games in 1965, the American Games in 1965 and 1966, and the Pan-American Games in 1967. He had also won Colombia's second race, the RCN Classic, in 1963, and was runner-up twice: in 1961, aged eighteen, and in 1967, by forty-three seconds.

But he was also a product of his milieu. In the absence of scientific coaching and international competition, it was his former Club Mediofondo team-mate Javier Suárez, Pugnose, the finest climber of his generation, who compelled Cochise to excellence. Suárez had been leading the 1962 Tour of Colombia by seven minutes when he had fallen heavily on the penultimate stage, between Manizales and Honda. He had refused to abandon and, in spite of his injuries, reached Bogotá to finish third overall, thirteen minutes behind the winner. He was fourth in 1963 and fifth a year later; as a member of Cochise's team, he exchanged his hopes of an overall win for the King of the Mountains title. In 1965, riding against Cochise, he finally took the Tour of Colombia, and added the first of two RCN Classics. A year later Cochise took his Tour title back by a quarter of an hour, and retained it in 1967 by five minutes; Suárez was second each time.

Cochise was a showman, Pugnose a mystic, a quietly-spoken man who would assume the lotus position at mealtimes and, beneath his brooding forehead and celebrated nose, measure out his wisdom in sculptured phrases. He had the appeal of the underdog, and an intense rivalry grew between his followers and those of Cochise. Colombia was polarized between 'Cochisismo' and 'Suarismo', and the division cost at least one life.

Suárez's greatest fan was Jorge Enrique Ospina, known to all as 'El Loco' – Crazy Ospina. Crazy had followed every Tour of Colombia since its inception. An expert car mechanic, he kept the caravan in motion. He ran errands, helped distribute food bags at the feed stations, and embodied the Vuelta a Colombia as much as the riders. At midnight on Sunday 29 May 1966 Crazy Ospina entered the Café Lido in Bogotá with two radio technicians. The alcohol flowed and Crazy bellowed his affection for Javier Suárez. When the group decided to leave, five men confronted them. Crazy was knifed in the stomach. His friends bundled him towards a hospital but Crazy died in the street. For Javier Suárez, Crazy's memory is still vivid; but he is under no illusions as to who was the finer rider. 'Cochise alone would never have had the discipline to become extraordinary. I could never have achieved what he did, but I forced him to be that good.'

Extrovert and noisy, Cochise was the centre of attention in any group of people. His clowning protected him from the considerable expectations that always surrounded him, and freed his freakish physical powers to function without the inhibition of introspection. By 1970 he had won thirty-four stages in the Tour of Colombia and five in the RCN Classic. He was indisputably the finest rider of his generation, perhaps the finest Colombian cyclist ever, and had a magnificent record abroad.

But his finest form was three years behind him. At the 1968 Vuelta fifteen minutes separated his seventh place from the winning time. He was second the following year by eleven minutes. An attack of hepatitis in 1969 deepened his decline. Once he had straddled mountains and stolen fire from the gods. Now his heroics belonged to an apparently inaccessible past. The cruellest month was April 1970: a brilliant twenty-year-old called Raphael Antonio Niño won the Vuelta. Niño was hailed as the new Cochise. The real Cochise, striving to become the old one, finished ninth, thirty-five minutes off the pace. Most of his Club Mediofondo contemporaries had retired; many hoped Cochise would preserve his legend by doing the same. He marshalled pathetic arguments for prolonging the agony. 'I remember how I used to climb,' he reflects. 'The kilos and the years weigh me down on the mountain stages. But we veterans remain a necessary part of the spectacle.' Still only twenty-eight, his flame was burning low. But secretly, a new athlete was pupating within him. Aided by the first professional coaching of his career, Cochise was concealing his own metamorphosis.

*

In October 1968 Cochise had been offered a professional contract by an Italian team named Germanavox-Vega. With his sights set on Olympic gold, Cochise had turned the offer down. Two months later the Germanavox-Vega team leader, a Dane named Ole Ritter, had set a world professional hour record of 48.666 kilometres in Mexico in December 1968. In November 1969 a member of the Germanavox-Vega coaching staff, Claudio Costa, left the team and travelled to Colombia, where he took personal charge of Cochise. His first victory lay in convincing the Colombian to concentrate on his track skills.

Like Ritter, Cochise combined the endurance of the road-racer with the speed of the track rider. At the 1965 World Championships in San Sebastian, Spain, Cochise had recorded the fastest time in the amateur pursuit; he had eliminated the Britons Brendan McKeowan and Hugh Porter before losing to the eventual winner, Holland's Tiemen Groen, in the semi-final. At the Mexico Olympics, too, he had been one of four riders to beat the old Olympic 4000 metres record.

Cochise and Costa had their first major appointment together at the 1970 World Track Championships at Leicester in England. To secure funding for the trip Costa talked up their chances: 'If the national sports council authorizes Cochise's journey to take part in the 4000 metres pursuit, he could win Colombia's first world title in any event.' The funding was forthcoming. Cochise even rode the second fastest time of the tournament. But freak August temperatures of 1°C acted against him. He was defeated in the quarter-finals by the reigning world champion, Switzerland's Xavier Kurmann. Cochise finished fifth overall; he was uncomprehending. He was receiving expert guidance for the first time in his life, yet his results were so poor that they were compromising the backing of Colombia's sports council. But during the championships Claudio Costa suggested a new project for his rider: an attempt on the world amateur hour record. Cochise took to the idea immediately.

The hour is unlike any other event. The aim is to ride alone as far as possible around a track in an hour. It is neither a time trial (held on open roads over arbitrary distances) nor a pursuit (in which two riders compete on the track over a prescribed distance, usually four kilometres). Nor is there a prize: the hour pits the rider against himself, voluntarily, for one reason alone – reputation. Attacking the hour on an open track is perhaps the greatest test in cycling. In a covered velodrome, where the atmospheric conditions are known in advance, preparation is far easier; in the open air the slightest change in conditions can destroy a record attempt.

The record had been broken twice the previous year. On 16 March Cochise's friend and rival, Mexico's Radamés Treviño, had ridden 47.213 kilometres. A month after setting his world record, Treviño had lost his life in a road accident while training. On 5 October he lost his record too, when Denmark's Olympic pursuiter Mogens Frey Jensen travelled to Mexico and rode 47.513 kilometres. Because the hour record was an ad hoc event that didn't fit into any recognized championships, the Colombian sports authorities refused to sponsor Cochise's attempt. In the absence of state backing, Claudio Costa had to find alternative finance. He contacted an Italian frame maker named Giacinto Benotto. Benotto had manufactured Ole Ritter's hour bike. The Italian agreed to provide Cochise with the bike and finance he needed for the record attempt.

On 21 September 1970 Cochise, Costa and Benotto met in Mexico City for the final preparations. The Mexican rain washed out days of trials. Only on 1 October, in wind and rain, did Cochise finally complete a twenty-five-circuit test at the Agustín Melgar Velodrome. His time was ten minutes six seconds, six full seconds outside world record pace – poor preparation for an event made impossible by the slightest weakness or self-doubt.

The ghost of Treviño and the shadow of Mogens Frey attended Cochise. Many years before, after his own hour record ride at Milan in 1942, Fausto Coppi had reflected, 'If only others could comprehend the meaning of sixty minutes of solitude to achieve the record.' But as Cochise told me, in the hour there are really two riders on the track: one of muscle, striving against the air, the other a phantom presence. 'You have a table of times, and your coach measures out your progress. He walks towards you if you are ahead of schedule, and away from you if you are behind. The phantom is in that table. You are racing against ghosts.'

On 3 October, Cochise rode for five hours between Mexico and Toluca. The following day, with the fatigue of those 180 kilometres in his legs, he rode a 2-kilometre trial at 47.850 kilometres per hour, and ten minutes later a 5-kilometre trial at 48 kph. On the fifth and sixth days he rested. On the seventh Cochise awoke to a cloudless Mexican sky. At 9.15 in the morning he arrived at the velodrome, accompanied by Costa and Benotto. He showered while his bicycle was meticulously prepared. Every turn of an enormous, sixty-eight toothed chain ring would advance him 7 metres 57 centimetres along the track. The front tyre was inflated to 10.5 atmospheres, the rear to 11. At 9.35 a.m. he rode onto the track for his warm up. Dr César Augusto Pantoja, Colombia's Ambassador to Mexico, arrived with the Embassy staff at 10.45. Costa gave the order at 11.12 a.m. local time. Three thousand spectators looked on as Cochise rolled over the white line and accelerated powerfully to a pedal speed of 106 revolutions a minute.

For a rider in good condition the first 10 kilometres of an hour attempt are a gift. The first five were fast: 6 minutes 11.2 seconds. Cochise stalked Frey's phantom. Costa, timing his protégé from the trackside, saw him too, 1.7 seconds ahead of Cochise. At 10 kilometres, the gap had widened to 2.8 seconds. Filling his lungs slowly through the nose, the Colombian pounded out an exquisite rhythm: at 15 kilometres, fine-tuning, Cochise had reduced the deficit to 2.2 seconds. At 20 kilometres he was tucked in at 1.1 seconds behind the Dane's schedule. After 25 kilometres Cochise had slipped back to 2.3 seconds behind schedule. Inexplicably, his relentless pursuit began to falter. 'From about 20 kilometres I felt a terrible ache in my legs. Then, at 30, I thought it was over. For ten seconds I had no strength to call on. I had to relax and rest on the gear. Claudio was walking backwards along the track.' The gap had become an abyss of 9.8 seconds. He rode the sixth set of 5 kilometres in 6 minutes 26.4 seconds where Frey had ridden 6 minutes 18.9 seconds. The crowd pleaded with him. Cochise was far behind schedule and losing sight of the record. Cochise tunnelled deep into his suffering. 'You can never alter your position on the saddle, so your crotch gradually becomes extremely sore, and pain accumulates in the buttocks and legs. Even your hands and forearms ache after gripping the handlebars for so long.' The plane of the attempt was shifting from the physical to the spiritual. Blocked by flashes of pain, Cochise sought another source of inspiration. 'I could feel millions of Colombians urging me on.' The static of desire crackled in the air around him. Conviction entered his mind. 'I had lost seconds, but I knew I couldn't fail.'

By 35 kilometres he had reduced the gap to 4.4 seconds. A roar engulfed the stadium at 40 kilometres – Cochise was suddenly ahead of schedule. He hammered out a furious cadence. The Colombian national anthem rang out, full of unexpected relevance: 'Enduring glory, immortal joy: hope is germinating in furrows of pain . . .'

After 45 kilometres Cochise was over three seconds ahead of Frey's ghost. He had three minutes eleven seconds in which to discover the body's breaking point. Costa gestured from the side, glowing. The timekeepers signalled fifteen seconds to go. Cochise accelerated mercilessly. The crowd delirium crystallized into a countdown: *five-four-three-two-one*. To mark the hour's end there was the definitive crack of a starting pistol, as though there had been an assassination attempt.

The record was his. It was the apotheosis of Martín Emilio Rodríguez. For the Mexicans, Cochise had raised the spirit of their lost champion, Radamés Treviño. Tears ran down Claudio Costa's face. Giacinto Benotto, the sponsor, embraced them both. There was an uncertain delay as the precise distance was calculated. Then an announcement broke the confusion: he had completed 47 kilometres, 563 metres and 24 centimetres: 39 metres, 45 centimetres more than the Dane.

Five days later, multitudes met at Bogotá's El Dorado airport to pay homage to the champion.

Stronger than ever now, Cochise began 1971 with a third Vuelta al Táchira victory, his prize a Ford car. His goal was now the world amateur pursuit title at Tradate, a small town in north-west Italy. In July, a month before his Italian appointment, Cochise won the individual and team pursuit titles at the Pan-American Games in Cali. He flew to Italy just five days before the championships. The absence from the amateur pursuit of the reigning Olympic champion Pierre Trentin (now riding professionally) and the 1969 and 1970 world champion Kurmann (with a broken collarbone) left Cochise the outstanding favourite. His hour record increased the curiosity of the press and the pressure on him to perform.

On 25 August he waited opposite the Czech, Milan Purzla. A fine drizzle was suspended in the air around them. The starting-pistol fired: the riders accelerated into a rainstorm. Two laps later, with

Cochise ahead, the race was suspended. When it resumed, Cochise was serene. He intimidated his rivals by defeating the Czech in the fastest qualifying time of 4 minutes 53.79 seconds. The closest contender, Denmark's Reno Olsen, was eight-tenths of a second slower. In the quarter-finals Cochise faced the slowest qualifier, Russia's Viktor Bikov. He rode easily, but still achieved the fastest quarter-final time of 4 minutes 54.45 seconds. The following day he met Poland's Jerzy Glowacki in the first semi-final. The Colombian brushed him aside with ease.

It was night in Italy but 4.17 p.m. in Colombia when the final began. Bogotá was grey and chill; elsewhere, the tropical heat had descended. A tense nation tuned into millions of radio sets. Every city centre in the land was paralysed as crowds congregated around televisions placed in shop windows. Cochise faced Switzerland's Josef Fuchs. After the first of nine laps, his advantage was 1.03 seconds. By the end of lap four the gap was 4.5 seconds: Cochise led by 50 metres or more. He held this distance for four more laps, before accelerating away on the final circuit to win by nearly 5.5 seconds.

Collective hysteria gripped Colombia. Enough tickertape to block streets for days spiralled down from the rooftops. Music and dance broke out. Klaxons sounded. Tens of thousands screamed 'Cochise' and 'Colombia' until they could distinguish between them no more. Celebrations lasted into the night. Few heard the telephone conversation between President Misael Pastrana and Cochise. But the following day his face appeared in full-page newspaper advertisements placed by Proexpo, the fund for promoting exports, an office of Colombia's Ministry for Economic Development. The text reads as follows:

> The Great National Challenge: Exports worth 1000 million dollars: Cochise accepted a great challenge and triumphed. Now the great challenge is yours, farmer, worker, public employee and entrepreneur…

> The country needs your efforts: we must export more mechanical goods, textiles and manufactured goods; pineapples, melons, tinned fruit and juices; wood and furniture; meat and many more international quality goods.'

Small print beneath the photograph acknowledged the 'voluntary co-operation by Martín Emilio *Cochise* Rodríguez, employee of Wrangler-Caribu, as a patriotic gesture for national development'.

Under Claudio Costa's tutelage, Martín Rodríguez had achieved the two greatest successes in the history of Colombian sport and some celebrity in the European cycling press. 'I cannot explain how Cochise lost so much time,' wrote Rino Negri of the Italian daily *Gazzetta dello Sport*. 'If he had come to Europe five years ago, he could have been a sort of Eddy Merckx.' In France, *Le Soir* christened him 'the South American Pelé of the bicycle, as fine an ambassador as *o rey do futebol*, [who] was worthy of his country's success at these world championships'. 'His future, uncertain at present, will probably take him to the next Olympics,' asserted the regional daily *Dauphiné Libéré*, 'where he should be the great favourite after the failure of many men who, logically, should have beaten him, as is the case with the Frenchman Darmet, the Italian Tonelli, the Czech Purzla and the Russian Bikov, whom Rodríguez vanquished with ease.' Cochise duly prepared for the ambition of his life: Olympic gold.

Two months after his world championship victory, however, his dream was shattered. A journalist named Edgar G. Senior, perhaps with designs on an International Olympic Committee post, had been collecting evidence of professionalism in Colombian cycling since Cochise's 1970 hour record, and had compiled a dossier for the IOC's representative in Colombia. The International Olympic Committee informed Cochise that he was in violation of Article 26 of the Olympic

Charter and would not be eligible for the 1972 Games at Munich. This article stipulated that athletes must receive no remuneration for or daily sustenance from sport, nor allow the use of their name, photograph or sporting abilities for advertising purposes.

At Tradate, when Cochise had won the world pursuit title on the Benotto bike that had carried him to the amateur hour record, he had been wearing the shirt of the Colombian national team. But in Mexico the previous year he had worn the logo of his sponsor, Benotto, on his cap and sweatshirt. Added to the evidence against him was the Ford car he had won at the Vuelta al Táchira and a photo published on the front page of *El Tiempo* the day after the record, showing Cochise in Benotto colours.

The International Federation of Amateur Cycling (IFAC) now suspended Cochise pending an investigation, and fined the Colombian Cycling Federation for non-payment of its subscription. On 26 February before a committee of IFAC and IOC members in Prague, a Colombian delegation argued that in Europe, too, amateur cyclists habitually wore logos. Their arguments only reinforced Cochise's guilt: he was unanswerably in breach of the article. On 30 May 1972 the IOC came to its final decision and excluded Cochise from the Olympic Games. A small book entitled *El Expósito* (*The Foundling*) was published about the affair. It refers to Edgar Senior throughout as Judas. The view was widely held.

But Cochise's was a crime of negligence committed elsewhere. Colombian cycling had always been resolutely amateur in order to compete at the Olympics. But it had never observed the formal requirements of Olympic amateurism. Nor had its own Olympic Committee sought to correct the discrepancy. Every rider since the Indomitable Zipa had received some form of payment – for competing, not training – from firms seeking publicity. Amateur was a euphemism allowing for occasional disbursements that never provided a living wage. Professional, on the other hand, meant Europe. Colombia simply had no resources to fund full-time athletes covertly though universities or the military on the American or Soviet models.

Two options faced Martín Rodríguez. One was retirement. The other, professionalism, had always been within his horizons. In May 1967, after his fourth Vuelta win, he had pondered, 'If only I could go back to Europe, where I learnt a great deal. It's one of the goals I've given myself: perhaps I'll achieve it one day.' And after the hour record, he had declared his intention to ride one more year as an amateur before joining a professional road-racing team, perhaps in Italy. Now the IOC had forced his hand. Claudio Costa spoke to his brother Piero in Italy, who in turn spoke to the great Italian rider Felice Gimondi. 'I was almost thirty,' Cochise told me, 'but my track title gave me a bargaining chip. It's ironic that my professional road-racing career began because of my victories on the track. I had been fourth at the World amateur road race at Montevideo in 1968, and ninth in the Olympic road race the same year. But those results never even registered in Europe. That was how hard it was for a Latin American to impress the Europeans.'

In Italy Cochise rode for Gimondi, but was freed to win token stages in two consecutive Tours of Italy. In 1973 the fifteenth stage from Florence to the seaside resort of Forte dei Marmi, just north of Viareggio, was rolling towards a sprint finish when, with two kilometres to go, Cochise roared out of the group. By the time the sprinters' teams had organized the chase, Cochise, curled into an aerodynamic teardrop, was plummeting towards the line. By the time the reigning world road-racing champion Marino Basso won the bunch sprint, Cochise had finished his celebrations.

Then in 1975, after 36 kilometres of stage nineteen, he joined a six-man breakaway. Crossing the finish line at Pordenone 129 kilometres later, Cochise set the record for the fastest Giro stage ever, excluding time trials. Days after his 1975 Giro stage win, Cochise partnered Gimondi to victory in another two-man time trial, the City of Verona Grand Prix. It was one of several events won in Europe by Cochise: a Grand Prix around the Italian town of Camaiore in 1973, a 1974 tour around the eastern Italian region of the Marches in July, and a Coppa Agostoni – a time trial relay – in 1975 with Gimondi and another team-mate.

Probably his greatest European triumph was in the 1973 Baracchi Trophy, a two-man time trial won with Felice Gimondi. In Italy the victory is remembered, if at all, as Gimondi's. Their director, Giancarlo Ferretti, one of the most respected technicians in the sport, puts it like this: 'Any clown could ride behind Gimondi and win the Baracchi.' But Gimondi takes a different view: 'I remember at the start I had to rein him in to impose the right rhythm, because the Baracchi Trophy is 110 kilometres, and you can't go flat out from the start. But he was strong; he performed his part down to the last detail. The Baracchi is a technical ride: normally you start off fast and struggle towards the end. We were in excellent shape all the way to Brescia, and that's how we won.'

Cochise only rode one Tour de France, in 1975, as a pure *domestique* – a team rider whose job was to partner and pace its star rider. 'On the Tourmalet in the Pyrenees, Gimondi lent on my leg to push himself up. Each time he did so, I went backwards. My job was to ride back up to him, and perform the same operation again and again. It was hard. Like any *domestique*, I was sometimes stronger than my leader, but I had to wait for him. I went with breakaways, but I couldn't ride to win because my leader was behind me. It was frustrating.' He finished twenty-seventh overall. As an athlete, Cochise had lost his identity. His triumphs were in the side-shows and circuses of professional cycling. He had become little more than a mercenary, a fate that would befall many of his compatriots in the future.

Today Felice Gimondi works for the bicycle manufacturer Bianchi, just south of Brescia, in northern Italy. When I met him there, he evoked warm memories of Cochise: 'He was a complete rider. Most Colombians have tiny physiques, ideal for the mountains but little more. Cochise could climb with great dexterity, but he could also pull the group along at 50kph on the flat. On the surface he was Colombian, but he had the characteristics of a fine European athlete. His experience on the track gave his pedal action formidable power. If a breakaway needed bringing back on the flat, you just gave him a signal and he would accelerate away, turning a huge gear. But he came very late. If he'd come to Europe aged twenty-two or twenty-three, he could realistically have hoped to become a team leader and achieve much more than his two Giro stages.'

Another of Gimondi's *domestiques* was the Dane, Ole Ritter, who had joined Bianchi in 1971: 'Cochise was excellent for the team, always in a good mood – one of the happiest riders in the peloton, always singing and joking. But he was a great rider, and if he'd been given the freedom to ride for himself, he would have won plenty.'

On 26 November 1975 Cochise and his wife Cristina boarded the cruiser Rossini at Genova and returned to Colombia. He renewed his amateur licence there and returned to competition. On 23 April 1980 he won stage ten of the Tour of Colombia. It was his thirty-ninth, and last, Tour of Colombia stage win, and it broke the record previously held by Ramón Hoyos.

In 1967, 1968, 1970 and 1971 Martín Emilio 'Cochise' Rodríguez Gutiérrez had been voted Colombia's Sportsman of the Year. At the end of 1999 he was elected Colombia's Sportsman of the Century – the result of the poll was a foregone conclusion. His remarkable innate abilities and the unique opportunities he had been given had established new standards for his nation's cyclists. He had taken Colombian cycling to the top of the world, and in the twilight of his career had become one of the finest riders in Europe. But that was in another country. If Cochise's achievements were unattainable, he had also suddenly become a remote figure. During the 1970s, while Cochise was abroad, Colombian cycling found a new idol.

7. The challenge of altitude

Catastrophic forces created the Andes. As brute rock, deformed and compressed, filled out its colossal architecture, tiny pockets of matter were tortured into more delicate geometries. Temperature and pressure, fused with duration, powered by discord, piled pyramid on polygon and replicated them into sequential harmony. On the other side of chaos, an unexpected paradigm of beauty appeared: emerald.

Far below the altiplano, where Boyacá's western arm drops towards the Magdalena River, the official emerald mines wash their scoria – their *guaca* – down into the valley. There, armies of fortune hunters, or *guaqueros*, sift through the slag for emeralds that slipped through the net higher up. Between 1963 and 1973, and again between 1984 and 1990, the roads here ran with blood. Fed by a subculture of fatalism, vicious infighting for control over the mines left thousands of dead. Today the violence is past. I spent enchanted days among the *guaqueros* who met me with broad smiles and quiet conversation as I waded over to them through the sticky grey dirt. Their finds are rare.

At nearby Chiquinquirá, at 2,590 metres, emerald dealers fill the market square. Generations have scratched away at the rock. For the inhabitants of Boyacá, mining – whether hidden crystals of beryl from the tenacious earth or nuggets of oxygen from the impoverished air – has added up to life. Above them the sky circles huge and slow, like a nation's mind.

The phenotypes of athletes, light-framed men and women with potent hearts and expansive lungs, people these poor heights. From the start the developing embryo must learn to suck the air's vigour: in Boyacá no one, irrespective of age, cargo or gradient, gets off to push.

When Cochise went abroad, Medellín slid beneath the horizon of Colombian cycling. Boyacá, Colombia's mining heartland, rose to displace it as the heart of the nation's cycling. Here, in the village of Cucáita – between Chiquinquirá and Tunja – another jewel was formed. On 2 December 1949 Raphael Antonio Niño Munevar, the man who would succeed Cochise, was born.

Niño would achieve a despotism that Cochise had never sought and even Hoyos never equalled. His headstrong personality drove him to discard the existing culture of Colombian cycling and impose a pitiless new order. An absolutist ruler at home, Niño was the poorest traveller of all Colombia's champions. Yet despite his consistent failings abroad, the conditions he created allowed those who came after him to compete in the finest international company. Born into peasant poverty, Niño also made bike-racing integral to Boyacá's identity.

When I tried to meet up with Niño, he missed two appointments and left me feeling like a nuisance caller. Our third rendezvous was in a dimly-lit suburb beside the north Bogotá freeway. Every dark street was guarded by spiked barriers. The intercom had been vandalized and there was no guard. A resident allowed me to enter but there was no one home, and to escape I risked emasculation on the gates. Eventually Niño arrived an hour or more late. Straight black hair hung unkempt over a long, hollow face. His careful courtesy didn't hide an instinctive distrust. Most athletes suppress the compulsion that drives them to compete. Not Raphael Niño: two decades after his retirement, you can almost hear the demons still drumming in his ears.

As a child, poverty had made him abrasive. Three brothers had died before he was old enough to learn their names. He had hated school and felt detached from his schoolmates. Some childhood happening too tiny to take shape as a discreet event – one of the unidentifiable occurrences that determine what we do with our lives – deposited in him an ambition around which he mustered the full might of his maladjustment. He wanted a bicycle. It had nothing to do with winning, competing or even riding, and still less to do with the Tour of Colombia. Reflected in the gleam and symmetry of a new cycle, Raphael Niño found both his lost dead and his future.

In his early teens Niño argued with his parents and left them for the capital. Lodging with a sister, he cleaned engine parts, coiled cables and hoarded his meagre wage. The day he bought his first bicycle he rode long into the night and returned home to his sister's railing. He crept into bed beside his nephews, indignant at having to leave his bicycle outside. He cleaned and greased it daily. On the steep slopes of Bogotá's eastern sierra he became a bicycle messenger. Some left after a day of suffering up those streets. Most left within a week. Niño stayed a year.

More arguments presaged another change of address: he moved in with another sister. He changed employer, doubled his wage and met a workmate named Raúl, who talked a lot and raced bikes. Niño went with him that Sunday in his work clothes and climbed the hill at La

Tribuna four times. The other racers, in cycling shorts and maillots, were impressed. When they asked him how long he had been training he told them the truth: 'This is my first time.'

Racing garments took another month of saving. He bought football boots and cut off the studs. He joined Cicloases, Bogotá's oldest club, and finished twelfth in his first race. In his second he was sixth; he carried the medal around for days and days. In his third race he punctured and abandoned – he was the only rider on a touring bike. He felt himself disintegrating with frustration. Overwhelmed by destructive impulses, he decided to give up cycling for good.

Two months later he heard Carlos Arturo Rueda's Tour of Colombia commentaries on the radio. By giving up his job he could collect his outstanding wages in one lump sum. With the sale of his touring bike he had enough to buy an unwanted racing bike cut-price from a cousin.

His new career began when he won his first race. In an unanalyzed ritual he pinned a map of Colombia to his bedroom wall and on it hung his winner's medals. Almost every Sunday he rode. Only mechanical problems kept him from victory. But unemployment meant hunger, and he knew he had to eat well to succeed as an athlete, so he took another job as a mechanic's assistant. Work started at seven, so Niño rose at three to train with two other cyclists, Pedro and Miguel – he has forgotten their surnames. One Sunday, Miguel's tyre became detached from the wheel on a fast descent. He fell, and a blow to the head killed him. Niño became afraid of descending at speed; the fear lasted years. Nevertheless, in January 1970 he won a stage and the General Classification of the Under-21 Vuelta a Colombia.

BETWEEN THE UNDER-21 Tour of Colombia and the elite event, due to start on 27 April, presidential elections took place. Soon the thread of Niño's life joined the tangled confusion of Colombian history. As he trained to meet the future, the country at large was concerned with an unexpected return to the past.

A show-trial and exile had done for General Gustavo Rojas Pinilla in the 1950s, but now, as the 1970 presidential elections approached, Rojas reappeared at the head of a populist movement: the People's National Alliance, or ANAPO. The National Front felt threatened. Rojas, it resolved, had to be defeated, whatever the price. The media ostracized him, leaving ANAPO only its own informal networks to pursue self-promotion. Still it grew. The outgoing President broke with presidential neutrality to rail against him. As the vote began, ANAPO claimed police harassment. Rumours spread of disappearing ballot boxes and shadows in the office of the central registrar. Yet early results on the evening of 19 April suggested an ANAPO victory. By 10.00 p.m. euphoria reigned in the Rojas residence, while the leading National Front candidate, Misael Pastrana Borrero, believed his cause lost. The General went to bed winning but woke up losing: early on 20 April, Pastrana had moved into a 0.1 per cent lead. According to the first count, the National Front's continuity had been preserved by less than 50,000 votes. Official figures gave Pastrana 1,571,249 votes; General Rojas had mustered 1,521,267. Electoral fraud was never proven, but Rojas had demonstrated that the system created to sideline him lacked the legitimating component it most vaunted: unambiguous popular support. Sixty-three per cent of his votes had come from the urban proletariat, a sector hitherto ignored by the state.

On 21 April rioting disturbed several cities. The army took to the streets and the threat of a coup hung over the country. ANAPO's campaign co-ordinator reacted to defeat with a coded warning: 'To defuse the explosive atmosphere produced by these events,' as the incumbent administration had requested, 'is beyond our means.'

Common sense suggested that the Vuelta a Colombia, due to

depart in less than a week, should be postponed. But the Chairman of the Colombian Cycling Association, General Marcos Arámbula Durán, disagreed. Teams representing Belgium, Italy, Russia, Spain, Switzerland and Venezuela had already embarked for Colombia. And in any case, aware of cycling's historical mission, Arámbula believed that the country needed the Vuelta now more than ever. 'In light of the political situation,' he explained, 'the mission of this twentieth Vuelta will be to soothe the nation, offering the populace distraction from the electoral results. It will be an instrument of peace between the people of Colombia.' For its international audience the Vuelta would focus attention, in Arámbula's words, on 'Colombia's achievements in the economic, social and cultural spheres, and on the road infrastructure'. Radio commentators were instructed to refer to the event as 'the Tour of Peace', and the Vuelta left Bogotá on schedule. And throughout the country, manual recounting of voting slips continued.

El Tiempo's Vuelta coverage included a daily diary by a journalist named Germán Castro Caycedo. Castro's almost sensual picture compares with the classic accounts of the Tour de France by Albert Londres or Pratolini's 'Chronicles of the Giro d'Italia'. As stage one descends from the chill highland plateau to the *tierra caliente* of Girardot, Castro observes its transfiguration:

> The Vuelta takes on a completely new face when the sun is shining. Higher up, 20 kilometres from Bogotá, mist fell on the caravan. Behind each curve the peloton seemed a procession of ghosts, mud-coloured, marching in silence.
>
> But approaching them through the dense fog we could make out a curtain of mud emerging from the group, rising a metre above their closely-knit heads.
>
> When the road is wet, the centre of the peloton is a storm of rushing water, as hundreds of wheels slice through the surface. It is as if a thousand leaves of paper, gummed down with half-dry glue, were becoming unstuck.

> Deeper inside this group of men, soaked through with sweat and mud, where they fight elbow-to-elbow, hip-to-hip, it is even worse. Every eye burns with the force of the rainfall. Look at the riders and you see their ruddy pupils. They are all weeping tears black with mud...

> The rain and mud make the race tougher still. Bicycle chains jam. Gears clog with clinging, damp sand. Their legs have to push harder to turn the pedals. Their wrists grip painfully at the handlebars, as the bike gradually loses mobility.
>
> Today we left Bogotá, through the rain and the cheering crowds... At Silvania the intense cold began to subside and in Fusagasugá a timid sun showed itself. Fifteen kilometres further down the road the heat began. Those of us accompanying the race tore off our coats and waterproofs. The mud began to trickle down our faces in lines, mixing with thick, running sweat. And so we reached the stage finish, sticky with sweat and mud. But at least the cold was behind us...

After two days of racing on the flat, European riders dominated the General Classification: they filled the top four places and seven of the top eleven. Four days later just two major climbs – the Alto de Guandalay (a 32-kilometre climb from the oppressive heat of low-lying Guandalay, at an altitude of 447 metres, to Ibagué, at 1,250 metres) and La Línea (from Ibagué to the chill of the 3,250-metre pass, a climb of 62 kilometres) – had decimated the European teams.

Castro convened a small group of European competitors and technical directors to try to grasp why foreign riders found racing in Colombia so close to impossible. The obvious starting point was the severity of the landscape. The Dutch considered it more extreme than anything found in Europe; the Swiss were amazed by the difference in altitude during individual stages; the Russians stoically claimed they had ridden climbs as steep as La Línea at the Tour of Yugoslavia.

arita
Malta
Pilsen

PREVIOUS PAGE: Ramón Hoyos Vallejo dominated the fifties, accumulating 38 stage wins on the way to five victories in Colombia's national Tour, and massive public adulation. His photograph even appeared beside holy images in the domestic shrines of Colombia's poor. [1]

ABOVE: 25 January 1958: Fausto Coppi (foreground, third from left) in the El Colombiano Classic. His race was ended by heat exhaustion. The great Italian, defeated by Hoyos that day, estimated that in Europe his vanquisher would have been a champion. [2]

RIGHT: The bromide fades on Honorio Rúa, between the gargantuan vehicles and the horsemen. Such was Colombia's isolation that, in February 1957, Rua had no idea his national hour record had come within a whisper of the world record. [3]

LEFT: Every settlement in Colombia, from the Macondo of García Márquez to the great towns and cities, celebrates its founders. In 1951, Ephraim Forero Triviño, the Indomitable Zipa, founded the Vuelta a Colombia, also starting a fine tradition in sports photography. [4]

RIGHT: Most of Antioquia's cyclists were the sons of peasant farmers or textiles workers. An exception is Santiago Botero, the son of a businessman and the holder of a university degree and a world time-trial championship bronze medal. [5]

LEFT: Unlike today's, the fifties riders never made big money. They used their fame in PR, or hired themselves out, like Hoyos, as celebrity drivers of *chivas* – reconditioned Chevrolet trucks used for mobile parties. [6]

BELOW: In July 1994, another Antioquian, Marlon Pérez, won Colombia's second world cycling title in the points race at the World Track Championships in Quito, Ecuador. The entire village of Támesis, near Medellín, welcomed him home. [7]

RIGHT: Roberto Escobar, a.k.a. Ositto, 'Bear,' ran his works team with a little help from his brother, drugs baron Pablo. At the 1981 Colombian tour, one of Roberto's staff, dressed in a bear outfit, was expelled for distributing free marijuana. [8]

ABOVE: Pablo Escobar used cycling to gain publicity for his political campaign to enter Congress. Pictured is Gonzalo Marín, a brilliant rider who was later murdered by Escobar's men. His shorts bear the motto: PABLO ESCOBAR, LIBERAL RENEWAL. [9]

LEFT: Standing beside Cochise Rodríguez (right), wheeled in for publicity purposes, is Rodrigo Murillo Pardo, who owned Joyerías Felipe, a jewellery chain that sponsored a highly successful team. But Murillo was really a major money launderer, and was murdered in February 1986. [10]

The drugs trade claimed many victims. Alfonso Flórez (TOP LEFT), winner of the 1980 amateur Tour de France, was murdered on 23 April 1992. Armando Aristizábal (TOP RIGHT) rode professionally in Europe before his body was found on a municipal tip in Medellín in 1987, hands bound, blindfolded, and showing signs of torture. Juan Carlos Castillo (BOTTOM LEFT) was arrested at Medellín airport in possession of a shipment of cocaine. He was absolved after investigation, only to be murdered on 23 November 1993. Raphael Tolosa (BOTTOM RIGHT) was arrested at Bogotá's international airport on 18 June 2001, departing for Costa Rica and the US with 125 heroin capsules in his gut, and $50, 000 of unlicensed emeralds in his luggage. [11-14]

RIGHT: The illicit velodrome where Pablo and Roberto Escobar held track meets in the late eighties. It's beyond repair now, subsiding on a Medellín hillside, but a constant reminder of the Medellín cartel's cycling connections. [15]

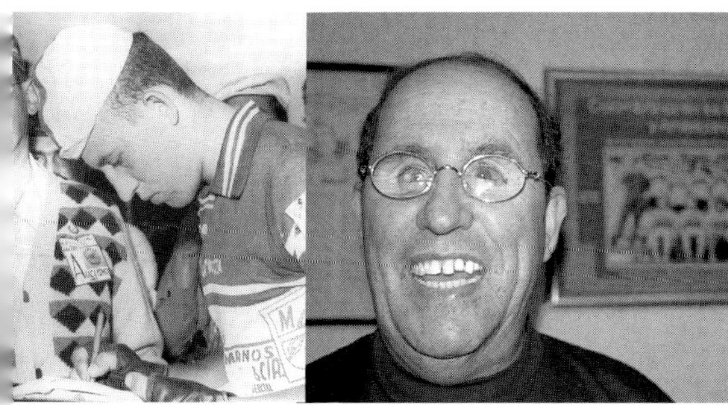

LEFT: Roberto Escobar, signing autographs during the 1965 Vuelta (FAR LEFT) and (NEAR LEFT) today, grinning through thick glasses, a legacy of the December 1993 letter bomb. Over his shoulder, a cycling photograph adorns his heavily guarded hospital room. [16-17]

ABOVE: The eruption of the Nevado del Ruiz on 14 November 1985 buried the town of Armero, leaving over 23, 000 dead and leaving hundreds of thousands homeless. [18]

ABOVE: The Fallen Lord in the Basilica of Monserrate, overlooking Bogotá, is just one example of the tortured, agonising religious images to whom Colombia turns in its times of need. [19]

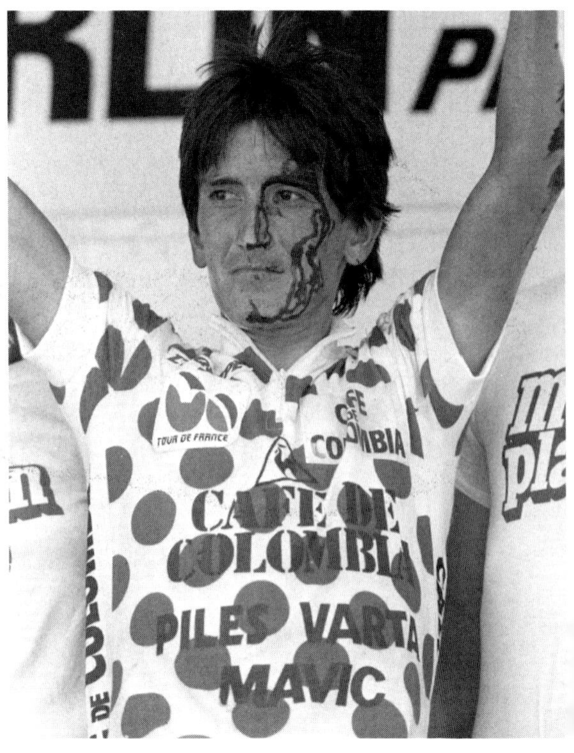

ABOVE: On 6 November 1985, M-19 commandos seized the Palace of Justice in central Bogotá. Over the following two days, the armed forces stormed the building, reducing it to rubble. Many of the nation's finest legal minds were lost. [20]

OPPOSITE: On his way to victory at St Etienne during the 1985 Tour de France, Lucho Herrera fell, sustaining a deep cut. Pictures of his bloody face soon took on a wider significance, capturing Colombia's tortured sense of self. [21]

ABOVE: Fabio Parra never enjoyed Herrera's popularity. Herrera was 'Lucho': Parra was simply 'Parra.' But Fabio Parra's third place overall at the 1988 Tour de France remains the greatest achievement of any Colombian cyclist. [22]

ABOVE: Sogamoso, the mecca of Colombian cycling. Cousins Iván Parra (far left, at front) and Chepe González (third from left, at front) are drawn irresistibly towards the heavens – caught on film in the Channel 4 documentary '*Kings of the Mountains*.' [23]

RIGHT: In the parish church of Morcá, Iván Parra prays to the Virgin of Morcá, patron saint of Sogamoso and of the town's cyclists. With his winnings, he helps finance the basilica's restoration. [24]

But other factors prevented them from focussing wholly on the racing. Jet lag, continual changes of climate, unfamiliar foods, indigestion, diarrhoea and vomiting, sunstroke, sleep deprivation and their relative inexperience made competing in Colombia a formidable task. By the standards of European amateur cycling the Vuelta was also extremely long, although the roads, said the Belgians (to Arámbula's ecstasies), were far superior to those at home. The Colombian fans, all the foreign teams agreed, were unbelievably passionate, but its cyclists simply had no comprehension of teamwork.

On the second day of racing *El Tiempo* commented, 'The idea of dubbing the XX Vuelta a Colombia the "Tour of Peace" has proven extremely well-judged, given the events of the last few days, during which the race was threatened with cancellation ... Indeed, in such circumstances reason itself dictated the necessity of the Vuelta. It will contribute (indeed, can be seen to be doing so) to dimming the public memory of its political preoccupations, and providing a motive of distraction.'

As they had during the 1964 Vuelta, the major national newspapers published front-page photographs from the competition, set among news stories of the curfews in force around Colombia. As the race swept across Colombia, curfews lifted in its wake. The Vuelta left Neiva, the capital of Huila. Two days later, as the riders reached Armenia, the Huila curfew was relaxed. On Sunday 3 May the riders descended from Riosucio to La Pintada, then climbed the Alto de Minas on their way to Medellín. The government associated itself with the race's sunny climate by dispatching Minister for Communications Antonio Díaz García to ride pillion on a scooter driven by Ramón Hoyos, who was commentating for Radio Caracol. Two days later, on Tuesday 5 May, the incumbent President Lleras declared that normality reigned. By Saturday 9 May overall race leadership was being hotly disputed between two riders from

Cundinamarca's 'A' team. The equality of the leading riders and the fury of their duel invited comparison with the recently concluded electoral campaign. In its sports pages Castro Caycedo could use the headline, 'Vuelta reaches its 19 April.'

The youngest of the leaders was Niño. He delivered his challenge to team-mate Francisco Triana on stage nine, the toughest of the race's thirteen stages and a nightmare for the Europeans. The route led from Medellín over the Alto de Minas to the village of La Pintada, and continued through Riosucio to a second mountain prize at the 2,200-metre Alto del Tigre. There, after nearly four hours of racing, Rafael Antonio Niño dropped Triana. Forty minutes later, after descending through a violent cloudburst to the stage finish at Anserma, Niño had gained nearly six minutes. Playing on his name, meaning 'child', *El Tiempo* ran the headline, 'Niño transformed into Giant.'

The following day – the penultimate stage – he lost his lead. The veterans, with Cochise at their head, locked Niño into the group and allowed Gustavo Rincón, another senior rider, to escape. The final stage from La Dorada to Bogotá, with the gruelling 36-kilometre ascent from Villeta to La Tribuna, would decide the 1970 Vuelta a Colombia. The vets, favouring a Rincón victory, contained Niño during the first two climbs of the day. But on the final ascent to La Tribuna, Niño found a way through. Further on he caught an escapee. Miguel Samacá was one of Colombia's most formidable climbers, and his collaboration guaranteed Niño's final victory. It was Boyacá's first Vuelta win. Miguel Samacá was third; two years later he became the second rider from the department of Boyacá to dominate the national sport in the 1970s. Like Niño, Samacá's royal road to the Vuelta a Colombia began as a bicycle courier for a drugstore. His barrel chest, indigenous features and improbable tolerance of pain gave him an extraordinary presence. But for now Niño was the national hero, and the day after the Vuelta finished, President-Elect Misael Pastrana held the obligatory public meeting with the new champion.

On 20 July, Congress opened. Thirty-eight senators and seventy-eight representatives refused to accept the election results. After the trauma of the elections, the technocratic president, Misael Pastrana, responded to the realities that had been highlighted by the campaign. Urban renewal took on a new urgency. The beneficiaries of his office, he declared, would be the proletariat, the marginalized, the homeless and the impoverished migrants to the cities. He announced a development plan to improve housing and the distribution of real estate in the towns and cities. In 1970 40,000 new houses were built under the national housing plan. It was hoped that the demand created by this construction boom would stimulate the entire economy, leading to lower rents and house prices. In recognition of Niño's Vuelta success the deeds of one of the new houses was presented to him.

In June 1971 Rojas Pinilla converted ANAPO into an independent socialist party, a 'Third Party' in Colombian political language. But the movement never again reached its electoral high of April 1970. By mimicking ANAPO's policies, Pastrana's programmes sapped the movement's popularity. But as soon as subsequent elections showed reduced support for the 'Third Party', urban reform was dropped from the government's priorities. At the 1972 congressional elections only a third of the electorate turned out. Liberalism took half of all votes cast, Conservatism a third, and ANAPO just 21 per cent. The movement began to collapse into itself. Many felt that the General had shown weakness in accepting electoral defeat. The movement's implosion was given greater force by General Rojas Pinilla's declining health. His daughter, María Eugenia Rojas de Moreno, was elected leader. Three days before the 1972 Vuelta a Colombia left Popayán, the majority of Colombians ignored the administrative elections of

16 April. Those who voted – 40 per cent of the electorate – supported the parties of the National Front. It was the end of ANAPO's flirtation with power.

The Pastrana years saw high growth but also high inflation, and in 1973 the economic crisis touched the Vuelta directly. Population flight from the countryside, encouraged by the demand for unskilled labour created by Pastrana's housing policies, had given Colombia an urban population of 13.5 million, with just 9 million left in rural areas. Many of the more recent arrivals were living in misery.

When stage one of the Vuelta finished at the town of Puerto Tejada in the Valle del Cauca, the riders were swamped by aggrieved locals, who forced them down broken streets into squalid ghettos. They wanted their lives to register on the national consciousness. The stage was annulled.

On the day of the Puerto Tejada protest, Cochise won his first European victory in the Cittá di Camaiore Grand Prix in Italy. Recent Camaiore victors – Eddy Merckx in 1971 and Roger De Vlaemink in 1972 – proved the calibre of Cochise's victory. 'A true champion won here today,' said Merckx. Colombia basked in Cochise's glory, even though Cochise and Camaiore seemed very far away.

Back at the Vuelta, meanwhile, Niño committed parricide. Between Riosucio and Medellín he destroyed Cochise's old record for the stage over the Alto de Minas. The difference was more than five minutes. Of the rest, only Samacá could finish within Cochise's old time; Pachón arrived third, five minutes three seconds after the winner. It seemed that nothing but an accident could prevent Niño from winning his second Vuelta.

On the penultimate stage the accident happened. Niño duelled with Samacá over La Línea. As they reached the closing kilometres of the stage, they were still locked together. Losing grip on the greasy road surface, Niño went down. Samacá seized his chance and sped off towards the finish. But Niño remained cool: he stood upright, checked his bike for damage, remounted, then smoothly accelerated to his body's limit. The fall had cost him time, but Niño was invulnerable. Samacá gained one minute ten seconds, but the Vuelta went to Niño by two minutes ten seconds.

Days after the 1973 Vuelta had finished, Niño had his chance to shine in Europe: he led a Colombian team in the Grand Prix de l'Avenir, the current manifestation of the amateur Tour de France. The event remained impossible to compare with Colombian events. The mountains were far from the start, and the fast flat opening stages through gusting winds required skills unknown in the tropics.

The alienation of the Colombian riders began at the prologue, a short team time trial. The Colombians predictably finished ninth out of eleven teams. On stage one across the Aubagne to Palavas-les-flots in the South of France, fierce sidewinds forced the Colombians out of the leading group. They had little experience of riding in protective echelons, taking turns to shelter from the wind. Even limiting their losses to ten minutes cost them enormous efforts. Niño ended the stage with knee pains; the following day Colombia's great hope, and by far the most accomplished rider in the team, abandoned. His disappointment fell into a pattern that was to last throughout Niño's career. His only victory outside Colombia would be a single stage in the Tour of Mexico. In his homeland he was unbeatable; abroad he was anonymous.

The challenge was now taken up by Abelardo Ríos, a young climbing specialist from Medellín. On the flat second stage from Pezenas to Argeles-sur-mer, Ríos attacked with the Spaniard Enrique Martínez, and followed him home in second place. One minute twelve seconds behind them, the mass sprint brought Luis H. Días in fourth. In the first mountain stage the following day, Ríos was second again, separated from a stage win by just half a wheel. He advanced six places in the General Classification to thirteenth place, five minutes fifty-five seconds behind the new race leader, Italy's Giambattista Baronchelli. As each day passed, Ríos and Luis H. Días advanced tentatively up the classification. By the end of the twelve-stage race, Ríos was ninth and Días tenth. All but Niño finished the race. After the ecstasies of Pachón's Mexican triumph and Cochise's world-beating, Colombia greeted its honourable losers coolly.

Niño's French disappointment didn't prevent him following Cochise to Europe to ride beside Giovanni Battaglin of the Jolly Ceramica team, one of Italy's most exciting prospects. Now a frame manufacturer, Battaglin's memories of Niño are ambivalent: 'When Cochise came to Europe, he surprised us. He was not only a complete rider technically, he was intelligent, excellent company and ballsy. I had a word with him about Colombian riders, and he recommended Niño. With Cochise's help we made contact and arranged to bring him to Europe. But Niño never adapted to life away from home, and it came out in his riding. Don't misunderstand me: in the mountains during the Giro d'Italia, he was strong and helped me a great deal. But I always felt he had an extra gear, one I never saw him use.'

Cochise remembers it as an unhappy season for his compatriot: 'In those huge pelotons of 180 riders, much bigger than in Colombia, he couldn't position himself. I'd drop back and bring him forward on my wheel. But when I looked back, he was gone. He couldn't hold his position. He was a fine rider, but he couldn't adjust to European racing. I advised him to return to Colombia. He still had a great future ahead of him. He was young.'

The journalist Germán Castro Caycedo met Niño in Rome that year: 'There he was with his long hair and hostile introversion. The Italians poked fun at him, they called him "Indian". You couldn't find a greater contrast between Cochise, the Antioquian, open, outgoing, comfortable in any surroundings, and Niño, the Boyacá peasant. No wonder he couldn't express himself on his bike.'

In November, Niño returned to Colombia for his final professional race, a five-day event around the Antioquian capital named the POC Classic, rightly billed as Colombia's greatest international event since the *El Colombiano* Classic of 1958. POC stood for Polímeros Colombianos, a manmade fibre manufacturer wholly owned by Coltejer. In 1972 the Polímeros Colombianos chairman, Luis Felipe Echavarría, from a dynasty of Catholic tycoons that dominated the Medellín economy, had sponsored a cycling team for the first time. More recently he had funded an expedition by a national quartet to Italy's amateur national tour, and sponsored a works team. Now he brought the cream of world professional cycling to Medellín. Eddy Merckx withdrew at the last moment due to injury. Giambattista Baronchelli, the winner of the 1973 Tour de l'Avenir, could not travel due to an injured elbow. But with those exceptions, Echavarría had assembled many of the leading professional cyclists to take on the local amateurs. The Spanish team Kas was led by José Manuel Fuente, third in the 1973 Tour de France. Fuente's team-mate Domingo Perurena was the reigning Tour de France King of the Mountains.

Naturally, the event was partly a showcase for Cochise, Medellín's greatest son. He brought Coppi's Italian successor Gimondi and the Bianchi-Campagnolo team. Giovanni Battaglin and Jolly Ceramica agreed to accompany Niño on his last race with the team. Battaglin recalls, 'If he'd stayed a second year, he would have improved. But he preferred to return home. And when we went to Colombia at the end of 1974, we saw him in his own country, where he was a different rider.'

Felice Gimondi was riding with Cochise. 'For the warmth of the welcome, the fans, and also the Colombian riders, it was an excellent experience. The downside was our performance. I had started the season wearing the shirt of the World Champion. A good Milan-San Remo, then a competitive Giro, but by November I was spent – we all were. So we didn't put up a terribly impressive performance for the Colombian fans. We'd arrived only two days earlier, and began the event almost immediately. I remember having difficulty acclimatizing to the altitude. From Medellín we went up to 3,000 or 3,200 metres. It was hard to wring the oxygen out of the air.'

Battaglin remembers his trip with fondness: 'We spent nearly a month in Colombia at the end of the season, in and around Medellín. It's a wonderful country. I loved it. The climate was remarkable: extremes of heat, cold and humidity. The Colombians were fired up; the European riders were tired. The first stage was a circuit ending in a bunch sprint won by Perurena. On each of the following stages there were three or four climbs. We only saw the Colombians at the starting line. We said goodbye, and saw them again in the evening. It was during the rainy season, and on the slippery roads our better bike-handling skills allowed us to make up time. But they reacted like men possessed.'

With just one flat stage and no time trial, the POC Classic was engineered to favour the local riders. Furthermore, it exposed the visitors to four classic routes known in intimate detail to every Colombian participant. The flat stage was the first: a circuit around Medellín, starting and ending at the POC factory. The Spaniard Perurena won it, with Colombia's finest sprinter Jaime Galeano Rua and Italy's Felice Gimondi in close attendance. A little known rider named Carlos Julio Siachoque was fourth. The second stage was the Vuelta a Oriente, the eastern circuit, leaving Medellín via Guarné (where Ramón Hoyos resides) and returning later in the day. A youngster from Boyacá named José Patrocinio Jiménez emerged to win the day. Perurena, Gimondi and Siachoque remained in the lead.

Stage three was a return ride to the village of Santa Rosa de Osos. Despite another Colombian victory, Perurena, Gimondi and Siachoque remained in the top three positions. The following day, on the alternative Vuelta a Oriente, via the terrible Santa Helena climb Gimondi succumbed to fatigue and lost ten minutes, while Perurena allowed Siachoque to gain four minutes and take the overall lead.

The race ended with the classic return to La Pintada. Race leader Carlos Julio Siachoque sealed his overall triumph with a solo victory. Colombians filled the first twelve places. Gimondi, second only to Merckx in the hierarchy of world cycling, would finish thirteenth. Perurena, another of Europe's giants, was the second overseas rider, in eighteenth place.

Niño, meanwhile, had abandoned on stage four. It was the end of his unhappy adventure with a professional European team. But the experience was not wasted. In Europe he had studied every aspect of team organization with cold detachment. He returned home with clear ideas about team finance, organization and tactics, and with them he revolutionized Colombian cycling. He found sponsorship from a major national bank, the Banco Cafetero. Then, as undisputed team leader, he hired his own *domestiques*, according to the European tradition, to ride themselves to breaking point for his benefit. If he had a puncture, they were paid to stop and give him one of their wheels. If he had a mechanical problem, they were paid to give him their bike. In return the collective team winnings were pooled and divided out equally.

The ruthless application of European tactics, combined with Niño's uncommon physical capacities, gave him success beyond compare. He won the 1975, 1977 and 1978 Vueltas a Colombia, and the 1975, 1977, 1978 and 1979 RCN Classics. In 1974 he was in Europe. A knee injury kept him out of the 1976 Vuelta and RCN Classic, when his team-mate José Patrocinio Jiménez won both titles. And in 1979 a heavy fall on stage one of the Vuelta ruined his Tour of

Colombia. He won six in all; absence and misfortune prevented him from winning eight or nine. Many connoisseurs in Colombia regard Niño as Cochise's lieutenant in the hierarchy of Colombian cycling. For a decade every other rider in Colombia scratched for crumbs beneath Niño's table.

Yet the margins of his victories were narrow: in the two-week Tour of Colombia he won by a minute and a half in 1970, two minutes in 1973, fifteen seconds in 1977, just over a minute the following year, and eleven seconds in 1980. In 1971, over four stages, Niño won the RCN Classic by fifty seconds; in 1979 over five, he won by thirty seconds. Cochise had won thirty-nine stages of the Vuelta; Hoyos thirty-eight. Niño only ever won thirteen. Colombian cycling had strength in depth. If Cochise had recommended Pachón or Samacá to Giovanni Battaglin, or if Patrocinio Jiménez had had the chance of a European apprenticeship instead of the introvert Niño, more Colombians might have broken into the professional scene by the mid-1970s. But it was his failure in Europe that allowed Niño to change cycling history: he returned to Colombia young enough to apply the lessons he learnt abroad and transform its national cycling culture.

COLOMBIA WAS CHANGING in other ways. At the end of 1973, when Niño was preparing to leave for the Old Continent for the first time, teasing advertisements in the Colombian press had begun to announce a mysterious remedy to a number of ailments: 'Depression? Failing memory? M-19 is coming.' 'Washed out? Listless? Wait for M-19.' On 17 January 1974 the final advert appeared: 'Today, M-19 arrives!' That chilly Tuesday the sword worn by Simón Bolívar when he entered the capital after defeating the Royalist troops was removed from a display cabinet in the Liberator's House in Bogotá. In place of the national icon a note was left proclaiming, 'Bolívar, your sword shall fight again.' It was signed 'M-19'.

The 19 April Movement, M-19, derived its name and its anger from the presumed electoral fraud of the 19 April 1970 elections. Part of General Rojas's decaying movement had crystallized into Socialist ANAPO. Some among its recruits, reinforced by former members of Tirofijo's FARC and its rival and contemporary, the National Liberation Army (ELN), formed the 19 April Movement, or M-19.

Convinced that the FARC and the other established insurgents lacked the vitality to transform the nation, a genial Caribbean named Jaime Bateman Cayón had founded the movement in 1973, together with ex-FARC militants, disillusioned leaders from Rojas Pinillo's National Alliance, Christian and student activists, and professionals. Bateman's charisma enthused Colombians unimpressed by either the longstanding guerrilla groupings or the status quo. Building a revolution, he said, has to be a celebration, engaging the deepest feelings and affection of the people. M-19 installed itself in the cities and gained the sympathy of the middle classes and the university-educated radicals alienated by the policies of President Pastrana. The Movement soon became identified with daring and imagination. Committed to personality, publicity and improvisation, M-19 was a guerrilla movement with style.

Niño's 1970 Vuelta had momentarily calmed the ghosts of the 1970 presidential elections, but with M-19 they rose to haunt the decade.

A deep pool of sympathizers was created for M-19 in 1975 after frost had decimated Brazil's coffee yield. International coffee prices had hit record levels and Colombia had experienced massive economic instability. Colombians had always attributed the weakness of the economy to the lack of foreign exchange, but the export explosion flooded the country with it and provoked price increases of over 40 per cent per annum. Economic chaos was the result. On 14 September

1977 a general strike began in Bogotá in protest. It degenerated into violence and left more than twenty dead. Some segments of society were visibly radicalized. The strike marked the beginning of a new period of violence; many Colombians saw in the events of 1978 nothing less than the return of the old Violencia. By the time the next President came to power that year, the National Front era should have been long dead. But President Julio Cesar Turbay Ayala's new cabinet enraged opponents of the power-sharing pact: it contained seven Liberals, five Conservatives and a hawkish new Minister of Defence demanding greater political influence for the military.

Turbay's was an age of impotence. Lacking any historical mission, he could do little more than attend the pressures of the strongest economic groups. Within a month new measures designed to clamp down on the guerrillas were unveiled, including increased sentences for kidnap, extortion, arson, armed assault and distributing subversive literature. When a former minister was murdered by an unknown group of radicals, the military launched a campaign of torture, disappearances and assassinations. M-19's response ridiculed the government and its repressive apparatus.

In October 1978 M-19 members rented a house in the north of Bogotá. Over the next three months shifts of diggers sunk an 80-metre tunnel that reached beneath a massive military arms dump. On the morning of 31 December the diggers broke into the arsenal. It took two days to lift 5000 weapons from under the noses of the army, and 55 gallons of vaseline to grease them for storage in safe houses all over Colombia. That the weaponry far exceeded anything the movement could use, and was recovered almost in its entirety soon afterwards, merely heightened the irreverence of the gesture.

In 1980 the audacity of M-19's actions reached a new pitch. At midday on Wednesday 27 February the Ambassador of the Dominican Republic in Bogotá was hosting a short cocktail party to celebrate the 136th anniversary of Dominican independence. From a shop in sight of the embassy, details of the guests' arrival were relayed to a safe house nearby. When a number of dignitaries were inside, the order was given, 'Let's go.' Sixteen members of the guerrilla organization M-19 surprised the ambassadors of the United States of America, the Vatican, Mexico, Uruguay, Venezuela, Brazil, Israel, Switzerland, Egypt, Haiti, Guatemala, Costa Rica and Austria, together with a number of commercial attachés, vice consuls, diplomats and wives. The former ambassador of Nicaragua, kidnapped by M-19 for a few hours twelve months earlier, was also taken. World headlines were already preoccupied by the fate of fifty-two American hostages held since November 1979 by Iranian students at gunpoint in the US Embassy in Tehran, where they would remain in captivity for 444 days. Now the fifty-seven hostages in Bogotá and their captors also prepared for a long wait. So began the greatest national crisis since 19 April 1970, and once again the Tour of Colombia would be intimately linked to its denouement.

The Colombian Cycling Federation had seen upheavals of its own in recent years. Through Raphael Antonio Niño, contact with European cycling had transformed every aspect of the sport in Colombia: from diet and preparation to contracts and finance. But the national cycling authorities had stagnated. General Arámbula Durán, growing old in an office that looked out over Bogotá city cemetery, was a spent force. At the Cycling Federation's general assembly in 1979, therefore, the regional representatives of the core cycling departments – Antioquia, Santander, Boyacá and Cundinamarca – broke away from General Arámbula's official body and constituted a rival organization, the Federation of Colombian Cycling. Their leader, and the instigator of the split, was a tactless, opinionated, imperious dreamer: Miguel Ángel Bermúdez – an industrialist and politician whose greatest gift was for making enemies. Things started badly. In

January 1980 the rival Federations organized simultaneous Under-21 Tours of Colombia. But before the elite Tour of Colombia, a second assembly ended the schism. Bermúdez became the boss and now nothing could stop him.

In his 1986 book *Un nouveau cyclisme*, Xavier Louy of the Société du Tour de France wrote:

> Solid, corpulent and with huge whiskers, Miguel Ángel Bermúdez has a pronounced taste for the official speeches... His personality leaves no one indifferent and has spiced up the dismal atmosphere of UCI meetings, due to his shortcomings in the art of diplomacy... At races, he is overcome by such emotion that the President of the Federation becomes a fanatical follower of Colombia... He is working passionately to make the Vuelta a Colombia one of the great events of the international calendar and to bring the World Championships to Colombia. With Miguel Ángel Bermúdez, Colombian cycling has a Federation that is going places... It is hardly surprising that Colombian cycling has an elite of thirty or forty international riders, some of whom are among the world's finest stage racers.

To be near Miguel Ángel Bermúdez is to be energized by the force field that surrounds him. After he had been elected Governor of Boyacá in January 2000, I sat all day in his office, as a stream of petitioners sought jobs and references and solutions to local disputes. Miguel Ángel had an instant answer, a joke and a smile, and no one left empty handed or feeling aggrieved. Within months political scandals had seen him hounded out of office. But back in 1980 Bermúdez needed all his bluster as the national crisis threatened his dissident Vuelta a Colombia, due to depart in April.

In the afternoon of the first day of the Embassy siege the Colombian Chancellor Diego Uribe Varel communicated with the Mexican ambassador Ricardo Galán, effectively opening negotiations with a guerrilla group for the first time in Colombian history. In the small hours M-19 stated its demands: an end to human rights abuses, freedom for political prisoners of all organizations, and $50 million. As a gesture of goodwill, the women in the embassy were freed.

On Sunday 2 March a yellow van with the doors removed drew up outside the embassy. There, government negotiators met with the M-19 negotiator Carmenza Cardona Londoño, known as Chiqui, accompanied by Ricardo Galán as a witness to the talks. In his later book about the siege, the leader of the hostage-takers, Rosemberg Pabón Pabón, alias Comandante Uno, described Chiqui as 'well tried in battle, disciplined, clear in our political vision, with great experience working with the lumpen proletariat in the poor parts of Cali and with indigenous communities; tender, happy, full of life – and a fierce fighter!' What most dismayed the government, he added, was to have to negotiate with a woman – masked, short and plump.

Five rounds of talks took place between 2 and 13 March; Chiqui reported back after each two-hour session to Pabón. On 9 March, between rounds, local elections were held throughout the country, with 70 per cent abstaining. The press reported visits by US and Israeli counter-terrorism specialists; the government reacted by censoring the media, local and international. Army helicopters buzzed the embassy while the armed forces cleared the area. The Chancellor issued a statement rejecting the freedom of prisoners out of hand, and a bloodbath looked imminent. But on 24 March negotiations recommenced. The government sought to wear down the guerrillas by keeping talks slow and inconclusive. When M-19's demands for observers from the Organization of American States and the International Red Cross to witness the trials of political prisoners were turned down, Mexico's Galán walked out. His protest forced a government U-turn: the observers arrived the next day.

Faced with the Embassy siege, the leaders of the Colombian

Cycling Federation argued that the Vuelta should be postponed. Miguel Ángel Bermúdez Escobar disagreed, and the seven major departmental cycling leagues went with him. Bermúdez brought in sponsorship from Sello Negro, the distillery of which he was managing director, and the Tour began on 14 April with a 4-kilometre evening prologue by lamplight through the town of Paipa, Boyacá.

Three days later both the Vuelta and the negotiations took an unexpected turn. During the individual time trial a sudden headwind threatened Niño's attempt to win a sixth Vuelta as he lost time against his greatest rivals. Meanwhile, a provocative Amnesty International report denounced Colombia's systematic violation of human rights through arbitrary detention and arrests, torture, assassination and disappearances, and noted the fragility of the rights to political representation, expression, association and movement. M-19 took the report as international corroboration of the grievances expressed in the embassy occupation.

On Saturday 19 April President Turbay Ayala accused Amnesty International of violating Colombian sovereignty, while Jaime Bateman, the M-19 chief, issued a new set of demands through the journalist Germán Castro Caycedo: an amnesty for 311 political prisoners, the lifting of the siege, suspension of martial law and a national dialogue with a constituent assembly to build Colombian democracy.

Niño, meanwhile, won his first stage of the Vuelta between Armenia and Buga. His greatest rival, a moustachioed hard man named Alfonso Flórez, responded the following Tuesday by winning stage ten. Two days later delegates of the human rights committee of the Organization of American States were appointed to take over the negotiations, and the occupation entered its final hours. The ransom demand had dropped to $1 million and free passage to Cuba.

As Niño powered to victory over the Alto de Minas on the Vuelta's penultimate stage from Supia to Medellín, the final arrangements for a peaceful resolution of the siege were made. Early the following day, Sunday 27 April 1980, after sixty-one days, M-19's occupation of the Dominican Embassy ended. The fifteen M-19 guerrillas and twelve of their hostages boarded a Cuban aircraft and flew to Havana. Minutes after boarding, the guerrillas surrendered their weapons to Cuban security agents. They were now no longer terrorists and hostages, but simply guests of the Cuban government.

The parting of the M-19 members and their former hostages showed few signs of hostility. Dominican Ambassador Diego Asencio told the press that relations with the guerrillas had been cordial and correct, and after the first seventy-two hours there had been no major problems. The Guatemalan Ambassador, Aquiles Pinto Flórez, had written a number of poems during the occupation. The Brazilian ambassador, Geraldo Do Nascimento, said farewell to 'Comandante Uno' with a warm embrace that lasted several seconds. Guatemalan consul Roberto Castañeda hugged one of the female guerrillas and pulled down her mask for a few seconds. The Embassy siege left no casualties. Of the sixteen guerrillas who held the Embassy, there were three couples, and two more couples fell in love during the siege. And the Mexican Ricardo Galán, it was rumoured, had fallen for Chiqui.

In Medellín, meanwhile, after fifteen days and 1,677 kilometres, Niño defended his eleven-second lead over Flórez and entered Medellín the first, and probably the last, winner of six Vueltas a Colombia.

On Monday 28 April 1980 Colombia's national newspapers juxtaposed pictures of an airliner landing overseas with the smiling faces of its finest cyclists. *El Tiempo*'s headline read, 'Jubilation as the drama ends.' Over the next decade it was to become a familiar formula.

Before it did, Niño retired. Not immediately: he rode for three more years. But his career had reached its natural end.

Sitting in a cold house in northern Bogotá opposite Raphael Antonio Niño, I suspected that, for all his victories and status, the medal he had won as a kid in his second-ever race, when he had finished sixth, meant more to him than all his trophies, and that if anything was recoverable from the past, he would choose that first touring bike. The day he bought it was the happiest of his life. He would give most things to have it back: to have that feeling back.

8. All the President's Men

KING COTTON DROVE the industrial revolution, but the energy powering Colombia's cyclists comes from Citizen Cane.

Only an expert eye can identify when the sugarcane is bursting with juice. When the moment arrives, the household mill is dosed with diesel – in poorer settings the mules are yoked – and the crushers come spluttering into life. The spongy fibres, ravished by savage metal teeth, yield up their honey, and from copper vat to copper vat the residue is boiled and reduced until the final elixir slops into the cooling mould. There it gently hardens into the pride of Colombian cuisine: *panela* or *dulce macho*.

There are also great industrial crushers that never stop – computerized mills of stainless steel with controlled spaces and sterile rooms. The appetite for *panela* is unending. Cut into cubes and dressed in banana bark, *panela* is sold in the best delicatessens, the dingiest roadside shacks or, in remoter areas, from the back of a truck.

The purest varieties are dark brown, although some *panelas* are bleached to a delicate yellow for consumers seeking a more refined experience. When the hot water hits it, it takes time to dissolve, and in the subsequent solution words and things unite: *aguapanela* is Colombia's staple drink. Steaming *aguapanela* with a grilled pancake of sweetcorn pulp – *arepa* – makes a traditional country breakfast, while in the coffee regions the local roast is timed to blend with the deep molasses taste of *aguapanela* poured through the filter. And when the flu spreads over the crowded highlands in April and October, piping *aguapanela* is served to the poorly. In the sweltering lowlands, by contrast, it is chilled and flavoured with lemon juice to provide respite from the cauldron heat. Cheap, satisfying and nostalgically sought by Colombians living abroad, *aguapanela* is an affectionate reminder of home, and a poignant symbol of its backwardness.

Ephraim Forero won the first Vuelta a Colombia washing bananas and sticks of *panela* down with flasks of tea. Even today, *aguapanela* sloshes about in the water bottles of Colombia's finest riders. Solid refreshment comes in the form of a gelatinous delight derived from red guayaba: *bocadillo*. Gnawed on the longest ride, *bocadillo* revitalizes the muscles and sharpens the mind with its citric sweetness. In September 1980 bolts of *panela* and *bocadillo* were shipped out to Paris with six of Colombia's finest riders. The goal? To bring to fruition the transformation spearheaded by Miguel Ángel Bermúdez, and establish Colombia as a global cycling superpower.

A visionary, an inspirational motivator and a man of limitless energies, Bermúdez bullied, cajoled and charmed his way towards the financial and political support to take a Colombian team to Europe and win the Tour de France. It was an outrageous idea, but one with firm foundations in the Colombian imagination. Colombia has always been in awe of its landscapes, especially the eternal, indomitable Andes. A concentrate of Andean severity flowed through its cyclists' veins: how could they not, ultimately, prove invincible? After all, only a puncture had spoiled the Indomitable Zipa's world championships in 1953, and at the Melbourne Olympics three years later, only inexperience had ruined Hoyos's title bid: he had timed his attack perfectly to cross the line first – before realizing that there was still a lap to go. In 1958 Hoyos had then crushed two of the finest riders on Earth, Coppi and Koblet; that they were at least semi-retired, and riding in conditions they had never experienced before, had little to do with it. Pachón had defeated the mighty Zoetemelk: if the Dutchman was just a kid, riding at altitude for the first time, that too was irrelevant. And in 1974 Siachoque had seen off Gimondi, Battaglin and the finest Spaniards; the Europeans, riding out of season, were tired and under-motivated, admittedly, but that was a mere detail! Even Cochise only went to Europe after years of semi-retirement. If he'd had his chance younger, he would surely have been another Coppi, Merckx or Hinault. It may have been a self-interested interpretation of the past, but the truth was that Colombian national riders had never had the opportunity to compete on level terms on the international stage of professional cycling. Now, however, a new generation was emerging, ready to take up the tradition and continue to Europe. An inverted avalanche of talent was roaring up the Andes.

In 1974 another Boyacá talent had appeared. In January, José Patrocinio Jiménez, 'Patro', aged twenty, finished sixth in the Vuelta al Táchira. In May's Vuelta a Colombia he was best new rider, and in November he had taken a stage win at the POC Classic. Patro was gaunt and handsome; the skin flowed close over his proud cheekbones. When you meet him now, two decades on, you still feel that at any moment he might dive out of the room, leap on a bike and sprint up the nearest hill. He was the finest Colombian climber of the 1970s, and finished runner-up to Niño in the 1975 and 1977 Tours of

Colombia and the 1977 and 1979 RCN Classics. In 1976, when Niño was injured, Patro replaced him in the Banco Cafetero team and won both events. He also won the mountains competition in the 1979, 1980 and 1981 Tours of Colombia. He rode his first Tour de France in 1983, years past his peak, and his performance there indicated that he might, in his prime, have competed with the finest in the world. Had it not been for Niño's tactical stranglehold, Patro might have matched him blow for blow. But as the 1970s ended and Niño's reign came to an end, another fine rider replaced Niño at the helm of Colombian cycling, and Patro started coming second to him, too.

Alfonso Flórez Órtiz was no physical match for Patro, and lacked his rival's heroic looks: Flórez was slight, hunched and cross-eyed, and only a remarkable determination made him a champion. Initially he showed little talent. 'He wasn't very good at all,' says Clímaco Guzmán, now a track coach in Flórez' hometown of Bucaramanga, who rode against him as a child. 'He didn't have the physique, he was graceless. We used to ride a regular circuit in Bucaramanga, which I normally won. When Alfonso began to ride, he'd ride like a lunatic, attacking on his own, getting caught, and attacking again.' But what Flórez lacked in innate ability he made up for in courage, intelligence and discipline, and in 1976 Cochise brought Flórez to Medellín to ride in the Vuelta. At Tunja on stage five Cochise fell ill and had to retire. As each day passed, Flórez got better and better, and he eventually won two stages to finish sixth overall. His talent was slowly flowering.

'Alfonso had unbelievable self-belief,' says Guzmán, 'in spite of his defects – in spite of everything. He was doggedly persistent, and became the best rider in Colombia. He became extraordinary. He was extremely intelligent on the road. His team manager only had to speak to Alfonso and he was guaranteed absolute discipline during the race. Alfonso was always talking, pointing, cajoling: "So-and-so! Go and win this Mountains prize"; "So-and-so! Keep your eye on him." He'd try to give the younger riders the opportunity to show themselves. And if there was a breakaway, all he had to do was nod his head and the chase was instantly organized. Alfonso was the undisputed *patron*. And his team won virtually everything. That's what he became: a magnate.'

In 1977 San Cristóbal in the Venezuelan Táchira hosted the World Cycling Championships. Flórez was selected to ride in a team that also included Pachón and Patrocinio Jiménez. By the time the road race approached its inevitable bunch sprint, Pachón and Flórez were in a leading group including the great Italian sprinter Claudio Corti. Corti won it; Flórez was the first Colombian to finish, in twelfth place.

But Flórez finally fulfilled his potential on the last day of the 1979 Tour of Colombia. His chief rival that day was his own teammate, a fine Antioquian rider named Gonzalo Marín. Marín and Flórez were similar in many ways. Both enjoyed brilliant campaigns in European amateur races. Both played key roles in opening professional stage racing to their countrymen. Destiny would also reserve a violent death for each of them.

Marín was the most agile rider of his generation. By spinning tiny gears he staved off muscle fatigue. And by slip streaming expertly he saved energy for the key moments. These skills had made him, at the age of twenty-two, the best new rider in the 1972 Vuelta – a race he could have won, had he not been forced to work for his team leader. In 1974 Marín was the most successful Colombian against fine European riders on Italy's amateur national tour, the Piccolo Giro, finishing second. And throughout the early 1970s he was far superior to Flórez, finishing fifth in two Vueltas, 1973 and 1975, and second in two RCN Classics, 1973 and 1974. But as the decade aged, Flórez matured, and throughout the 1979 season the two riders traded blow for blow. By the morning of the Vuelta a Colombia's final stage, Marín was wearing the leader's jersey, albeit with a lead of just one second. Then Niño attacked: Flórez, Marín's team-mate, went after him, and the two-man breakaway built up a huge lead. Flórez was dragged away by Niño's attack to overall victory over his team-mate Marín.

His victory brought talk of betrayal and retribution, of huge losses by Medellín's betting mafia, of executioners contracted and released. Death threats were delivered. Flórez' wife Marta, nursing their new-born daughter, fielded menacing phone calls. The word was that the drug baron Pablo Escobar himself intervened to cool tempers at fever pitch. Subsequently, as Marín's career wound down, Flórez' years of iron discipline and clear vision forced him, and Colombia, into the world spotlight.

In the early 1980s the Tour de France was still for professionals only: for amateurs its organizers ran the Tour de l'Avenir. No Colombian had competed in the Tour de l'Avenir since 1973, but with only weeks to go before the start, Colombia managed to secure an invitation to the 1980 event – at the expense of Venezuela, who had already been invited.

With just four weeks to prepare his riders, time was against the team director Raul Mesa. To have any chance of success, the Colombians required something like a miracle: but of those, they had never been short. France, meanwhile, awaited Latin America's giants with bated breath. When the giants failed to show, and the diminutive figures of Patrocinio Jiménez, Alfonso Flórez and Rafael Acevedo disembarked instead, awe dissolved and pity took over. The new Olympic road-racing champion, Sergey Sukhoruchenkov, who was looking for his third consecutive victory in the Tour de l'Avenir, would eat their frail physiques for breakfast.

The pessimists were soon reassured. In the team time trial

Colombia lost over five minutes to the victors, Czechoslovakia. But on day four Flórez joined a ten-man breakaway that gained over five minutes on Suku. The Russian didn't care: he was marking Patrocinio Jiménez. They had ridden against each other at the Tour of Cuba, and Patro was the only Colombian he credited with realistic title hopes. But in April, Flórez had lost his Vuelta a Colombia title by just eleven seconds – to Niño; he had brought a terrible hunger to France, and now began to ride away with the race. After judiciously joining the winning breaks day after day, as evening drew in on day five he became the first Latin American ever to lead a European stage race.

It became a contest of wills: on the flat Flórez gritted his teeth; in the mountains he darted into the sky. His overall lead expanded to six minutes. But on stage eight Suku rocketed away from the field and led by four minutes at the foot of the final climb, La Joux Verte. Flórez kept his nerve: ascending with ruthless delicacy, he ate into the Russian's advantage and crossed the col less than two minutes behind. On the final descent into Morzine the two men squeezed such speed from the mountain air that their adhesion on the spiralling road edged towards zero. The heavier Suku, lurching downwards in a glissade on the limits of control, could only claw back a few seconds.

Day after day the Russians launched fierce depradations: Suku glowed with a champion's pride, staring down defeat. Given more time, he might have made up the deficit. But on 21 September 1980 Alfonso Flórez rode into Paris as champion.

It was a defining moment for the Colombians. With *panela*, *bocadillo* and Alfonso Flórez, Miguel Ángel Bermúdez' dream was becoming reality. The victors' reception at Bogotá was like the return of a World Cup-winning football team. Crowds hundreds of thousands strong greeted their riders and director along the route leading from the airport to the President's palace.

*

Over the following years Colombia attained encouraging results in Europe's elite amateur events. In 1981 Raphael Acevedo won the mountains competition at the Tour of Slovakia, and Patrocinio Jiménez, runner-up in the William Tell Grand Prix in Switzerland, finished third in the Tour de l'Avenir, open to professionals for the first time and won by the Frenchman Pascal Simon. Sukhoruchenkov was second. A year later Colombians won the Tour of Valsesia, in the shadow of Monte Rosa, Italy; came second in the amateur Giro d'Italia; and took third and fourth positions in the Tour de l'Avenir. A foundation of consistency was being laid.

Meanwhile, the RCN Classic was fortified into the home front of Colombia's assault on the citadel. Anxious to score points over its rival Radio Caracol, RCN expanded its race budget and invited the greatest cyclists in the world to participate. The Europeans treated the event as altitude training; the Colombians benefited tactically and morally by racing against and beating professional riders. In 1982, for instance, the international star was Pascal Simon, riding for Peugeot. He won two stages and finished fifth overall. Victory, however, fell to the Colombian who would become the best climber of the decade anywhere in the world.

Bogotá rises early, and the road to Fusagasugá was already snarled with traffic. Out of the city, smooth asphalt replaced the pot-holed cement, and we snaked southwards, losing 920 metres in altitude. The air filled with generous warmth. Every half-mile we passed a cyclist coming the other way. This was the Alto de Rosas, one of the great climbs of Colombian cycling, and the final ascent in many Vueltas a Colombia. It had once been a favourite training route for the man I was going to meet. The taxi driver was thrilled to learn our destination, and glowed with admiration as Luis Alberto Herrera Herrera greeted us at the door of his office in the garden town south of the capital where he grew up.

'Lucho' Herrera speaks quietly and in volleys that quickly tail off into silence. He belongs to Colombia's peasantry: unassuming, jovial and of few words. His childhood, he told me, was spent playing among the trees on these hills. His mother gave him his first bicycle to get to school. There he was told that his physique was too fragile for an athlete. It was an impression that fooled his adversaries throughout his career. It couldn't have been more wrong. With local riders, he climbed the Alto de Rosas, then rolled back down to climb it again and again. It was here, on the final stage of the Under-21 Tour of Colombia in 1980, that Lucho dropped the overall leader Martín Ramírez, himself a brilliant climber with a fine career ahead of him, and won the mountains competition. But it was on stage five of the 1981 RCN Classic, over Colombia's most legendary climb, La Línea, that Herrera exploded into domestic cycling. As ever, his bird-like frame and tiny limbs seemed too delicate to withstand the stresses of the stage, yet he rode away from the formidable trio of Niño, Flórez and another brilliant youngster, Fabio Parra, to win – even though in the General Classification he could only finish sixteenth. 'I was still a newcomer,' he observed.

However, in 1982, when he and his team attacked on stage seven, near Manizales, the European riders – even the main attraction, the Tour de l'Avenir champion Pascal Simon – were left standing. Herrera took over the leader's jersey and held it until the race finish at Medellín, where he also won the final stage. And in September 1982 he won his first international race, stage ten of the Tour de l'Avenir, between Dinvoc-les-Bains and the ski station at Morzine, earning temporary ownership of the King of the Mountains jersey.

Lucho Herrera and his rivals Fabio Parra and Martín Ramírez held Colombian cycling in their hands. An aura of optimism settled over the nation, and the unexpected prospect of civil peace brightened its radiance. For in November 1981 the first of an important series of peace commissions was convened, and the following year a new president, the Conservative Belisario Betancur, had been elected on a platform of peace talks. A survey he had commissioned suggested that 80 per cent of Colombians either sympathized with, were tolerant of or indifferent to the various guerrilla movements. Known simply by his distinctive forename, Belisario had to negotiate a political minefield to achieve a ceasefire from all the major guerrilla groups.

In April 1982, before negotiations could start, a light aircraft carrying M-19's charismatic leader Jaime Bateman to Panamá hit a violent storm and disappeared. Bateman's remains were not discovered until the following year. The electric typewriter lying next to his decaying remains was the only clue to his identity. In November 1982, between the death and its discovery, an amnesty was passed freeing 400 prisoners held for political crimes. The talks with the FARC and M-19 could begin.

The future looked bright. But the present was pandemonium. Since 1981 a slump had been corroding the economy, wearing down public services, spreading unemployment, undermining incomes and inflating prices. Less than a third of the population remained in the countryside. The remaining 19 million had flocked to the towns and cities, which were swelling with unplanned growth. Colombia had failed to invest in its human capital. By the mid-1980s Korea and Taiwan, which had had similar educational standards to Colombia in the 1950s, were attaining standards twice as high. Cycling exhibited the nation's underdevelopment as profoundly as wider social processes. In advanced Western nations and the Eastern bloc, the resources invested in national sports systems had long since replaced individual effort as the key to athletic success. By the late 1960s sportsmen and women from developing nations were increasingly crossing national boundaries to train: African track and field athletes, for example, were exploiting – and being exploited by – athletic scholarships in American universities. But the success of Colombian cycling still depended more on individual tenacity than national planning. 'Most of Colombia's athletes were produced by nothing but their own will-power,' sports scientist Dr Juan Darío Uribe told me in Medellín. 'The State never organized programmes to realize the potential of this country. Most cyclists were from the lower social, cultural and economic strata: many had suffered malnutrition in early childhood – a key period in an athlete's life. Miguel Ángel Bermúdez took a group of cyclists who had never had access to proper medical advice or sports medicine to compete in a completely different climate, and these men won our first victories in Europe.'

Raphael Mendoza, former cycling correspondent for *El Espectador*, rode in the Colombian team cars throughout the 1980s. When Colombia's international riders were first given medical check-ups, he was amazed at the results: 'For a long time there was considerable opposition to health checks. When they were finally held, the reasons for the resistance became clear: some couldn't stand on one leg, others couldn't perform basic co-ordination tests. And these were the very best riders – the ones selected for the national team!'

Just three years after Bermúdez had had his dream, he finally sent a team to the Tour de France. The event organizers had broken with tradition by declaring the 1983 event open. Amateur teams from beyond cycling's European pale were invited: the USA, Russia and East Germany. Colombia, too, was on the guest list. For Miguel Ángel Bermúdez it was an unmissable opportunity, and he needed 35 million pesos. But it was the worst time in decades to be looking for handouts: in 1982 six of Colombia's greatest industries – Coltejer, Fabricato, Avianca, Tejicóndor, Colmotores and Paz del Río – had reported losses totalling 5.64 billion pesos.* Bermúdez asked seven major Colombian businesses for 5 million pesos each. Of the seven, only one, the battery manufacturer Varta, gave a positive reply. The project looked to be foundering until Varta's managing director took a massive gamble by agreeing to underwrite the entire budget. So began an expedition Colombia has known ever since as 'The Great Adventure'.

Two of Colombia's great riders of the past, Ruben Darío Gómez and Cochise, were hired to direct the team, and the Colombian media prepared for a feeding frenzy. No less than thirty-five journalists travelled to France, with Radio Caracol planning to broadcast every racing moment for the first time in Tour history. In Bogotá and beyond, the national dailies and all the media were saturated with coverage. Neither Fabio Parra, the 1981 Vuelta winner, nor Lucho Herrera made the team – both rising stars were still considered too young – but the Colombian team was nonetheless full of promise, and former Avenir champion Alfonso Flórez was touted as a dark horse.

By the time the peloton hit the Pyrenees, however, ten days of interminable flat stages, long even by Tour standards – 299 kilometres one day, 257 the next, 222 a few days later – had drained and

* The Colombian domestic economy is dominated by two conglomerates run by major public figures. Julio Mario Santodomingo and Carlos Ardila Lulle are Colombia's sole entries in the *Forbes* magazine list of the super rich, and they divide many key economic and cultural activities with perfect symmetry. Santodomingo owns the Caracol radio and TV network; Ardila Lulle owns Radio Cadena Nacional (RCN), Caracol's principal rival. Santodomingo owns the Bavaria brewery, dominating the beer market; Ardila Lulle's Postobón brand controls the lucrative soft drinks market. Santodomingo owns Avianca, the Colombian international airline; Ardila Lulle acquired Coltejer, the textiles firm, in the mid-1970s. Of Colombia's sixteen Division One soccer teams, eight are sponsored by Santodomingo companies, and the remaining eight by Ardila Lulle brands. Especially in the 1980s, the rivalry between Caracol and RCN worked in favour of cycling, as RCN pushed its own event, the RCN Classic, to become Colombia's premier international cycling race, while Caracol bought the rights to the Vuelta a Colombia.

demoralized the Colombians. Two individual time trials penalized them one at a time, and the team time trial on stage three punished them collectively. Flórez, in particular, suffered with the pace and the cobblestones. Much had been expected of him, but by the morning of the first mountain stage, ten days and 1,600 kilometres into the race, he had had enough.

The road out of Pau, however, led up into the Pyrenees. As Flórez abandoned, his co-leader Patrocinio Jiménez launched a long-range attack, and in the company of Scotland's Robert Millar spent the day at the head of the Tour de France.

Patro had already met Millar. The Scot had travelled to Colombia twice before with Peugeot to ride the RCN Classic. There he was a pushover. But in this alien environment the tables were turned. Near the brow of the Peyresourde, the final climb of the day, Patro was pushing a much bigger gear than the Europeans, and Millar dropped him. On the descent into the town of Luchon, Patro faded into fourth place. Nevertheless, he had won enough mountains points to end the day leading the King of the Mountains competition. It was a moment of enormous significance to the Colombians: never before had a Colombian, and a Colombian amateur at that, worn the Tour de France mountain leader's talismanic polka-dot jersey.

Three days later he was ready to attack again. While he was sharing the stage lead with France's Gilbert Duclos-Lassalle, it emerged that the previous day's stage winner had failed a dope test. The peloton announced a go-slow in protest, and Duclos-Lassalle persuaded the Colombian to relent, thereby sacrificing his efforts. Nonetheless, Patro spent five days in the polka-dot jersey, finished third on the classic climb up the volcanic Puy-de-Dôme, and sounded Colombia's intentions for the future.

It was gruelling for the South American amateurs. Five of the ten Colombian starters had abandoned by the time the race reached the

Alps. One evening five European riders, convinced that Patro could reach the podium, offered him their services – for a price. Cochise's reaction was necessarily realistic: 'It would have been a waste of money. Pride would never have allowed the professional European riders to let an amateur South American win the Tour de France.'

Yet Patro wasn't the only Colombian to impress on the national team's first professional Tour. His team-mate Edgar Corredor, another Boyacá-born rider, finished third on Alpe d'Huez and again at Morzine, and ninth in the mountain time trial. Corredor, nicknamed 'Condorito' ('little condor') after a cartoon character to whom he bears a bizarre resemblance, was the only rider to beat the eventual winner, Laurent Fignon, in every mountain stage. On the climb into Morzine, Patro punctured, losing time and his hopes of a top ten finish, and when he fell in the Champs Elysées, Condorito overtook him as the highest ranked Colombian. They were sixteenth and seventeenth overall.

The Great Adventure had been a qualified success. The Colombians' Achilles' heel was the same as ever: the flat stages had cost Condorito over twenty of his twenty-six minute disadvantage. Still, Colombia could be proud. Impressed by their performance, European soigneurs purloined specimens of their exotic *panela* and *bocadillo* to examine them for miracle ingredients.

And although the sponsorship bill had eventually ballooned to nearly 60 million pesos, Varta's gamble had paid off. Hitherto Colombians had habitually referred to batteries as 'Ever Readies', but after the 1983 Tour, Varta added 11 per cent of the Colombian national market to its sales, and changed the national vocabulary. In the core European market it had also been a publicity coup for Varta's German mother company, whose sole acknowledgement of the fact was to buy the Colombian delegation lunch at a Bois de Boulogne brasserie.

9. Snow White and the Renault fours

EL DORADO INTERNATIONAL in Bogotá is like any major airport: crowds rush in, magnetized into queues, atomized into particles, and drift, like dust agitated by airport static, across the departures area until finally they are squeezed out through the terminal ports and into the waiting aircraft. On Tuesday 5 June 2001 El Dorado ground staff were preparing the 8.35 a.m. flight to Mexico City for departure. Across the terminal corridors national security agents exchanged imperceptible signals. Dry lips, swollen eyes and the sweat streaming down his neck – despite the regulated temperature – were clear signs of their suspect's sleepless night and early-morning fear. As the target approached the security gate, a uniformed agent stepped forward discreetly. 'Sir, you're carrying drugs.' Resignation replaced the man's hypnotized gaze. 'Yes. I've swallowed some capsules.' At a nearby clinic he was x-rayed, given some castor oil, and subsequently passed forty heroin capsules. Gustavo Wilches Tumbía was the 154th carrier caught at El Dorado in 2001. Few had made the national press, but this was one arrest that couldn't go unnoticed.

In 1990, after several years as a professional rider, Gustavo Wilches had completed the most prestigious double in Colombian cycling: victory in the RCN Classic and the Vuelta. Between then and 1992 he competed in Europe, riding three Tours of Spain and numerous smaller events. He went on to travel between Costa Rica and Mexico, competing for smaller teams until his retirement in 1998.

Wilches had been a famous name in Colombia's national sport long before Gustavo's double; he was the second of four brothers known with affection as the Wilchery. The top ten finishers in the Vuelta the year Gustavo won it included two more Wilches. Marcos, the third of the brothers, took the points title, and the eldest, Pablo, the mountains. Indeed, Pablo rode in three Tours de France, and was considered by the venerable Jacques Anquetil, victor in five of them, to have the potential to win at least one. But Pablo's career reached its zenith in 1987 when he chastened the almost invincible Lucho Herrera to win the Tour of Colombia. A year after Gustavo's double, he matched his brother by taking home the trophies of both the RCN Classic and the Vuelta a Colombia, but when mid-race dope tests showed traces of nandrolone, he was stripped of both. The youngest of the Wilches, Ricardo was no champion but a solid *domestique* for the Postobón team. At the time of Gustavo's arrest Ricardo was serving a prison sentence in Mexico for drug-related offences. Gustavo should have known better.

The arrest soon dissolved into the white noise of Colombia's daily news – massacres, murders and violent crime. Two weeks later another former cyclist was apprehended. On the afternoon of 18 June 2001 Rafael Antonio Tolosa was arrested boarding a flight to San José, Costa Rica, with an onward connection to New York. He was carrying

125 heroin capsules in his stomach, and had no export licence for the reported US$50,000 of emeralds in his luggage. At his home in southern Bogotá nine more pellets containing heroin were found. Tolosa must have abandoned these only when his sated gut could take no more. The discomfort must have been agonizing.

Like Gustavo and Ricardo Wilches, Tolosa was part of cycling's Elysian realm. He had been part of the Great Adventure, riding the 1983 Tour de France with Varta. All three men had been duped by the oldest confidence trick of all: the promise of easy money. Predictably, none even came close. Gustavo Wilches, with his smaller load, might even have been an unknowing fall guy, sacrificed to allow another carrier to slip by unnoticed.

The drug cartels had compelling reasons on paper for wanting to recruit cyclists. Credible as travellers and accustomed to airports, they are also used to physical punishment – transporting cocaine and heroin in the gut is a gruelling ordeal. The carrier, or 'mule', must prepare for weeks, swallowing progressively larger eggs to habituate his gullet and stomach. On the morning of the operation, he (or, more frequently, she) rises early. It can take between eight and ten hours to swallow a consignment. Forty-eight hours or more follow, during which the mule can neither eat nor drink, so that fatigue, hunger and dehydration complicate the routine stresses of air travel. Should just one capsule rupture, the dose of narcotics is potentially lethal. Even those with the rare physical and psychological attributes to carry the load and fool the guards are not guaranteed their lucrative rewards. Violence is the only insurance, and the wholesalers usually have that in abundance. Countless mules are left penniless or dead. The drug trade is not for freelancers.

Most travellers would consider the odds too high. But early retirement from the glamour of international sport into a life of restricted opportunity imposes its own perspectives, and if some ex-sportsmen risk occasional incursions into the criminal underworld, it is hardly surprising. In any case, long exposure to an environment where the drug barons were familiar faces, and their fantastic wealth seemed unrealistically attainable, could erode a man's judgement. For many years the cycling milieu in Colombia was just that. Explore it, and a quite different version of three decades of history appears.

THE FOUNDATIONS FOR Colombian cycling's cocaine connection were laid in the 1960s, when the black market attained enormous dimensions and marijuana cleared the path for more profitable products. As the decade ended, Pablo Escobar Gaviria, born 1 December 1949, was managing a network of petty thieves stealing gravestones from the cemeteries of the wealthy for sale in Panamá.

Pablo laundered the profits in a bicycle-hire business in the Medellín suburb of Envigado, abetted by his cousin and partner Gustavo Gaviria. The gravestones were dispatched to the Atlantic coast to be shipped out; the return journey brought him contraband bicycle parts. This modest operation was the embryo of a criminal empire that would make Pablo Escobar one of the world's wealthiest and most wanted men – and also a hero to many of Medellín's poor. Here was a man born with nothing, like us: with nerve, self-belief and defiance, he became someone.

According to an associate of Pablo now serving time in a Madrid prison, Pablo, Gustavo and Pablo's elder brother Roberto used to deliver groceries by bike to elegant houses in the El Poblado suburb on a steep Medellín hillside. Afterwards they would plummet downhill at top speed and talk about the Tour of Colombia. By the mid-1960s Pablo and Gustavo were graduating through the ranks of organized crime. Roberto Escobar, on the other hand, was one of Antioquia's finest cyclists. He won international medals for his country, and occasionally even defeated Cochise. In the mid-1980s, when the source of Pablo's wealth became public knowledge, Roberto too retired, into a clandestine existence as his brother's devoted shadow. Pablo is dead now, his criminal career curtailed in December 1993 when he was gunned down by police on a Medellín rooftop. As for Roberto, armed guards keep watch outside his private room in a Medellín clinic.

I arrived early for our appointment. The ground floor bustled with patients and visitors, but few were aware that Pablo Escobar's brother was three floors above. Prison guards in bulletproof jackets shuffled bored outside the door to his room, submachine guns rattling on hospital trolleys. A journalist had given me a telephone number. I had dialled it, imagining it would connect me to a prison administrator or warden's office. But in an instant I was speaking to one of Roberto's helpers, and then to 'Osito', the Bear – Roberto himself.

I sat in a hospital waiting room as a stream of visitors came and went. René Higuita, the extravagant goalkeeper of Colombia's national soccer team of the 1980s and early 1990s, emerged from the room with a woman on each arm. Higuita had himself been a potent symbol to Medellín's disaffected youth, having learned to block shots in the poor north-western neighbourhood of Castilla, where slogans on its walls proclaimed, 'Higuita for President.' Then a television news crew from Mexico arrived to film a long interview on the subject of Roberto's book, *My Brother Pablo*, published that week. Roberto was using the publication to reveal the identities of politicians and generals who, he claimed, had benefited from Pablo's subsidies – including Peru's President Fujimori and his intelligence chief Montesinos. Finally, the guards confiscated my camera and tape recorder and I was allowed to enter.

I was greeted by a face pocked with black scars. Sixteen days after Pablo's death, a letter had reached Roberto at Medellín's Bellavista Prison. The envelope, he claims, was official Prison Service stationery.

He was holding it up to the light when it detonated. The blast blinded him (some vision has since returned) and destroyed the hearing in his right ear. If he'd been looking down at it, he says, it would have blown his head off. Roberto Escobar was tired but charming. He listened patiently with his left ear and suggested I go back on Monday. 'Dress as a doctor,' he said.

The night porter at my hotel provided me with a nurse's chemise and some constructive criticism. But when I phoned on Monday morning, I found Roberto would be unavailable. Monday became Tuesday; Tuesday, Wednesday; and eventually I arranged to pass by on Friday. By then I had a detailed account of Roberto Escobar's career as a cyclist and team manager, and a list of questions. I waited in a nearby bar until a big 4x4 arrived. Roberto greeted me as I stepped into the hospital lift on the ground floor: I had slipped inside the security cordon. With camera, tape-recorder and photocopies of press reports dating back to his cycling career, I entered his lair.

It was then that I learned Roberto Escobar doesn't take questions. In the cramped cell of his hospital room he delivers a monologue that conjures a version of the past in which he appears as an innocent victim of State persecution. The history presented in these interviews, and his book, is sanitized to suppress any detail that could allow his enemies in the police or DEA to perpetuate his confinement. But between his official autobiography, the recollections of those who knew him and contemporary press coverage lies the truth about how cocaine hijacked a sporting milieu.

'I was nine or ten when my mother bought me my first bike,' recalls Roberto. 'We lived 25 kilometres from the nearest school. To get there by foot I used to leave home at 4.00 a.m. I was never home before 8.00 in the evening. But with the bike I could load Pablo into the basket over the back wheel and be at school in no time. On the way there I used to see Ramón Hoyos and Honorio Rúa on their training rides. When Hoyos took on Coppi and Koblet in 1958, I waited on the Alto de Minas to see them pass. The flapping of their shirts fascinated me: that was how I fell in love with cycling.'

His nickname came about like this. 'I remember taking part in a race around Medellín in cataclysmic conditions. Cochise and Javier Suárez had escaped, but I broke across to them. By the time I caught up with them I was covered in mud from head to toe. The radio commentators didn't recognize me. All they could say was that I looked like a bear. The mud washed off in the shower, but the nickname stuck for the rest of my life.'

Roberto was Cochise's team-mate at Dr Vinicius Echeverri's Club Mediofondo: he rode Ramón Hoyos bicycles and wore the colours of the Mora Brothers, a big electrical firm. Between 1964 and 1968 he rode three Vueltas a Colombia and four RCN Classics. He won a gold medal at the Bolivarian Games in Guayaquil in 1965, the same year's Vuelta al Oriente, and in 1966 was ninth in the first Vuelta al Táchira. He represented Colombia in the first Panamerican Cycling Championships in Chile, and at the national championships won a bronze medal in the 100 kilometres team time trial with Cochise. After Cochise and Javier Suárez, Roberto Escobar had become Antioquia's third rider: 'I won thirty-six races one season – more than Cochise or anyone else in the region. It's still a record.' In 1968 Caribu jeans offered him a place in Cochise's team at the Vuelta a Colombia, but then at the last minute withdrew the offer. After being selected for the Tour of Mexico, only to be told twenty-four hours before the flight that he had been replaced by someone else, he decided to retire as an athlete.

Roberto took a job repairing radios and televisions for Mora Brothers, but the cycling exerted an irresistible pull. He began to coach, and took Antioquian teams to compete in Panama, Ecuador and Venezuela. In 1975 he went to live and coach in Manizales, the capital of the department of Caldas. There, he also opened a small factory producing bicycle frames. He had added a 't' to his nickname ('"Ositto" looked more Italian') and Bicicletas Ositto – Bear's Bikes – was born.

It was when Roberto was living at Manizales that the trajectory of his life intersected with that of his younger brother. Pablo had heard about the cocaine trade for the first time in September 1974 while serving a prison sentence for car theft. Pablo Escobar moved into small-time cocaine smuggling in 1975. Until then, Americans had run the business. In 1973 ninety-three foreign nationals had been arrested attempting to export cocaine. By the mid-1970s, according to a US survey, nearly 5.5 million Americans had tried cocaine. They were paying between US$30,000 to US$60,000 a kilo; in Colombia it was less than US$6,000.

Two years later, after another spell in prison for drug-trafficking, which ended when the main witnesses were murdered and investigations ran dry, Pablo began to transport large quantities of coke to the US. He became a dollar millionaire and a minor local celebrity: at least once in the late 1970s he presented the trophy to the winning rider of the Classic of Antioquia. And, seeking legitimate outlets for the money his criminal activities were generating, his contribution to cycling went further.

The obvious choice would have been a cycling team. But first the Bear's Bikes logo appeared on a stable of racing Renaults and Porsches. Motor sport was Pablo's passion: he had raced on motorbikes and had taken lessons in car-racing. Before competing he smoked a small amount of marijuana to enhance his perception. 'Pablo loved cars,' Ositto told me. 'He drove a black Mercedes and a white Porsche convertible. He imported them from Germany. High speed fascinated him. He probably owned the first electronic fuel injection system in the country.' In the 1979 season Pablo was fourth in the

Renault Cup, despite missing the last three rounds; business commitments didn't always allow him time for his hobbies. His wife, Victoria Eugenia, sponsored by Bicicletas Ositto, competed in the Class 5 Improved Touring Car category of the Departmental Championship, driving a BMW. The Bicicletas Ositto vehicles were rarely off the podium. Escobar kept his cars in perfect condition, sending to Paris for spare parts and adding the latest devices. When he went to Bogotá to compete, he rented a suite on the first floor of the Hilton and travelled to the capital in his private helicopter. He also drove his Porsche in mountain time trials. Pablo promoted the races in the press and radio, and brought employment to the race track. After the races one weekend, keys to luxury BMWs and Mercedes were distributed, and invitations were issued to a party in Escobar's luxury pad. Titbits – female, liquid, shredded and powdered – were provided alongside the canapes, although Escobar himself was never seen drunk or euphoric, and could melt away unnoticed. The following day some of the guests visited Escobar's offices to thank him. On leaving they read a notice on the door saying, 'The telephone number and address of this office must be given to no one; repeat, no one.' In 1980 Pablo returned to the autodrome and the world of racing, but with less dedication and regularity, until he finally abandoned the sport.

In the colours of Bicicletas Ositto, a Colombia entry also entered the Daytona 500. Pablo and Roberto travelled to the US to watch, and also to explore new distribution networks.

While Bicicletas Ositto was making its mark on the history of motor sport, the power struggle in the Colombian Cycling Federation that split the cycling community cast Roberto Escobar as part of the old guard and *persona non grata* for Miguel Ángel Bermúdez, who looked for a pretext to have him dismissed from his coaching post at Caldas. He found it in Roberto's visit to the 1978 World Cycling

Championships in Bonn. There, equipped with a tiny Kodak 110 camera and accredited as official photographer for Colombia's *Mundo Ciclístico* magazine, Roberto found the crowds of photographers, wielding two or three cameras and a collection of huge lenses, taking pictures of him. 'I thought they had mistaken me for someone else. But they were just fascinated by this pathetic figure from poor little Colombia covering the world championships with a Kodak Instamatic.'

But his absence breached his contract with the Caldas Cycling League. And on his return Roberto had lost his job. Now he turned his energies to launching the Bicicletas Ositto cycling team. With the backing to hire the best, Bicicletas Ositto was ready to race in 1981. The technical director was Ruben Darío Gómez, and the team leader Manuel Ignacio Gutiérrez, the winner of the 1975 Vuelta de la Juventud, runner-up in the 1980 Vuelta al Táchira, and Niño's greatest *domestique*. 'The factory employs thirty-five engineers,' Osito told the press, 'and produces every type of bicycle, with sales all over the country. I've always wanted to sponsor a team, and it makes sense as a means of publicizing Bicicletas Ositto bikes. I love cycling and I want to give something back to the sport.'

Roberto claims today that his team was self-financing. But this is certainly false: factory visitors noted a huge gap between their expectations and what they found. Ephraim Forero, the Indomitable Zipa, drove one of his protégés to Manizales to meet Roberto. 'When we got there, all we found was a tiny bike workshop. It didn't add up.' 'No one knew at the time,' adds Samuel Cabrera, in 1981 the best young rider in the Vuelta. 'Not directly. You wondered how a little company like that could sustain a team at all, let alone one as strong as that, because Bicicletas Ositto was a monster.'

Gutiérrez, now free to ride for himself, proved his abilities in the 1981 RCN Classic. On the final stage Alfonso Flórez accelerated away from the peloton, dragging Gutiérrez, Fabio Parra and

Patrocinio Jiménez along in his wake. Flórez won the stage: on his wheel, Gutiérrez gained two minutes on the previous leader and won the race overall. It was Bicicletas Ositto's finest hour.

During the race a staff member of the Bicicletas Ositto team was witnessed handing out marijuana to other members of the caravan. The race organizers investigated the accusations but found no proof. The affair was forgotten until the morning of stage thirteen in April's Tour of Colombia, when in the coffee-producing town of Pereira one of the team's mascots handed out free marijuana to the crowd. This time he was caught and thrown off the tour. Roberto pleaded *lèse-majesté*: 'I had dressed two actors up in theatrical bear costumes to hand out miniature teddy bears for publicity purposes. They gave a teddy bear and a Bicicletas Ositto shirt to the owner of RCN during a television interview – great publicity for us, but it created a lot of jealousy. So all sorts of stories were invented to discredit us.' But a masseur working at both races told me, 'Roberto, Pablo and their entourage followed the RCN Classic and the Vuelta from a small "chiva", a customized jeep that was enveloped in a cloud of marijuana smoke. They made a welcome show of largesse by handing out 50,000 peso notes to the soigneurs and team auxiliaries.'

In 1981 Bicicletas Ositto sponsored the Colombian national team at the Tour of Cuba. 'Although it may appear differently from today's perspective,' argues a respected sports journalist who joined the team to cover the Tour of Cuba for RCN radio, 'at the time Pablo and Roberto Escobar were perfectly respectable figures in social and sporting circles. Roberto was a distinguished Colombian industrialist sponsoring the national team in good faith. He came to enjoy the racing, support his riders, and nothing more. Just one more member of the team.' This was the official line. But another member of the entourage on that trip told me, 'Pablo was looking for new routes to get coke into the US. The purpose for the trip was for Roberto to explore the viability of using Cuba as a possible slingshot stopover, and that's what he did.'

The Federation's obstructionism aggravated the hostility between Roberto Escobar and Miguel Ángel Bermúdez. This peaked during a race in 1982. Bermúdez left his car at the roadside near La Pintada. Quickly, during his absence, a bomb was installed and the car destroyed. Soon afterwards, the Bicicletas Ositto cycling team disappeared from the national cycling scene.

Bermúdez took a principled stand against cocaine money entering Colombian cycling, but Pablo Escobar wasn't the only drug lord funding a team. In 1979 three members of the Droguería Yaneth team had finished in the first ten of the Vuelta a Colombia. In 1980 and 1981 the drugstore's twin, Perfumería Yaneth, sent a team to the Vuelta al Táchira. And in 1982 Manuel Ignacio Gutiérrez, the former Bicicletas Ositto leader, won the Giro de Valsesia in Italy for the same team. But as their riders concentrated on achieving excellence on the road, Droguería and Perfumería Yaneth were laundering the drug money of José Gilberto Rodríguez Gacha, also known as 'the Mexican'. By 1984 Rafael Tolosa – the second of the riders arrested at El Dorado International Airport in 2001 – was riding for Perfumería Yaneth.

The Mexican controlled the department of Cundinamarca for the Medellín cartel. He was its military chief and the mastermind behind the campaign of violence later known as the 'dirty war'. He was close to Pablo Escobar: when Pablo bought property on the west bank of the Magdalena River, the Mexican bought land to the east. Shortly before the police hunted him down and assassinated him from a helicopter fitted with night sights in December 1989, details of seventy-seven companies dedicated to laundering the Mexican's fortune were found in a Bogotá office. They included livestock, construction and investments in sport, especially football.

As Colombian cycling gained respect from the professional peloton in Europe, the RCN Classic had begun to invite European riders. In the relative calm of the early 1980s, some of the finest riders on Earth had travelled to Colombia to prepare at altitude for the Tour de France. During these prestigious international events the sky grew dark with the helicopters of the narcos.

Escobar's ambition was to be recognized as the true friend, mouthpiece and defender of Medellín's poor. Sport was an instrument for extending his empire of affection and *omertà* He made fabulous handouts to footballers who played well at the matches he attended, and his door was always open to the nation's top cyclists, like Martín Ramírez, a brilliant time triallist and stage racer, who remembers joining Pablo for dinner in 1984, during a training camp near Medellín at his estate, the Hacienda Nápoles. The Hacienda, which sprawled over southern Antioquia, Caldas and Santander, formed the centre of the Escobar empire. Several Tours of Antioquia had stages that finished there, and the caravan parked up overnight on Escobar's land.

But also at Hacienda Nápoles was the zoo Pablo opened, which in 1982 became the most visited tourist attraction in Antioquia, attracting 40,000 visitors per month. Entry was free. 'It was an absolutely normal day out for day-trippers,' says Martín Ramírez, who took his family there as tourists. But there are other explanations for the zoo's existence. One was a rumour perpetrated to put potential investigators off the trail. It said that the cocaine packets were impregnated with elephant and giraffe dung to repel the sniffer dogs, according to the superstition that dogs were instinctively repelled by the smell of the excreta of animals superior to them in the food chain. The truth was rather different. In the US the narcos kept safehouses bursting with billions of dollars of cash. Transporting it to Colombia demanded great ingenuity. Escobar imported animals for his zoo through Miami. Cages were built with a double-bottom, and beneath the droppings massive sums of cash were packed. Escobar brought in his own money and that of the other cartels, charging 6 per cent for each shipment.

Pablo and Osito also had their own velodrome built in the El Poblado neighbourhood of Medellín. According to a police colonel who commanded the surveillance operation on Pablo Escobar – a former cyclist – 'The great Alfonso Flórez would assemble teams to ride for Pablo and Osito's pleasure, and they would bet fabulous sums on the outcome. The riders were handsomely rewarded.' The velodrome is still there, 460 metres above the town's most prestigious shopping mall, the Tesoro, and clearly visible from the road. I squeezed through a gap in the main gate and walked around the track. After ten years of neglect it is subsiding now and soiled with cow pats. Beside the entrance an italic sign reads 'Assisi' – Escobar always chose Italian place names.

The velodrome was for the Escobars' private delight: for the poor of Medellín they provided floodlighting and stands for local football grounds through Pablo's pressure group, 'Civismo en marcha', 'Public spirit on the march'. Its activists planted trees and laid paving in Medellín's poorest neighbourhoods, and gave prizes to local artists. The movement's newspaper, *Civic Medellín*, had environmental leanings and a 40,000 circulation. It was funded by advertisements for Bicicletas Ositto, Depósito Cundinamarca, and other Escobar enterprises. *Civic Medellín* was run from Flat 708 in the Apartahotel Antaño, a building in the Jesus the Nazarene neighbourhood. It was the first of many high-rises built by the Medellín Cartel. The roof was adorned with a heliport.

Pablo's philanthropy also financed a campaign named 'Medellín without slums', building decent housing for the indigent population subsisting on Medellín's refuse tip. A second cousin of the Escobars was living in the filth. Above the Medellín suburb of The Miraculous Virgin, east of the city centre, therefore, Pablo had 800 bungalows put up for the slum dwellers, rent free. The city authorities tried to re-baptize the Pablo Escobar housing complex: they call it The Willows. But its residents resist and continue to call it by its founder's name. Like any number of suburbs in Manchester, Milan or Moscow, 'Pablo Escobar' is not a place to be visited without a local guide: this can be a no-go area. But I climbed its steep slopes with a local journalist and met warm, open residents happy to invite us into their homes. I was surprised not to find a picture of Pablo on the wall. 'I do have one,' an ageing tenant told me discreetly, 'but I keep it in my purse and use it only when I need it.' After his death, Pablo became the object of a cult, and today, venerated by many of the residents, he hears their prayers in times of need.

In life, however, Pablo Escobar became a familiar figure on the Tour of Colombia, appearing at the roadside on a shiny Vespa, a brand associated with cycling in Colombia since Ramón Hoyos returned home from the Rome Olympics with the Piaggio franchise. When the Tour distances were too large to cover by Vespa, a helicopter would transport Pablo and Roberto to the stage starts.

These were happy years, and as Pablo and Roberto frolicked over the countryside by land and air, a generalized optimism shone over the nation. Bermúdez' Tour de France project had started auspiciously, and in parallel with it the peace process was raising hopes that guerrilla insurgency might soon belong to the past. However, President Belisario Betancur's peace plans were flawed: despite the drugs trade's close links with insurgency, the peace process made no reference to the cartels. If Colombia had become the international host of the drugs trade, it was not simply because of the trade in contraband. The guerrilla presence had made it possible to open enclaves in which drug manufacture could establish itself without the intervention of the armed forces. Indeed, the cartels even paid the guerrillas for surveillance and protection of the drug processing areas.

The air of expectancy that hung over the negotiations and the national sport was part of a growing divergence between image and reality. New pretensions – political now – on the part of the drugs cartels emerged in the months before the 1982 presidential elections. In Medellín, Pablo Escobar launched a political movement, the Movement of Liberal Renewal, and financed the campaign of a politician named Jair Ortega Ramírez in order to be named his designated proxy and enjoy parliamentary immunity. He had 'Pablo Escobar, Liberal Renewal' printed on cycling shirts and shorts; through his brother Roberto, he distributed them among Medellín's most prestigious riders. Ortega and Escobar were elected to the Congress of the Republic in May 1982. For the first time cycling, politics and drugs had been explicitly mixed.

Courageous journalists began to risk their lives by denouncing the entry of the drug lords into the networks of political power. And as Colombian national life became a stage for men whose towering statures allowed them to be referred to by their first names alone – Belisario, Pablo, Lucho – faceless, hooded figures began to move among the shadows. Belisario's presidency saw an unprecedented growth in paramilitary organizations. The first, a group calling itself Death to Kidnappers (MAS), had appeared in November 1981. Financed by over 200 drug bosses, it employed 2000 armed men to hunt down and execute those involved in kidnapping, especially those to the political left. Some serving members of the armed forces were later linked to MAS. The paramilitary organizations benefited from a strategic alliance between the military and the drug traffickers which until 1989 was virtually overt – the narcos opened a paramilitary training school in Puerto Boyacá, for example, employing British and Israeli mercenaries. In September 1983 Escobar's movement had the audacity to promote a debate over the use of drug money in Colombian politics. Escobar saw himself as a successful businessman who was merely exploiting a pre-existing, and almost infinite, market.

The new Minister for Justice, Rodrigo Lara Bonilla, crossed swords with him, and showed a video of an ABC television documentary that revealed the source of Escobar's wealth.

In March 1984, with the full co-operation of Rodrigo Lara Bonilla, a gigantic coca refinery deep in the Amazon known as Tranquilandia was captured by Colombian police in conjunction with the US Drug Enforcement Agency. Homing devices hidden in a cargo of seventy-two barrels of ether, a necessary ingredient in the chemical production of cocaine, led the DEA to the complex of ten laboratories set deep in the jungle, capable of producing 5 tonnes of cocaine a week. According to the US Ambassador, Tirofijo's FARC was paid to guard its laboratories and airstrips. Two helicopters and an aircraft carried Colombian police and DEA agents to Tranquilandia, where they confiscated 4 tons of cocaine and 15 of paste, 10,000 tanks of petrol and ether, three twin-engined aircraft and a helicopter, and arrested forty workers. Carlos Lehder, the director of the complex and head of a drug-funded political movement in his native region of Quindío, escaped into the forest.

On the evening of 30 April 1984 twenty-five 45mm rounds, fired by the pillion passenger on a powerful motorbike, blew the life out of Rodrigo Lara Bonilla as he travelled home in a chauffeur-driven Mercedes. The killer was twenty years old. His pilot, sixteen and a hardened smoker of the cocaine-base bazuka, had already been imprisoned fifteen times and weighed scarcely seven stone. They had been trained in the skills of motorbike execution in a school in Sabaneta, Medellín, funded by the narcos. Lara Bonilla's murder was on Pablo Escobar's orders, and it unleashed a dirty war that lasted a decade and caused international scandal.

THE 1984 VUELTA started days later. In earlier conjunctures, when history's tides had churned up massive movements of people, or the institutions of State reached crisis point, the Vuelta had provided a way back to reason. It had been the nation's conscience. After this singular act of terror, it suddenly seemed irrelevant.

Three domestic teams, all sponsored by Varta, wrestled with a formation sponsored by a dairy named Gran Via Milk. Gran Via was led by Fabio Parra and 'Pacho' Rodríguez – another youngster with roots in Boyacá. Pacho finished second, with Parra third, six seconds behind him. The winner was Lucho Herrera of Varta 'A'.

After a long domestic season, the shock of the Lara Bonilla assassination and a gruelling Vuelta, Varta's riders were now committed to the eight-day Criterium du Dauphiné Libéré, the traditional warm-up for the Tour de France. The Société du Tour de France had made it quite clear that absence from the Dauphiné would cost the Colombians their place in the Tour. The Dauphiné Libéré was a little-known event in Colombia, despite the fact that its roll-call of victors included some of cycling's greatest champions: Bobet, Anquetil, Merckx and Hinault. Miguel Ángel Bermúdez even told Pacho, with Pablo Wilches the core of a makeshift team, 'It's just a little race in the mountains. You can win it.' An unlikely scenario given a field that included many of the world's finest riders, including Bernard Hinault and Pascal Simon of France, the American Greg LeMond, Scotland's Robert Millar, the Irishman Stephen Roche and Australia's Phil Anderson. Two other Colombians, Patro and Condorito, professional now, were competing for the Spanish team Teka.

After stage three, when a French rider named Guy Gallopin raced to a fifteen-minute lead, a Colombian victory seemed less likely still. A day later Pacho and his team-mate Pablo Wilches attacked the first mountain. It was a typical Colombian approach, and caught the Europeans off-guard. Just behind them, two more Colombians, one of whom was Martín Ramírez, were in hot pursuit. All but Pacho were caught on the descent. Despite losing his chain and vital seconds, the Colombian crossed the finishing line first in Saint Julien de Genevois. It was there that the Colombian community of the south of France celebrated in a rare display of national pride. Never before had a Colombian amateur defeated professional riders. Pacho was in second place; Gallopin, despite losing over seven minutes of his lead, still seemed unassailable.

The following day, a kilometre from the stage finish at Chambéry, four Colombians and three professionals were leading. A ninety-degree turn with 400 metres to go interrupted the flow, and the Frenchman Michel Laurent burst out to snatch victory. Pacho, however, was second. As time ticked away, he chattered nervously to the press. After seven minutes seventeen seconds, Gallopin had not arrived. The Colombian was marched off to the podium and dressed in the yellow jersey of the race leader.

The following day the private laws of Colombian wish-fulfilment displaced the public realm of verisimilitude: Pacho rode away to victory again. It was impossible, unthinkable, absurd. But perhaps inevitable. Weeks before, with Lara Bonilla's murder, Colombia's morale had hit absolute zero. The mysterious logic that attracts Colombia to life's extremities seemed to govern Pacho's preposterous triumphs. He led Bernard Hinault by three minutes fifty-six seconds. Martín Ramírez, fourth, was a further sixteen seconds behind. With two days to go, Colombia hardly dared celebrate.

Then news filtered through: suffering unbearable knee pains, Pacho Rodríguez had abandoned. The new leader was Bernard Hinault, the most formidable rider in the world. And on the penultimate day of racing he was on the attack. The Frenchman crossed the first four mountains of the day alone. Martín Ramírez resolved to defend his podium place. 'But I also knew that if I could win back sixteen seconds, I would wear the race leader's jersey for a night. The following day there were two stages: Hinault would inevitably defeat me in the second, a time trial. But I could at least wear the jersey in the morning.' There were cars ahead of him. Drawing closer, he discovered Hinault, running on empty. 'I passed him in silence. As I climbed, the world turned to snow. I entered a state approaching ecstasy. I'd never seen a snowstorm before. I was climbing and suffering, but laughing too. I felt stronger and stronger, and eventually reached the stage finish on Alpe Rousset. By the time Hinault crossed the line, I was race leader by twenty-two seconds.

'The following morning, on a short stage before the final time trial that would decide the race, I had only one team-mate left to protect me: Pablo Wilches. I rode the entire stage on Hinault's wheel. He responded by braking hard to make me fall, while his team bombarded me with elbows and fists. They said the Colombians were cheats; they were angry about something I couldn't understand. But they were wasting their time. I was race-hardened and paid them back in kind. The stage finished as it had begun. I had a twenty-two second lead over the finest time trialler in the sport.

'I didn't want to face Hinault's team at lunch. I had food brought to my room, but I couldn't eat anyway. I put my feet up until two hours before my start time. I rode out onto the race route to examine the time trial profile. It started with a 6-kilometre climb. I knew I'd have to gain time on Hinault before the brow, and then try to hang on the descent and the final flat.

'Waiting on the starting ramp, my only thought was to use up every ounce of energy. I wanted to finish the stage exhausted, knowing I'd given everything.

'I started fast. My team-mates were waiting at the col with a stop watch. I had gained seconds on Hinault. I plummeted down the other side. There were no further time checks, and on the final flat I just tried to maintain my cadence. But when I crossed the line, the faces told me I'd won.' Ramírez had finished third in the stage, five seconds faster than Hinault, who was fifth. When these five seconds were added to his overall lead, the Colombian had won the Dauphiné Libéré by twenty-seven seconds.

There were street celebrations all over Colombia. Ramírez dedicated his exploits to Colombia. In so doing, he triggered a bizarre exchange between the master propagandists of M-19 and the Colombian government. In a press release datelined 'Bogotá, June 1984', M-19 wrote:

> These exploits have invariably been achieved by children of the common people. Today, overflowing with happiness, we welcome home these young men whose courage has made the world look at Colombia's cyclists with respect. Together with thousands of our fellow Colombians, M-19 applauds Martín Ramírez, Francisco 'Pacho' Rodríguez, Pablo Wilches, Armando Aristizábel, Reynel Montoya, Alirio Chizabas and Luis Herrera: riders who, in the cold and the snow, defeated Hinault, Lemond, Simon, Anderson, Fignon – the cream of European professional cycling.
>
> When President Betancur telephoned to congratulate him, Martín Ramírez was right to tell him: 'Our athletes need constant recognition, not solely in their moments of glory.'
>
> Good on them, and good on the common people of Colombia who feel they are their own kin. Like the majority of Colombians, they were brought up and triumphed on a diet of aguapanela. Their fame was earned by sweat and, at times, by begging for support from sponsors. Their bicycles, before they bore them to the highest summits, were first indispensable tools of labour. They have climbed high . . . from very low.

Belisario was equally aware that the success of Colombia's cyclists provided important ammunition in the propaganda war. He responded with a Presidential Decree:

> The President of the Republic of Colombia, by virtue of his constitutional and legal faculties, and considering the following:
> That the national government seeks to encourage and improve the performances of Colombians who enhance the nation's image on the international stage;
> That the sport of cycling enjoys a great reception and popularity in all sectors of the community;
> The Colombia's cyclists have achieved displays of singular merit on various occasions;
> That in light of the above, and sensitive to the feelings of the Colombian people, cycling should be encouraged;
> decrees:
> Article 1. The national government considers cycling a sport of special significance in Colombia, and in promoting Colombia abroad. Consequently the government, by means of the Colombian Institute of Youth and Sport, and the relative regional sports administrations, shall encourage the practice of cycling, as a recreational activity and in the organization of competitions and sporting events in all their forms, in accordance with the regulations emitted to this effect.
> Article 2.This decree shall take effect from the date of expedition.
> To be communicated and implemented. Bogotá, 11 June 1984.

It was belated recognition for a sport that had done much to keep Colombia whole over the previous three decades, even if by this time many of the nation's finest riders were accepting offers from foreign teams to ride for foreign masters. By Tour time the French team Système 'U' had snapped up Ramírez, while Pacho and Pablo Wilches went to Marc-Zeep-Savon Mondial Moquette-Splendor.

By comparison the 'official' Colombians, with their lonely Varta logo and 'Colombia' jerseys, looked decidedly undersold. Alfonso Flórez had lost the leader's job to Lucho Herrera. Herrera had already won Colombia's RCN Classic, his third consecutive victory, against Pascal Simon, Marc Madiot, Robert Millar, Charly Mottet, America's world champion Greg Lemond, and Laurent Fignon, the reigning Tour de France champion. The professionals, who now routinely came to Colombia every year for altitude training before the Tour de France, had performed better than in the past. Lemond had taken the leader's jersey after his Renault team dominated the team time trial, Mottet and Fignon had won a stage, and Pascal Simon had once again been the best non-Colombian, finishing twentieth overall. Herrera had followed up by dominating the Vuelta a Colombia.

The 1984 Tour de France started as it had the previous year: ten days on the flat, then a Robert Millar win in the Pyrenees putting a Colombian in the picture – Herrera finished second. He crescendoed to second place in the mountain time trial on stage seventeen, and the following day exploded into Tour history at Alpe d'Huez.

It was a classic stage, ending at a destination where no French rider had ever triumphed. Now two of France's greatest ever champions, Laurent Fignon and Bernard Hinault, were determined to enter history.

Robert Millar led over the day's first climb; Patrocinio Jiménez reeled him in and took the second mountain prize. Then Hinault went to the front for the first time, with Fignon in tow. Over the third mountain Herrera led with Fignon, to be caught in turn by Hinault with 20 kilometres to go. Hinault's advantage was thirty seconds when Herrera made his move. He dropped his fellow travellers, dispatched Hinault by nearly four minutes and prevented Fignon from becoming the Alpe's first French victor, to win by forty-nine seconds. On the other side of the world people took to the streets. Alpe d'Huez was Colombian: Herrera was the first amateur to win a Tour de France stage. It was another step on the path towards greatness.

But the exertions took their toll: the day after the Alpe d'Huez win, Lucho was on the point of abandoning. He stayed in the race and finished twenty-seventh overall. Patro, fifteenth overall, was the highest placed Colombian when the Tour reached Paris. And after their Colombian preparation, the European professionals had performed brilliantly at the Tour de France: Millar was fourth, Lemond third, and Fignon first after five stage wins. Martín Ramírez and Lucho Herrera returned home with still more valuable experience.

They arrived in a country almost overcome with hope. Within days of their triumphant arrival, on 23 August 1984, one of the rebel bands, the EPL, signed a truce and cease-fire with the government. The following day, in the village of Corinto in the Cauca region, M-19 followed suit. A member of Belisario's Peace Commission, the brilliant Colombian novelist Laura Restrepo, describes the signing and the euphoria that followed it in her book *History of a Betrayal*. Remarkably, this defining moment in Colombia's political struggle found its point of comparison in cycling:

> The guerrillas were walking an inch above the ground . . . A rank-and-file combatant was telling a journalist: "Before we arrived we knew we were going to meet girls, dance and drink beer, but we could never have imagined a reception like this. It's like when we were kids and we went out to greet the cyclist Rubén Darío Gómez after he'd won the Vuelta a Colombia. That's how they greeted us."

10. Café de Colombia

COCAINE, *PANELA* AND political chicanery had already touched cycling. In 1985 another of Colombia's characteristic ingredients entered the equation. Coffee had long been the nation's prime export; now the industry was looking to expand internationally. With Colombia's cyclists beginning to figure on the front pages of the European and Latin American press, the National Federation of Coffee Growers joined Varta Batteries as co-sponsor of the national twenty-two-man cycling team.

It was the culmination of a promotional strategy that dated back to 1960, when a New York advertising agency had created a fictitious character named Juan Valdez to personify Colombia's coffee growers and manual labourers. In 1982 Juan Valdez, his donkey and the Colombian mountains in the background appeared as a triangular logo to denote supermarkets' own-brand coffee produced from Colombian beans. By 1985 the

'Café de Colombia' trademark was well positioned in North America, and the Federation wanted to reinforce its image in Europe. After only two years of cycling sponsorship in Europe, more than thirty brands there were using solely Colombian coffee.

The athletes behind this success were no longer plucky amateur underdogs: at the start of the 1985 season Miguel Ángel Bermúdez had introduced professionalism. But when the Varta-Café de Colombia riders went to May's Vuelta a España to prepare for the Tour de France, they found a Colombian on a Spanish team challenging for overall victory.

The year before, Edgar Corredor and Patrocinio Jiménez had finished fifth and seventh riding for the Spanish team Teka. Now it was Pacho Rodríguez, on another Spanish team, Zor, who led the Latin American attack. It did not go down well. The Varta-Café de Colombia riders, especially Fabio Parra, reportedly spurned Rodríguez. Local journalists deepened the enmity by spreading the falsehood that Rodríguez was seeking Spanish nationality.

The Colombians' collective cold shoulder had its roots in the previous year's Dauphiné Libéré. 'I massaged Pacho the night before he abandoned the race,' the Colombian Cycling Federation's national coach Roberto Sánchez told me. 'There was nothing wrong with his knees. He was in excellent shape, at least until about 10.00 p.m., when there was a knock at the door. It was a leading French rider with an interpreter. Pacho left the room to speak to him. We didn't think any more about it.

'The following day, one kilometre into the race, Pacho abandoned. I know nothing about money changing hands. But Pacho Rodríguez was never again invited to ride for Varta or Café de Colombia.'

At the 1985 Tour of Spain, however, Pacho wasn't for sale, and after seventeen stages and eighty-six hours on the road, just ten seconds separated him from the leader, Scotland's Robert Millar. With only 375 kilometres to go, the Spanish press, and the director of Millar's Peugeot team, Roland Berland, agreed that the race was as good as won. On the final mountain stage Miller and Rodríguez scrutinized each other for signs of weakness. Pacho attacked twice on the first climb and twice more on the second, but the Scot went with him. Cancelling each other out with equal ability, they allowed a Spanish rider named Pedro Delgado, six minutes thirteen seconds behind Millar in the General Classification, to launch a long, speculative attack over the roads he used to train on.

Delgado led his breakaway partner, José Recío, down descents he knew intimately. By promising Recío the stage win, he secured his compatriot's collaboration.

As Delgado sped away to an enormous lead, Javier Mínguez, the director of Zor, took a decision that cost his team leader any chance of victory: he ordered his team not to attack. He was deliberately sacrificing Rodríguez' second place to ensure that a Spaniard would win the race. By the time Pacho and Millar crossed the line, Delgado had made up his disadvantage and taken a lead of thirty-six seconds. Mínguez explained to disbelieving Colombian journalists, 'As things stood, Pacho was destined for second place and Millar for the title. Anything was preferable to allowing Millar the victory. Delgado had gained a considerable advantage: it pained me to hold Pacho back during the last kilometres, but it was necessary to prevent Millar from reaching the pantheon of champions. Have no doubt: I was the artificer of Delgado's victory, and I don't regret my decision.' Of 170 starters, just 101 finished a race held over narrow, slippery roads with poor surfacing. *El Tiempo* wrote, 'The Tour of Spain isn't human, according to many of the cyclists, like the old Tours of Colombia won by the heroes.'

Lucho Herrera, meanwhile, had abandoned the Vuelta a España early. As preparation for the Tour de France, his race programme took him home to ride the Vuelta a Colombia, which he won, defeating Fabio Parra by thirty-three seconds. Then he resolved to dominate the mountains competition in the 1985 Tour de France.

Over the stage four pimples of Brittany he was already fighting for points. But by week two Bernard Hinault, who had won the Giro d'Italia in May, threatened to make the Tour a one-horse race with a big time trial win. When Hinault attacked on the race's first Alpine climb, only Herrera could stay with him. All day they shared the lead, sweeping across the mountains to the ski resort of Avoriaz. Herrera consolidated his King of the Mountains lead with the stage win. Hinault's second place put real distance between him and his rivals for the General. Next day, Herrera spent eight-and-a-half more hours at the helm. After 296 kilometres over the Colombière, three intermediate climbs and the Côte de St Nizier, he took second to team-mate Fabio Parra, who'd won the toughest stage of his first Tour de France.

But the most dramatic episode of the 1985 Tour de France came forty-eight hours later at St Etienne. Leading on the final descent, Lucho Herrera skidded and fell. Blood poured from his face as he limped in to take the stage. The wind separated the blood flow into rivulets that swept down his face. Moments later Hinault sped into a collision that sent him head first into the tarmac. Nose fractured, eyes blackened and scalp dripping with blood, he too crawled over the line. Herrera didn't know about Hinault's injury until they met in hospital.

The wounded survived, although breathing difficulties restricted Hinault's overall victory to one minute forty-two seconds. Herrera set a record points total for the polka-dot jersey. The manner of his triumph, his seventh position overall, and the emergence of Fabio Parra made the 1985 race another step forward for Colombian cycling.

Colour photographs of Herrera's tribulations were published in the Colombian press. Television footage of Herrera's darting breakaway was broadcast repeatedly, imprinting on Colombia's collective memory the image of lava flows of blood flowing across his face. The sentimental cast of its Catholicism and the morbid tendency of its national character found their supreme expression in cycling. In Lucho's tiny physique, bloody features and tortured victory, Colombia saw itself reflected more faithfully than ever.

Over the following months new waves of violence and tragedy hit Colombia, and the image assumed lasting pathos as a generalized picture of its suffering.

AT 11.30 A.M. ON Wednesday 6 November thirty-five M-19 guerrillas erupted into the Palace of Justice in Bogotá. Flanking the Plaza Bolívar, where the Vuelta a Colombia traditionally started, the white-stoned modernist building was the home of the Supreme Court of Justice and the Council of State. On its façade were carved these words: 'Colombians: arms gave you independence, but laws will give you freedom.' The interlopers intended to stage another of M-19's symbolic pranks: they would compel the highest court of justice in the Republic to conduct a show-trial of the Betancur administration, which stood charged with betraying the peace process. The President was accused of signing the peace accords in bad faith, excluding the general population from the talks, repeatedly violating the ceasefire and pursuing economic and social policies that prejudiced the peace, incited popular discontent and violated national sovereignty. However, like many M-19 operations, it was a prank stained with blood. To gain access the guerrillas had to murder security guards. They entered with a sizeable arsenal.

The armed forces were immediately straining at the leash. The Canton Norte arms theft in 1979 and the seizing of the Dominican Embassy in 1980 had humiliated them before an international audience. By 1975 hard liners in the military had already begun to displace the more democratic chiefs, and the government was allowing them increasing autonomy in matters of public order. Arbitrary detentions and torture were becoming commonplace, although murder and disappearance were not yet as common as they would be. Their response was immediate and disastrous. By 12.25 p.m. seven tanks were positioned in and around the Plaza Bolívar. At 1.55 p.m. they led a major frontal assault. The national television stations broadcast incomprehensible images of a tank climbing the Palace of Justice steps and firing 57mm shells inside.

The fighting lasted until early afternoon the following day. During the night, flames burst out of the building. The law library and the palace archives, which contained priceless historical manuscripts dating back centuries, were consumed by fire. So too were files containing the details of ongoing investigations; among the millions destroyed were the dossiers documenting Pablo Escobar's criminal career.

At 2.20 p.m. on Thursday 7 November the armed forces declared the building under control. The dead included eleven magistrates of the Supreme Court of Justice, twenty-nine other functionaries and secretaries, eleven members of the armed forces and three private individuals. Of the M-19 guerrillas, just one came out alive. Twelve more individuals simply disappeared, wholly annihilated, it is assumed, by the heat. The military wished to underline that 244 hostages escaped.

Seven days later a massive natural disaster outscaled even the man-made tragedy of the Palace of Justice.

The Nevado del Ruiz volcano hadn't erupted since 1845. In September 1985 the Colombian National Geological Service detected signs of activity. A month later it submitted detailed reports to the government, with a hazard map showing mudflow routes. Eruption, it predicted, was imminent. At 10.22 p.m. on Wednesday 13 November, before any action had been taken, the Nevado del Ruiz exploded. A holocaust followed.

The town of Armero had been built on the Nevado's lower slopes. Five times its townsfolk had cheered the arrival of the Tour of Colombia. In 1955 the first stage of the Vuelta a Colombia had finished there with a Ramón Hoyos victory. Eleven years later Javier Suárez had won the stage. The Vuelta had returned in 1969 and 1975, and in 1977 Raphael Niño had won what was to be the Vuelta's final visit. It would never go back now, for by the morning of 14 November 1985 Armero no longer existed. Millions of tons of mud displaced by the erupting volcano had turned an entire town into an underground cemetery, where 23,000 victims are still interred. Photographs of survivors dragged from the mud depict haunting figures barely recognizable as human.

Meanwhile, on the Friday and Saturday between the Palace of Justice massacre and the Armero tragedy, a little-known track racer from Bucaramanga, Ephraim Domínguez, had set three world records. On Mexico's La Magdalena Mixhuca track he rode 10.778 seconds for 200 metres with a rolling start, 27.897 seconds in the 500 metres with a rolling start, and 1 minute 5.2 seconds in the standing-start kilometre. Under normal circumstances street parties would have celebrated his achievements. But in a country mourning so many dead and such vicious passions, they scarcely registered. It was only the following year, in December 1986, when Domínguez travelled to Bolivia and improved on his times at the extreme altitude of La Paz that his achievements were finally recognized.

In September 1985 Martín Ramírez had repeated Flórez' feat of 1980 by winning the Tour de l'Avenir, no longer an amateur event, but limited to riders aged twenty-five and under. Colombians won the team, mountains, competitiveness and best *domestique* categories. But in the aftermath of November's disasters, a general pessimism descended over the nation: suddenly, victory only seemed possible against amateurs and the young.

The mood continued into 1986. In the Tour of Spain, Fabio Parra was Colombia's best performer, yet he could only finish eighth. Lucho's third successive Vuelta a Colombia triumph deepened the national identification with his minuscule figure, but in the Tour de France he could only manage twenty-second, nearly an hour behind Greg LeMond, and second to Bernard Hinault in the King of the Mountains competition, despite completing the Alpe d'Huez climb six minutes ten seconds faster than the Frenchman. Perhaps the Colombians' minds were on other things: at Alpe d'Huez, Lucho and the Colombian team had placed volcanic rocks from the Nevado del Ruiz in a monument to thank France for its humanitarian assistance after the Armero disaster.

Ironically, the nation had been more visible than ever at the Tour. Two Colombian teams, Café de Colombia and Postobón, had entered the Tour, and Café de Colombia had also sponsored the King of the Mountains competition. Samuel Cabrera, formerly Martín Ramírez' faithful *domestique* but now riding for the Spanish Reynolds team beside a youthful Miguel Indurain, was the highest placed Colombian, eleventh overall. For Alfonso Flórez, twenty-seventh, the 1986 Tour de France was his last. Questions were asked at home: could the *escarabajos* ever win in Europe without spending the whole season there? Would they need European *domestiques*? Tragically, the violence that followed the Palace of Justice massacre made the answers irrelevant.

After the definitive failure of Betancur's peace efforts, vigilante groups in Pereira, Cali, Medellín and Bogotá launched frenzied campaigns to clear the streets of delinquents. The authorities connived. Already the victims of urban society, Colombia's prostitutes, homosexuals and beggars were now hunted down in shameful acts of social cleansing. Urban delinquency and government corruption peaked, and there was talk of two Colombias – one institutional, the other at the margins, finding its only means of expression in violence. Since 1986 violence has caused more deaths in Colombia than any other single factor.

Betancur's policy of peace had effectively created the conditions for the violence to spread. The guerrilla groups had restructured, found new forms of finance and formed an alliance, the Simon Bolivar National Guerrilla Co-ordinator. The 1984 ceasefire did produce a new and legal political party: the Patriotic Union (UP), sponsored by the FARC and the Communist party – but it became an easy target for paramilitary forces, which had grown exponentially. By 1987 there had been 600 UP members murdered; three years later this figure had doubled. The ELN and the FARC gave up fielding their own candidates and adopted politicians from the traditional parties whom they could subjugate to their will.

The armed forces recovered their full autonomy at the very moment that the drugs trade began to finance sectors of the military to eradicate the guerrillas from their territories. The lines distinguishing political, drugs-related and social violence blurred and disappeared. In 1987 the commanders of one guerrilla front, fearing infiltration, murdered more than 200 of their own troops. Purges like this drove ex-guerrillas over to the drugs traffickers or the paramilitary, or into petty crime, and created a drifting community of mercenaries.

Paradoxically, compared with other Latin American economies besieged by the international debt crisis, throughout the second half of the 1980s Colombia enjoyed relative economic stability. 'The economy is going well; the country is going badly,' people said. The years 1947 to 1954 had also been a time of great prosperity, sustained by rapid growth of the coffee economy and an upturn in international prices. It, too, had been an era of unrestrained savagery.

The idea of history as a straight line of unrelenting progress culminating in a revelatory event of life-changing proportions now seemed discredited and absurdly utopian. Success for Colombia's cyclists, however sought after, had ceased to soothe the nation's soul. It wasn't that Colombia didn't want to win: it yearned for victory. But in this new context cycling had suddenly entered the essentially onanistic domain of the sports fan. Not only was it frivolous, it was also a long way off.

Yet 1987 was to see the Colombians' greatest achievement yet. The protagonist was Lucho Herrera, the strategist behind him was Café de Colombia team director Raphael Antonio Niño, and the event was the national tour of Colombia's colonial motherland, Spain.

On the morning of 4 May, Lucho was in the red jersey of the mountains category leader and in fourth place overall. The race left the Spanish resort of Santander for the lakes of Enol and Encina in the Covadonga national park. Herrera measured his efforts over the first four climbs on the stage. When he reached the foot of the Lagos de Covadonga – Spain's Alpe d'Huez – he pulled away from his rivals with exquisite ease. The stage and the leader's yellow jersey were his. He was the first Colombian to wear the leader's jersey in one of the three-week European grand tours. His greatest rival, Ireland's Sean Kelly, ended the day in second place, thirty-nine seconds behind him.

Kelly recovered the leader's jersey in the time trial around Valladolid, but his forty-two second overall lead was too slender to protect him from the Colombian's prowess in the mountains. Lucho didn't need to wait: unbearable saddle sores forced Kelly to abandon on stage nineteen and Herrera took over the race lead. His strongest rival now was Germany's Raymund Dietzen, in second place.

When news of Kelly's abandon became known, Dietzen's team directors sent his team on a frantic chase after the forty-five seconds of time bonuses available on the stage to close the gap on Herrera. Niño bided his time. With 20 kilometres left, on the second category climb at Alto de Navalmoral, Lucho was restive. At last, Niño unleashed him.

Lucho exploded away from the peloton, dragging along the Frenchman Laurent Fignon in his wake. They reached the stage finish at the Adolfo Suárez Velodrome in Ávila alone. The Frenchman won the stage, but it was Herrera, now unassailable, who took the 1987 Vuelta a España and the King of the Mountains competition for Café de Colombia. It was Colombia's first title in a major tour.

Colombians had filled four of the top ten places. The riders sponsored by Manzana Postobón, led by Martín Ramírez, won the team competition. Triumph in the colonial mother country still held a special savour. But Colombia was not at war with its colonial past: it was at war with itself. To placate its angry gods, Herrera took the trophy on a pilgrimage to the Virgin of Chiquinquirá, Colombia's patron saint.

Throughout the rest of the summer the Colombians achieved unprecedented consistency. Herrera's mountain lieutenant, Henry Cárdenas, finished second to the Frenchman Charly Mottet in June's Dauphiné Libéré. In the ten-day Tour of Switzerland, Fabio Parra finished third, just eight seconds behind the victor, Andrew Hampsten of the United States. In the Tour de France, Lucho Herrera won his second King of the Mountains title and fifth place overall. His Café de Colombia team-mate Fabio Parra was sixth.

These were omens for what was to come the following year. After Herrera had won his fourth Vuelta a Colombia and devastated all-comers in the Dauphiné Libéré, Pedro Delgado predicted that Colombia's climbing genius held the key to the 1988 Tour de France. The winner, he said, would have to stick with Herrera in the mountains.

But he said nothing about Fabio Parra, whose tactical awareness had already led him to fifth place in the Tour of Spain. Now it gained him consistent high placings in France. And after an easy win into Morzine, it was clear that Parra posed the most serious Colombian threat. Next day was Alpe d'Huez day, and for once, after dragging the group within sight of Delgado and his Dutch breakaway companion Steven Rooks, Herrera cracked. With another powerful Dutchman, Gert-Jan Theunisse, glued to his wheel, Parra launched a series of attacks. Each time the camera-bikes frustrated his attack. When he kicked for the last time, a motorbike blocked his way again and his impetus was spent. Rooks stole away to win the stage. Parra finished fourth, at the back of the group he had led away. On the Tour's greatest ascent the traffic had denied him a level playing field. But he had climbed the classification, and by stage fifteen, when the Tour left the Alps, Parra was in third place overall. There he stayed, with Herrera two places behind, for seven more stages and a further 1,126 kilometres, and he was still there as the knot of exhausted athletes finally reached the Champs-Elysées and the race's end. Thirty-seven years and six months after the Indomitable Zipa had won the first Tour of Colombia, a Colombian was standing on the podium of the Tour de France. Decades of Colombian longing were at last becoming reality.

11. The sense of an ending

AND YET AS the cyclists scaled ever greater heights, the country plumbed the depths of misery. Violence was now so commonplace in Colombia, depravity so quotidian, that they had become indifferent components of everyday life. During 1988 a new manifestation of degeneracy emerged, comparable only to the worst excesses of the Violencia of the 1950s: indiscriminate massacres of peasant groups by paramilitary forces. Between 1988 and January 1989 more than eighty slaughters took place. In January 1989 a team of lawyers investigating just one massacre was itself exterminated.

Cycling was peeling away from reality. In the 1989 Vuelta a España, Colombians dominated the early stages. By the end of stage fourteen they filled five of the top eight places. On stage sixteen Spain's Pedro Delgado seized the leader's jersey. Fabio Parra lay third, one minute and one second behind. The following day, attacking on the final climb after six hours in the saddle,

Parra clawed back fifty-nine seconds. He was just two seconds down. Twenty-four hours later on the short, mountainous stage from Cangas de Onis and the ski station of Branillín, Parra repeatedly tried to shake Delgado off, but Ivan Ivanov, a Russian riding for the Soviet team sponsored by Alfa Lum, led the Spaniard back. Over the final four kilometres, enveloped in cloud with torrents pouring from the sky, Ivanov led Delgado to the stage finish. Parra, exasperated, was third. The gap had opened to three seconds and the Vuelta had left the mountains.

In the final time trial Delgado gained another fifty-four seconds on Parra. One decisive stage remained: a 189-kilometre stage over five major passes. Parra attacked with two Colombians as Delgado ran short of energy and team-mates. Ivanov again shepherded Delgado home. Though there was still a stage to come, the race was now effectively over. And there would be two Colombians on the podium. In third place was Oscar de Jesús Vargas of Manzana Postobón, who also won the mountains and the combined categories. Varta-Kelme was the best team. But although Parra had finished the stage twenty-two seconds faster than Delgado, it was the Spaniard that had won the Tour of Spain by the minuscule margin of thirty-five seconds, and relegated the Colombian to second.

There was controversy but it counted for nothing. Colombian delegates complained that Spanish TV bikes had helped Delgado, and on the morning of Delgado's triumphant procession into Madrid, a Colombian television cameraman filmed him handing Ivan Ivanov an envelope. But the Spaniard explained, 'I was just giving him my address.

However, although their results were better than ever before, all was not well with Colombian cycling. Its greatest cyclists no longer seemed to belong to the nation. Foreign dollars bought them off and they disappeared overseas. The national tour could no longer bring together the cream of Colombian sport. Then, just sixteen days after Parra and Vargas finished the Vuelta a España, Colombian cycling was dealt the most serious blow.

At Wembley Stadium in May 1988 Colombian soccer had taken an important evolutionary step. Gary Lineker's goal had put England one-up, but then a fine defender named Andrés Escobar headed an equalizer. For much of the game the Colombians' rhythmic, one-touch football had electrified the evening. England manager Bobby Robson rated them better than Brazil. Now, on the evening of 31 May 1989 at El Campín stadium, Bogotá, the soccer champions of Paraguay, Olimpia, brought a two-goal lead to the second leg of the Libertadores Cup final against the Medellín team Nacional. At half-time the score was goal-less. Forty-two seconds after the restart, the Colombians had reduced the deficit to one goal. Twenty-six minutes later Nacional's Andrés Escobar began a move that ended with a high cross headed home by Alveiro Uzuriaga. Despite relentless Nacional pressure, the aggregate remained even until the end of ninety minutes.

After seven penalties each, the scores were still level. Then Olimpia's eighth flew wide. Nacional's Leonel Álvarez stepped up, and hammered the ball towards the right-hand corner of the goal. The Olimpia goalkeeper had already leapt the other way. Atlética Nacional were champions of South America.

In René Higuita and his deputy Oscar Córdoba, Colombia had two of the finest goalkeepers in the game. With Andrés Escobar marshalling the defence and the orange beacon of Carlos Alberto Valderrama Palacio dictating the pace from midfield, Colombia began to beat its neighbours at their favourite game. Colombian football began to acquire an international reputation. Cycling and football, which appeal to such different temperaments, had been rivals since the 1950s. In an economy that offered limited sponsorship possibilities the two sports could co-exist, but only temporarily.

At the 1989 Tour of Italy, Lucho Herrera completed his stage-race curriculum vitae by winning two stages and the mountains competition. But he made no impression on the race for overall victory, finishing only eighteenth in the General Classification. At the Tour de France the Colombians were almost invisible. Herrera finished nineteenth; Parra abandoned during week two. Then the 1980s ended, and with them something uniquely Colombian died. The internationalization of Colombian cycling had been inevitable. It was an aspiration that dated back to the 1950s, and Bermúdez, however genial, was a symptom, not its cause. But by aspiring to European glory Colombia had inadvertently accepted Europe's claim to be the sole arbiter of world cycling. The Tour of Colombia, once the supreme popular expression of Colombian nationhood, had become a provincial side-show in a global system. The utter uniqueness of its landscapes and talents was denied. No longer equal to itself, Colombia was now an anonymous province in a multinational empire.

At his modest bike shop in Bogotá I met Sammy Cabrera, one of the great *domestiques* of the decade. 'In the European climate,' he told me, '*aguapanela* becomes sticky and stops you salivating. It's hard to breath. We began to replace *aguapanela* with chemical supplements from France: they had the advantage of weighing very little. And *bocadillo* we replaced with energy bars containing nuts and raisins. In the end we were importing European products into Colombia. We stopped taking *aguapanela* and *bocadillo* to Europe altogether.'

Colombia now entered one of the most profound social and institutional crises in its history. Beyond city limits the peasant massacres continued. Within them the drugs bosses responded to the threat of extradition to the US by launching a bloody offensive against the state. By the time Antioquia's Governor and Police Chief were gunned down in July and August 1989, murder itself had lost the power to shock. Each act of violence was intended to convey so many meanings to so many different parties that its essential barbarism was obscured. Confused by each indecipherable strategic exchange, public opinion could not cohere into an active social force.

At least the economy had been structurally sound. But on 3 July 1989, when the International Coffee Pact collapsed and the global coffee market lost its protected status, that security also ended. Prices plummeted by 60 per cent overnight. The value of wheat, barley, potato and maize also fell, condemning 7 million Colombians, three-quarters of them in the countryside, to extreme poverty.

Colombia's coffee producers – mostly smallholders selling their harvests to the National Federation of Coffee Farmers – reacted by increasing production to record levels. Their income merely continued to slump, and with it the value of their only capital: land. This was neo-liberalism, an international manmade disaster, and its effects on Colombia were quickly compounded by another, this time natural, calamity. The coffee blight broca, negligible in the late 1980s, had spread to 25,000 hectares by 1990. Six years later 600,000 hectares were affected.

Neo-liberalism had taken hold of Latin America unchallenged by global rivals. The Soviet system was falling apart, throwing Cuba into crisis; the Sandinistas were defeated at the polls in Nicaragua; in El Salvador the peace process was gathering momentum. Colombia's violent left was deprived of its former legitimacy-by-association. But after the decimation of the Patriotic Union, laying down its arms held few attractions.

In any case, the guerrillas were fighting vicious territorial battles with the army, local paramilitary groups and the drug lords. No longer able to offer an ideological alternative, they began to seek an economic one. Like the paramilitary and branches of the Armed Forces, some guerrilla columns found it in the drug trade.

On 18 August 1989 Luis Carlos Galán, the leader of the Liberal

Party and the favourite to win the forthcoming presidential elections, was assassinated. It was a turning point. President Virgilio Barco declared war on the drugs traffickers and re-introduced extradition. The narcos responded with attacks on symbols of the international stranglehold that choked Colombia. A massive bomb destroyed the DAS headquarters in Bogotá; another brought down a plane from the fleet of Avianca, the national airline. At the end of December the police hit back by hunting down the drug lord Gonzalo Rodríguez Gacha – 'the Mexican' – and gunning him down from a helicopter fitted with night sights. The execution was filmed from the air and broadcast on national TV.

Colombia was fragmenting economically, militarily and politically, and the principal victims were the peasant farmers who had produced Colombia's main crops and greatest cyclists. The coffee crisis also put a sudden end to Colombia's insignia cycling team. Café de Colombia continued to sponsor an amateur team, but in 1993 this, too, was discontinued. And with the narcos no longer able to make their public displays of largesse, the drug money ran out as well. Cycling, the sport that had always offered healing metaphors, was starved of funds.

In faraway Europe, Herrera and Parra were still the leading Colombian riders. But cocooned back home in Colombia, the new generation was quietly developing. On Wednesday 10 February 1988 its principal personae emerged. It was the evening after stage five of the Under-21 Tour of Colombia. Álvaro Mejía Castrillón, twenty-one, had taken the leader's jersey two days earlier. Hernán Buenahora, aged twenty, had jumped into second place by finishing the stage nearly a minute ahead of the pack, and lay five seconds behind, while Oliverio Rincón, also twenty, was two seconds further back.

At the race's close the following Sunday, these were the podium finishers, although not quite in that order: Mejía consolidated his advantage by winning the 35-kilometre time trial by over a minute. Rincón moved into second place, with Buenahora – twenty-two seconds behind – third.

Álvaro Mejía's remarkable natural talent would counterbalance his indiscipline for half a decade. His career and that of Rincón, the other great rider of his generation, were cut to similar patterns. Buenahora followed a different path, sacrificing personal glory and mislaying his ambitions in the ranks of a big European team. But all three were spirited out of Colombia to compete for international honours and lost to the domestic scene, which needed riders of their quality more than ever.

Mejía, a charismatic figure with film-star looks from Pereira, had emerged during the previous year's RCN Classic (he was third behind Fabio Parra). In 1988 and 1989 he used the final time trial to make up lost time, and won captivating races both times. Mejía was Colombia's most complete rider since Cochise. When, in late spring 1993, he signed for the US team Motorola, he joined Lance Armstrong, already World Champion and destined for a striking future. Today, after cancer, a remarkable comeback and spectacular victories in three Tours de France, Armstrong is the finest rider in world cycling. And he still holds Mejía's talent in enormous esteem: 'Álvaro was probably one of the greatest natural talents I've ever seen. He could climb like a Colombian and ride real good against the clock.' Coming to cycling from the world of triathlon, Armstrong hadn't been aware of the established Colombians like Herrera and Parra. But Mejía gained an immediate reputation among the Motorola riders. 'He went over to Italy and trained with Andy Hampsten. Remember, Andy was an important rider: it was only a year since he finished fourth in the Tour, and Mejía skinned him. Andy couldn't even stay on his wheel. I don't think anyone got inside his head. No one at Motorola spoke Spanish at the time, and he didn't speak English. In some ways Álvaro was just one of the stranger guys I've been around, but in a nice way. Always wore a lot of clothes. When the heat was scorching, we'd see him training in gloves. I could never understand it.' Mejía, already dark skinned and perhaps fearing racism in the white European peloton, hated the sunlight on his skin.

In 1991 in the tour of the Spanish region of Galicia, Mejía led Ryalcao-Postobón to the team prize, and in the individual classification defeated one of the hard men of cycling, the Russian-speaking Latvian, Piotr Ugrumov, by twenty-four seconds. In 1992 he won the Tour of Murcia, and the following year the Vuelta a Catalunya – beating Induráin and Rominger, the finest time trial riders in the world, at their favourite discipline. And in 1994 he was champion of the Paris-Nice. Yet at the greatest events he always seemed to miss out by tiny margins. At the 1991 World Road Racing Championships he was fourth, and he was fourth again at the 1993 Tour de France. 'Sure, he could have been more aggressive,' says Armstrong, 'but perhaps he was just smart enough to know his limits. He signs for Motorola late spring of '93, gets on the Tour de France team, and until the last time trial he's second. He ends up fourth – not even on the podium. It must have been a big blow; maybe it affected him.' Sports psychologists speak of the athlete's fear of winning: Colombians bring it up whenever Mejía is remembered. But Lance Armstrong's explanation is more concrete: 'He was racing at the same time as Miguel Indurain, which eliminated everybody.'

During the 1995 Vuelta a España, Mejía fell and broke his collarbone. He missed the World Championships in Duitama, Boyacá (Oliverio Rincón's home town), and then the Motorola team found itself without a sponsor. Mejía continued to train but couldn't find a contract. He eventually agreed to ride for the low-budget Colombian Petroleum team. His career slowly petered out. As recently as 1998 he was talking about making a comeback. 'He probably could,' says

Armstrong. 'He's a wild guy.' Yet for all his talent, Mejía never won the Tour of Colombia. It would have been a blight on a lesser rider's career record, but if anything, it was Colombia's national tour that was diminished.

His greatest Colombian rival, Oliverio Rincón, did inscribe his name on the Vuelta's list of champions. In 1989, like Niño and the Indomitable Zipa, he won the national tour at his first attempt. But unlike the all-rounder Mejía, Rincón's sleek limbs were forged for cruel mountains. He concealed his steel behind an easy smile and squirrel cheeks.

Soon afterwards he joined the Spanish team Kelme. In 1991 he won the best young rider title at the Vuelta a España and the Dauphiné Libéré. He finished the year by winning the Escalada a Montjuich in Barcelona. In 1993 he left Kelme to join Javier Mínguez, Pacho Rodríguez' old director, at Seguros Amaya. It was his finest season. Before the Tour de France, Rincón took stages in the Tour of Aragon in Spain, the Vuelta a España itself, and finished second overall in the Dauphiné Libéré. At the Tour he won the gruelling mountain stage from Perpignan through the Pyrenees to Andorra. Like Cochise, he had travelled to Europe to ride for a foreign team. Like Lucho Herrera, and with Lucho's inarticulate shyness, Oliverio won stages in the three great Tours, France, Italy and Spain. And in 1994 he scored Colombia's 100th win in Europe by winning the Classique des Alpes in France.

But this is what Colombia's European campaign had achieved: a bland statistic. Not through lack of talent. Mejía was briefly one of the world's top five riders, and Oliverio was good enough to finish fifth in the 1995 Giro d'Italia. But the tremendous depth of talent that the coffee bonanzas and the fervour of the 1980s had fostered was blocked. Only athletes of freakish physical gifts could now break into European cycling. Bermúdez' great plan had withered. There was as much raw ability as at any time in Colombia's history, but finance, support and direction were missing. And even Mejía and Rincón followed in the footsteps, not of Herrera and Parra, but of Martín Ramírez. Like him, they both had prodigious physical capacities; like him, they left Colombia young, enjoyed moments of irresistible power and threatened the summit of world cycling. Yet all, ultimately, belong in the footnotes to their respective eras. All underachieved and retired before reaching thirty, conquerors of tiny kingdoms, peripheral both to the great rivalries of global cycling and the history of their own country.

In their own country, life, like coffee, had become cheap. In March 1990 Bernardo Jaramillo, the presidential candidate of the Patriotic Union, was assassinated. The following month the plane carrying M-19 leader Carlos Pizarro to a campaign meeting was brought down. The politicians accepted the thesis of the guerrilla, that the violence was a political problem. They opened the doors of a new assembly to the whole of civil society to draw up a new constitution. Even the guerrillas were invited, in exchange for re-incorporation into the legal political system.

M-19 had already disbanded. The EPL and other, smaller groupings joined them. The EPL rapidly converted itself into a new political party, Esperanza, Paz y Libertad – Hope, Peace and Freedom – and established an alliance with M-19. Six months later, in the special elections for the Constituent Assembly, the alliance's leader, an engineer educated in England named Navarro Wolff, gained nearly 30 per cent of votes cast, and became one of the three co-chairmen of the assembly convened to re-write the constitution.

But those who hoped that paper guarantees and inclusive intent would staunch the bloodshed were disappointed, for Colombia's violence, which has always evaded analysis, has its roots in the same compulsive, almost fanatical spirituality that also powers its cyclists. The Colombian gunman wields his weapon like the cyclist and his bike: with the same ambition, the same amalgam of humility and arrogance, power and desperation – the same devotion to a greater ideal, and to escape. Some channel their energies into sport and art and honest labour, and keep their homeland whole; others pursue the forces of disintegration.

And disintegration characterized the start of the 1990s. In September 1990 the guerrillas launched a campaign of operations against the Armed Forces and the economic infrastructure. The Army, meanwhile, taking its military supremacy over the rebels for granted, occupied the operational headquarters of the FARC's Eastern Block. With negotiations going nowhere, President Gaviria ordered an attack on the enclave housing the FARC secretariat at Casa Verde in La Uribe. On 9 December, to coincide with the election of the National Constituent Assembly, it was bombarded and captured.

The occupation of La Uribe was presented as a decisive stage in the defeat of the guerrillas. In reality, the parity of forces between the military, their paramilitary cousins, and the guerrillas was perpetuating the stalemate and made any decisive victory unlikely. The occupation merely led to a powerful offensive by the FARC and the ELN. Maps printed in the national press depicted a noose tightening around Bogotá – this was the nightmare haunting Colombia. The government and guerrillas met for talks, but between each round, military confrontations took place, and overtures ended when a former government minister was kidnapped and assassinated.

In April 1992 two of the benevolent presences who had staved off national disaster for so long sang their swan song. Fabio Parra took over the leader's jersey in the Vuelta a Colombia by winning the final time trial. The following day he celebrated victory in Bogotá: it was his final Vuelta and his last professional win. In April Lucho Herrera won stage four of the Tour of Aragon in Spain. Remarkably, Colombians filled the first seven places on the stage. Three days later, the race concluded at Zaragoza. There Herrera, too, celebrated the final victory of his career. Then, with a crash, not a whimper, they bowed out: Lucho Herrera fell and abandoned his final Vuelta a España, and Fabio Parra did the same in the Tour de France. Their careers were effectively over.

On 2 December 1993 in Barrio Los Olivos, west Medellín, another 1980s icon fell. According to the official police version, Pablo Escobar was shot as he tried to escape over the rooftops. His brother Roberto claims it was suicide. From the wellspring of urban myth sprang the story that Escobar's death had been faked: he had paid a huge sum of money to a lookalike with AIDS, who allowed himself to be mown down in order to relieve his mother's financial problems. The rumour condensed the traits of tragic excess and tenderness publicly associated with Pablo Escobar. His tomb became a place of pilgrimage. Some Sundays over 2000 devotees visit. In the tombstone inscription some have read winning lottery numbers. An indigent Ecuadorian named Perfomante Solórzano visits every day to confess his tribulations. Thanks to Pablito, he claims, he is regaining sight in his blind right eye.

The deeds of Lucho Herrera and Fabio Parra, the villainy and humour of Pablo Escobar, the finest years of Valderrama and Higuita – all receded into the same mythical memory.

At the great stage races of the 1980s European competitors had coveted the lavish resources of the Café de Colombia teams.Their team coach was celebrated as the most luxurious in Europe. Now, with finance from Varta, Café de Colombia and Postobón dried up, European teams moved in to fill the space. Kelme, the Spanish clothing manufacturer which had employed Parra and Vargas, turned to Colombians as *domestiques* for its Spanish leaders.

However, after contributing to Colombian cycling in the 1980s and 1990s by developing local riders and keeping interest in the sport alive, the Kelme team found themselves embroiled in a contract scandal. In 1997 the time trial specialist Victor Hugo Peña claimed he had been forced to sign a contract in which the period – agreed verbally – had been left blank, and then manipulated after the event. Other riders came forward, claiming similar experiences. Just months after Kelme's owner José 'Pepe' Quiles had provided, free of charge, cars, bikes, time trial wheels, the team doctor, masseurs and mechanics for the Colombian delegation at the 1996 World Championships in San Sebastian, Spain, his contribution to Colombian cycling was suddenly the object of suspicion. But foreign teams who get involved with this vulnerable world, perhaps intending to do good, find it easy to exploit, even inadvertently. Colombia is rife with stories of European teams that pay Colombians a fraction of their team-mates' salaries, fail to make obligatory social security payments, settle wages either late or not at all, use Colombians as guinea pigs for new doping products, or employ nationalistic, not sporting, criteria in team selection and strategy, with the consequence that cycling, originally a means of national introspection and then a form of national assertion, suddenly exposed Colombia to all its post-colonial insecurities and suspicions.

The relationship between Colombian riders and European contractors embraces a complex range of power relations: between country and city, peasant and lawyer, mind and body, colonial metropolis and periphery, and between the internationalism of European cycling – where Swedes, Poles and Czechs skip across borders to compete with Spaniards, Italians and French from an early age – and the introverted pool of cyclists in far-off Colombia, occasionally thrashing the Venezuelans or Costa Ricans before their local sponsors spend a season's budget on a trip to two or three insignificant Portuguese events, to gain experience and a few scarce UCI points.

After the big budget Kelme, the international team most closely identified with Colombian cycling has been a modest Italian team (registered as Colombian since 1995) called Selle Italia, sponsored by one of the bike industry's biggest saddle manufacturers. Selle Italia relies on the genius of an exquisitely dressed Italian named Gianni Savio for coaxing funds from small sponsors, and Savio has become an institution in Colombian cycling. More than thirty Colombians have passed through his teams since he first saw Lucho Herrera at close quarters on the 1985 Tour de France.

Early in 1991 Savio visited Colombia for the first time, and won the Cucutá Border Classic with Leonardo Sierra, a native of the department of Santander who had moved across the Venezuelan border illegally with his parents. It was only when Sierra was conscripted for the national team that the Venezuelan authorities noticed his statelessness and gave him the necessary documents. Like US national champions Fred Rodríguez (born in Bogotá) and George Hincapie (born in the US of Antioquian parents), Sierra was one of Colombia's great cycling exports, and a product of Savio's expert eye.

By contrast with Kelme, a huge vessel that allowed its Colombians to sink or swim in its towering wake, Savio's nurturing style encouraged unregarded riders to explore their limits. For instance, Hernán Buenahora, who had emerged with Mejía and Rincón, finished sixth in the 2000 Giro d'Italia, when he was already past his prime at thirty-three. For eight seasons Buenahora's abilities had been squandered as an eternal *domestique* lost in Kelme's crowds.

Buenahora lacked Mejía's pure speed or Rincón's explosive acceleration, but had perhaps greater racing intelligence and a work ethic that made him good enough, even as a *domestique*, to finish tenth in the 1995 Tour de France. Victory in the 2001 Vuelta a Colombia, with four mountain stage wins, including the stage ending on the Escobero climb near Medellín – one of the most feared in a nation of extreme ascents – rounded off his career.

But Selle Italia's greatest moment was achieved by Nelson Rodríguez, 'Cacaíto', in the hardest stage of the 1994 Tour de France, into Val Thorens. Cacaíto was another fine athlete who virtually never rode in his homeland. He went to the Seoul Olympics with Varta's sponsorship, then as an amateur won the Tour of Martinique against French, Australian and Swiss competition. A great success in Spain, Cacaíto joined Kelme-Varta in 1989 as a *domestique* for Fabio Parra and got them both a thirty-second sanction in the Tour de France for pushing him up a 6–7 kilometre climb. But after two unappreciated years with Kelme, he accepted Savio's offer to join Selle Italia. He was twenty-four years old. 'For the next six years I spent January to October alone in a hotel.' In 1994 he lost the Tour de France stage finishing at Lens by a hair's breadth. 'The following day I was offered 10 million lire not to attack.'

In 1992 the RCN Classic momentarily regained its international aura when Claudio Chiappucci finished second, the best ever performance by an overseas rider. Chiappucci led an all-star Carrera Jeans team that included Russia's Vladimir Poulnikov and the Italians Fabio Roscioli and Alessandro Giannelli. The Dutchman Johan Bruyneel, later Lance Armstrong's technical director at US Postal, was eighth at two minutes fifty-five seconds.

But the increasingly rare rallies of Colombian cycling paled against the achievements of the national soccer team. Coach Francesco Maturana had instilled a distinctly Colombian style: rhythmic, dynamic, one-touch football that became known as tic-tac. On 5 September 1993 tic-tac gave Colombian football the finest ninety minutes in its history. In Buenos Aires, Maturana's men faced the 1986 World Cup winners and 1990 losing finalists, Argentina. A Freddy Rincón goal gave Colombia the lead at half time. Tino Asprilla scored five minutes after the interval, Rincón scored his second after 73 minutes, Asprilla did the same two minutes later, and finally, with six minutes left, Adolfo 'the Train' Valencia netted Colombia's fifth. In Bogotá the celebrations verged on mass hysteria. Rivers of alcohol-lubricated, gun-toting revellers fired into the air and at anyone who threatened to disturb their ecstasies. There were sixty-seven murders, fifteen killed in road accidents and 725 injured. After the match Colombia's assistant manager Hernán Darío Gómez said to Francisco Maturana, 'Pacho, now you've done it. We're going to have to be world champions.' Pelé named Colombia among his favourites for the 1994 World Cup. With a covert war going on in the Colombian countryside, football, with its fortress-like stadia, its screaming crowds turned inward on themselves and its short time span, was ousting cycling.

Argentina's rout was a publicity coup for Bavaria beer, which had signed a sponsorship contract with the Colombian national team until 2001. A current affairs magazine noted that 'this major investment can only be compared with massive sponsorship by the Ardille Lulle Organization, and specifically Postobón, of Colombian cycling'. It sounded like an obituary.

Of course, Colombia didn't win the World Cup, or even get through the first, group stage. A 3–1 defeat by Romania set the tone, and after losing 2–1 to the USA, Colombia abandoned all hope. Overwhelmed by the occasion, or by the burden of expectation, the Colombians returned home ashamed.

And when football began to wane, Colombia, especially the young, turned to motor sport, with its high-octane alternative to cycling's timeless meditation on pain and abstention. Motor sport was not entirely without roots here – Colombia's first motor race, the Colombia Cup, had been held in 1941 between Bogotá and Cali, and Roberto José Guerrero, son of Roberto Serafín Guerrero, the Argentine cyclist and coach to Honorio Rúa, had competed in Formula One. But it was Juan Pablo Montoya's victory in the 500 Miles of Indanapolis in May 2000 that generated national hysteria.

Montoya had been national go-kart champion six times between 1981 and 1991, and his time at the driving school of Vic Elford, who had trained Alain Prost and Michael Andretti, drew a glowing reference from Elford: 'I'd never seen such quality. Montoya was exceptional.' In 1995 he had travelled to Miami in the freezing hold of a cargo plane carrying a consignment of flowers to pursue his ambition to be a racing driver. He was runner-up in the British Formula 3000 championship in 1997, and won it the following year. Williams F1 took him on as a test driver, and then throughout 1999 the nation thrilled as he dominated the Formula CART-Fedex series in the United States. On 31 October 1999 Montoya sealed his victory by finishing fourth at Fontana. For him and for Colombian sports fans, it was the enticements of Formula One, not cycling, which filled the immediate future.

12. Blindspots

THE 1990S HAD BEGUN WITH a series of macabre murders that shocked the cycling community. What had begun as a few individuals supplementing their income with drug money was to become the financial dependence of the whole cycling community. Alberto Duarte Bernal was an early casualty.

Known as 'Chispitas' ('Firecracker') for his explosive climbing, Duarte had great technique, turning tiny gears with a quick cadence. At the 1970 Tour of Guatemala, Chispitas finished fourth overall and won the mountains category, beating a Spanish rider named José Manuel Fuente, who subsequently won two Vueltas a España and finished third in the 1973 Tour de France. But Chispitas's friends say he was also an adventurer, and when he associated with the Escobars, it led to his untimely demise.

After his cycling career had ended in the late 1970s, Duarte had joined the customs service at Bogotá's El

Dorado Airport as manager of airport customs warehousing. By applying selective blindness to certain packages passing through his jurisdiction, it seems Chispitas was able to supplement his earnings. And that was a mere stepping stone to a more lucrative career transporting cocaine cash from the US to Colombia.

In 1982 by pure coincidence a fellow rider who grew up with Chispitas in the town of Bucaramanga, Clímaco Guzmán, met his former team-mate on a flight to Panama. 'He was travelling with a large suitcase,' Guzman told me. 'I remember he had stolen a blanket from the plane, and when he opened it to put the blanket inside, I could see the suitcase was empty. He spent a few days in Panamá before taking an onward flight to the United States.' In Houston, Duarte was detained in possession of a suitcase containing a massive sum of cash for which he had no convincing explanation. Remanded in custody for fifteen months while investigations took place, he was eventually released and returned to Colombia. On his arrival he told a chilling tale. During his months in prison, he claimed, he had been forcibly restrained and injected with HIV+ blood. His killers allegedly told him, 'Go back to Colombia and die.'

Duarte was arrested on another occasion in Costa Rica, under similar circumstances. Again, no evidence could be found and he was released. 'Years later I bumped into him in Bucaramanga,' says Guzmán. 'It must have been 1986. I offered him *aguardiente*, but he refused. "I don't drink any more. I've calmed down a lot." You couldn't tell there was anything wrong with him. But he knew.'

Chispitas died of AIDS on 28 December 1990. Two years later AIDS also killed his widow.

THROUGHOUT THE 1980S Pablo Escobar's wealth, and the violence of his relations with the state, contaminated Medellín. The poorest parts of town rapidly flooded with hi-tech weaponry and bounty hunters seeking Escobar's one million-peso reward for every policeman murdered. Kidnap and murder became everyday instruments for negotiating small disputes. Rival gangs fought futile wars for territorial control over impoverished suburbs. The brutality had two competing outcomes: a generation of nihilistic teenagers resigned to an early death, coexisting with a crime economy initially run by the narcos but increasingly with a life of its own. Juvenile gangs in inner city slums, initially armed and contracted to settle accounts between drugs bosses, degenerated into independent bands of assassins.

Meanwhile, Pablo and Roberto enjoyed their cycling in their heavily-guarded velodrome. Their associate Gonzalo Rodríguez Gacha, alias the Mexican, also had his own team, and by 1985 the finest team in the country had suspicious backers.

The Joyería Felipe cycling team and its sister, Almacenes Felipe, were the playthings of Rodrigo Murillo Pardo, ostensibly a wealthy entrepreneur with business interests that included importing watches from Panamá. But Felipe had more in common with Roberto Escobar's team than just riders (Tolosa and Gutiérrez had joined Felipe when it was founded) and success (Felipe's riders dominated the 1985 Vuelta a Colombia, winning seven of the twelve stages). There was also the source of their finance, for Murillo was one of the three brothers who were also Medellín's greatest money-launderers.

The Betancur administration had implemented two policies that made money-laundering child's play. The first was to release US$200 million of foreign debt bonds, issueable to the carrier but transferable by simple endorsement. The second was to create a gold subsidy, the Bank of the Republic being authorized to acquire gold from Colombian citizens at a few dollars more than the highest international price. What the Murillo brothers did was simply to buy gold abroad on behalf of the drugs cartels and sell it to the bank for cash. To front their massive transactions they opened branches of

Joyería Felipe in Medellín, Cali and Cartagena, the principal centres of the drugs trade.

The Joyería Felipe dream was shattered at midnight on 17 February 1986 when two vehicles ambushed Rodrigo Murillo's BMW as he left a Medellín night club. Seven gunmen burst out bearing state-of-the-art weapons, and surrounded the partygoers. Murillo offered no resistance; no shots were fired and two days later the kidnapping had still not been officially reported to the police. A fortnight later, Murillo's corpse was found in a shallow grave with six bullet wounds but no other signs of torture.

Four months later Murillo's brother José Jaime watched two former 'Joyería Felipe' riders, Israel Corredor and Reynel Montoya, allow their Postobón team-mate, local boy Antonio Londoño, to win Colombia's first national road-racing championship for professionals. It was the last thing Murillo saw alive. At 3.00 p.m. the same day two assassins strafed José Jaime's Daihatsu camper with bullets. The second Murillo died instantly.

The Joyería Felipe cycling team passed into another incarnation. It was bought by a Cali-based sponsor and changed its name to Punto Sport Catalina, a bikini brand. But the change of identity did nothing to end its association with violence: behind Punto Sport Catalina was a dangerously exotic figure. Hugo Hernán Valencia had been employed as a bicycle courier for a drugstore, something he shared with a number of major drug dealers of the 1980s, like the leader of the Cali cartel, Gilberto Rodríguez Orejuela. He also used his bicycle to compete in the local tourist bike league, his dream being to compete with Colombia's greatest riders.

In a matter of years Valencia's life was transformed. He funded an ostentatious new church and a modern football stadium for his village. He purchased ranks of luxury cars and an apartment in an exclusive quarter of Bogotá. Valencia's crude extravagance led him to support a number of beauty queens (three candidates enjoyed his hospitality before one pan-American pageant) and then to acquire a stake in the Punto Sport Catalina bikini brand, a major sponsor of beauty contests. His parties were legendary: he would invite famous Puerto Rican salsa bands to entertain his guests, who could also feast their eyes on his sumptuous art collection. He boasted over a thousand pairs of shoes. His sexual excess was satirized in a virtually pornographic novel called *El Divino* by a major Colombian author, Gustavo Álvarez Gardeazábel. During the 1984 Vuelta his hometown of Zarzal, where he owned several large ranches and a state-of-the-art karting track, hosted the departure of stage ten. A successful cycling team was the logical next step in the exhibition of his fabulous wealth.

In 1984 former Bicicletas Ositto leader Manuel Ignacio Gutiérrez complained that Miguel Ángel Bermúdez was persecuting him. After winning stage one of the 1984 Vuelta and donning the leader's jersey, death threats arrived at Gutiérrez' home in Medellín. Whatever the truth, Gutiérrez was moving in dangerous circles. From Roberto Escobar's team he had moved to Perfumería Yaneth and then to Joyería Felipe. In 1986 he retired from racing; his first job off the saddle was as technical director of Punto Sport Catalina. His assistant was Armando Aristizábel, a former Café de Colombia rider who had assisted Martín Ramírez and Lucho Herrera to their finest performances in Europe.

El Divino, Gardeazábel's *roman à clef*, was published in 1983, four years before Valencia's appropriately bizarre demise. On 12 March 1987 the Punto Sport Catalina team prepared to start stage two of the Clásica a Itagüi in the south of Medellín. One of its riders had won the first stage: taking into account the prologue time trial, his teammate Reynel Montoya was wearing the leader's jersey.

A journalist who had travelled to Medellín to commentate on the

Tour of Itagüi for RCN told me, 'On the first day the Joyería Felipe riders came to the race start, but the car carrying team director Aristizábel never arrived. We waited while they tried to trace the vehicle, but it was soon clear that Aristizábel had been kidnapped.'

At 7.30 a.m. Valencia, his bodyguard, John Jairo Cartagena, the team's technical assistant, Armando Aristizábel, and a cameraman, Jorge Figueroa, were kidnapped. At 2.30 p.m. a corpse discovered on a municipal waste pit was identified as that of the bodyguard. Thirty-one 9mm rounds had been fired into it. A ring, watch and bracelet had been removed from the corpse. The left hand was handcuffed. Two men and a woman had been seen dumping the body from a green Renault. The police said that the kidnapping bore all the hallmarks of a drugs cartel operation. The trail went cold.

Waiting for further developments, the press observed that Aristizábel had no sources of income substantial emough to explain the luxurious Mercedes Benz he drove. A close friend of Armando Aristizábel told me, 'He was a good friend and a good rider. No champion, but he could have earned a good wage as a *domestique*. I tried to convince him to get out of organized crime, but he was having a good time, with plenty of money to spend. He invited me to join him, but I told him it wasn't for me.'

At 2.30 on the morning of Monday 6 April, Hugo Hernán Valencia's corpse was found on the waste pit where his bodyguard had been found slain. There were eight bullet wounds and further signs of torture. The body wore a blindfold. Later that morning a taxi driver discovered two more dead males, hands bound, with torture wounds and many bullet holes. They too had been blindfolded. They were identified as the cameraman Figueroa and the former international cyclist Armando Aristizábel.

Punto Catalina Sport's Reynel Montoya had won the Itagüi Classic. His team-mate Manuel Cárdenas had taken the points title and the Punto Catalina Sport riders collectively the team prize. But by then Valencia's interest in cycling was long past.

Between August and October 1990 Pablo Escobar's military commander John Jairo Velásquez Vásquez, alias Popeye, confessed to 'knowledge of the kidnapping and death of señor Hugo Hernán Valencia, together with three cyclists, in the city of Medellín'. It was one of Pablo's kills.

IN NONE OF these cases did the athletes concerned have any idea that they were funded by drugs money: as a rule, they had no personal stake in the drugs industry. There were, however, exceptions.

Neither Alfonso Flórez nor his great rival Gonzalo Marín went into team management. Both opened bike shops. Marín's store was called Chalito's. Alfonso joined Antioquian coach Raúl Mesa and Abelardo Ríos in a store named Arios Bikes. But under cover of their bike shops, both worked for Pablo Escobar.

By the late 1980s Medellín Airport had become too dangerous for shipments of cash and cocaine. Cargoes had to be driven to Cali airport, and Marín was rumoured to be on Pablo Escobar's payroll, organizing transport. It was lucrative but dangerous work, and when a large cash payment to two intermediaries went astray, Marín was held responsible. On the morning of 25 April 1990 he was waiting for his young son before the Man & Woman beauty salon on 10th Street and 34th Avenue, when three vehicles skidded to a standstill and eight heavily armed assassins burst out. As Marín scrambled for refuge in the salon, a deafening burst of gunfire rang out. The cyclist and two passers by lost their lives.

THE GREATEST COLOMBIAN cyclist to get involved in the narcotics business, however, was Alfonso Flórez. The race nights he organized at Pablo and Roberto's private velodrome weren't Alfonso's only link with the Medellín cartel, although his precise involvement remains a topic of speculation. But Flórez also had a reputation as a ladies' man, compensating for his looks with wit and innuendo, and it appears that these emotional cravings, combined with the company he was keeping, caused his downfall.

The police colonel who had commanded the surveillance operation on Pablo Escobar, a former cyclist who had ridden alongside Flórez in the early 1970s, told me how he had tried to save his old friend's life. 'Alfonso was friendly with a known gangster. This associate discovered that his wife was seeing another man, and decided to execute his rival. What he didn't know was that the other man was his best friend Alfonso Flórez. My unit used to monitor phone calls between members of the Medellín mafia, and from one conversation it transpired that Alfonso Flórez' life was in immediate danger. I called him. "Alfonso, you're involved with some dangerous people." But it was too late: he was dead within minutes.'

The police who attended the scene, at the traffic lights where Medellín's 65th Avenue meets Pichincha Street, opposite the landmark Exito hypermarket, were puzzled by the absence of bullet holes in the vehicle, his wife's Mazda 323. The four bullets that killed him were fired at point blank range: the assassin may have been in the vehicle with Flórez. It was Thursday 23 April 1992.

According to the colonel, 'It was only when the hitmen informed their paymaster that the job was done, at such-and-such a time and place, that he learned the identity of his wife's lover.' A former national newspaper reporter added, 'Alfonso's lover was also involved with one of the Gavirias, Pablo Escobar's cousins. The woman was told: either you kill him, or I kill you both. She decided to save herself.'

IN JUNE 1991 with the DEA, the FBI and the police forces of half the world on his back, Pablo Escobar had negotiated a deal with the

Colombian government. He, his brother Roberto and the rest of the Medellín cartel would surrender themselves to the state in exchange for a custom-built prison complex and guarantees that there would be no extradition. 'Better a grave in Colombia,' wrote Pablo, 'than a prison cell in the USA.'

He had already chosen the site for the prison complex: a grove sheltered from air attack and with a natural escape route through the hillside to its rear. Pablo and Roberto had played there as children and knew the terrain better than any policeman.

Roberto wasn't a wanted man. According to his own account, he had to invent an offence to gain access to a prison cell and his brother. He handed himself in on 21 June 1991 in the company of another cartel member, Gustavo González Flórez (murdered in Medellín's Bellavista Prison on Good Friday 1993).

Life inside the Escobar's prison complex, which became known as the Cathedral, bore little resemblance to conventional prison routine. Among his other luxury items, Escobar had a full-size football pitch built. The colonel told me, 'He celebrated the feast day of Las Mercedes, the patron saint of prisoners in Colombia, by inviting the three professional football teams of Medellín to play at the Cathedral – including players like René Higuita, Fausto Asprilla and Andrés Escobar.

'To accommodate the full-size pitch, a vast concrete platform was built at a cost of millions of pesos. A variety of turfs, some imported, were laid, but none satisfied Pablo. Eventually, a fine-grain aggregate of ground fish bones was commissioned, at incredible expense.'

Pablo acquired a regular service bus, filled it with bodyguards, and in a driver's coat and cap took the wheel. In this way the man who once offered to pay off Colombia's foreign debt with his cocaine fortune in exchange for a pardon could cross Medellín incognito.

On 22 June 1992 Pablo, Roberto and eight others left the Cathedral definitively. Threats by the Cali cartel to bomb the Cathedral from the air were followed by troop movements below the prison site. Fearing assassination or extradition, Pablo led his confidants through a breach in the escarpment behind the buildings, and into the uncertain life of fugitives. Roberto Escobar told me, 'I put on my Bicicletas Ositto cap and walked slowly down the corridor. It was the end of the 396 most special days of my life, a beautiful interlude that allowed me to share profound and sincere moments with my brother, during the last months of his existence.'

In the interests of his own security Roberto Escobar, accompanied by Popeye, again surrendered himself on 8 October 1992. Pablo remained at large until December 1993, when he was finally gunned down by police.

Incidents related to the Escobars continued to affect Colombian cycling through the 1990s. With the Colombian police, the White House and the hoodlums of the Cali cartel baying for Escobar's blood, on 6 September 1993 a hit squad funded by the Cali cartel known as the Pepes – or 'P-Ps', for 'Persecuted by Pablo Escobar' – murdered former cycling coach Ricardo Zea Salazar. Zea had been a close friend of Roberto Escobar, administering his cattle and horses. In the 1960s and 1970s he had travelled all over Latin America with Colombian national teams, and before Claudio Costa's arrival in 1969, he had been Cochise's coach.

In the last week of January 1993 the Pepes detonated a series of bombs beside Escobar properties, which included several high-rise residential blocks put up in the 1980s. One of these, a building named 'Habidules de la Toja', housed Pablo Escobar's mother, Doña Hermilda. An adjacent block named 'Altos de Campestre' housed his son Juan Pablo. Sandwiched between the two lived a young cyclist named Santiago Botero with his family.

At 10.00 at night on Wednesday 27 the Pepe's detonated a car bomb outside the Habidules de la Toja. The windows of the Botero residence were blown in. Five minutes later a car pulled up before the building opposite and Doña Hermilda, unhurt, climbed in. The bombers returned the following Saturday; that midnight a more powerful device exploded. It blew Santiago Botero to the floor. A fraction of a second later a second bomb, intended for Escobar's son, went off on the other side of the house. Half of the Botero home was destroyed, but by a miracle Santiago was unhurt. Botero grew into one of the finest cyclists on earth, winning the King of the Mountains title at the 2000 Tour de France and a bronze medal in the 2001 world time trial championship.

Meanwhile, cocaine smugglers began to use the cover of official teams travelling abroad. On 24 October 1991 a team of ten Colombian cyclists, claiming to be sponsored by the American Commerce National Bank, landed in Rome. Two of its members, Marco Antonio León Castro and Oscar Ivan Valencia, were cyclists of some repute: León had won two stages of the 1982 Vuelta de la Juventud, and had ridden with Café de Colombia in Europe, helping Lucho Herrera win the 1987 Tour of Spain. The rest were youngsters, led by their manager, José Alirio Salas, fifty-two.

As they waited in the airport for their hotel transfer, a detachment of armed police surrounded the men and hurried them towards a checkpoint. It was there that the cocaine secreted inside their bicycles was laid out before them.

The colonel told me, 'They were Superala bikes which screwed together. The frames had been filled with cocaine. The riders themselves didn't know anything about it. They were well paid, but they were used.'

Five months later they were sentenced, the cyclists to five years and four months, the coach to fourteen years. In January 1993 León and Valencia were transferred to a high security prison, where they remained until 15 October 1993. With three years of their sentence left to serve, they were granted expulsion from Italy.

A team with a rather higher profile, Postobón's international operation, came close to suffering a similar scandal in 1991. Raúl Mesa was technical director of the Postobón team in the early 1990s. One of his riders was Juan Carlos Castillo, the winner of the 1984 Under-21 Tour of Colombia. He had represented Colombia at the Vuelta al Táchira, the Tour of Switzerland, the Tour de l'Avenir and its professional cousin, the Tour de France.

Mesa told me, 'Castillo was a strong rider on the flat. His job was to protect Lucho Herrera on the long, windy stages before the major tours reached the mountains. In 1991 the Postobón team was leaving for the Tour of Murcia in Spain. A suitcase was searched and a consignment of cocaine found. The case belonged to Juan Carlos Castillo. It set off a tragic chain of events.'

After a lengthy detention in Bogotá's Model Prison during investigations, Castillo was tried and absolved. One Thursday afternoon in November 1993 Castillo, aged twenty-nine, visited the town of Pereira. Traced by an unknown telephone caller, a meeting was hastily arranged in nearby Chinchiná. Parking where 8th Street meets 11th Avenue, the subject waited in the evening dark. A passing vehicle slowed and a single bullet was fired. At Saint Mark's Hospital, Chinchiná, Juan Carlos Castillo was dead on arrival. There were leads, suspects and known motives, but no arrests.

Years later, Carlos Ardila Lulle, Postobón's patron, sat next to Santiago Botero on a flight to Europe. He confided that the Castillo scandal had led him to withdraw funding for the Postobón team at the end of 1993.

As the 1990s passed, the number of narcotics-related incidents involving cyclists shrank. Cycling budgets had never been large enough to interest the money-launderers: only enthusiasts got involved. But in 1996 another of the finest riders of the 1970s was added to the list.

At midday on 22 November, Bogotá anti-narcotics police discovered a tonne of 95 per cent pure cocaine in an apartment at 3rd Street and 15th Avenue, just a few blocks from the Metropolitan Police headquarters. The stash was buried in a shipment of coffee to camouflage its odour. Around them the drugs police found certificates, shirts and trophies from the brilliant athletic career of the former Perfumería Yaneth rider Carlos Julio Siachoque.

Staff at the offices of Siachoque Investments informed the press that the director had left for lunch at 2.00 p.m. He was finally picked up six months later, during the following year's Vuelta.

Three days later five more carriers were arrested at El Dorado International Airport. They claimed to be cyclists travelling to an event in Cantabria, Spain, and bore false Colombian Cycling Federation documents. Inside their bicycle frames 20 kilos of cocaine were discovered.

Other murders may be added to this dossier. On 30 April 1995 a former Kelme rider, José Vicente Díaz, was murdered in Tunja; police investigations suggested a drugs connection, although the crime was never solved. On 8 August 1999 Elkin Darío Rendón, a Medellín cycling coach, was shot from a passing car as he cycled near the town. Once again, a drugs connection was suspected.

But the moral to be drawn is not that cycling became an important means of laundering drugs money – it didn't. The narcos entered cycling because they were fans. It was a way of showing off and of competing with each other. Relatively few riders entered the drugs industry. The fate of those that did proves that the only way out is into a hole in the ground. Or a prison cell – and what exquisite justice, to subject a man who once soared over Colombia's immense landscapes to such oppressive confinement. Today Roberto Escobar sweats away his detention on an exercise bike. Into the darkness of his blindness, the memory of mountains and the infinite sky must seem a source of light as intense as the flash of a bomb, brilliant even to his unseeing eyes. He pedals towards them, getting nowhere, suspended in time and space.

13. Unnecessary interference

It was not a major operation: three men, masks and handguns. They had tracked their quarry out here, to the marshland of Pantano de Vargas in rural Boyacá. Relative isolation was enough. At 2.33 p.m. they exploded into the cottage, waved pistols at two young children and bundled their father outside. Cowering at the window, his wife saw him swallowed by a waiting vehicle that sped away. Behind it rose a cloud of uncertainty.

At the centre of Duitama, the town that had hosted cycling's 1995 World Championships, a sculpture depicts Oliverio Rincón crossing some imaginary threshold, arms raised to a greater power. He had been visiting his parents, ten minutes away, when he was snatched. Thirty-one but already retired (too much riding – too much *success*, too young), the man known simply as Oliverio had been a pure Colombian climber. When news of the kidnapping became public, the streets of Duitama and Bogotá filled with crowds demanding his release. Colombia's leftist subversives had never before touched the sport. The violence that had finally invaded the last *locus amœnus* of Colombia's conscience came unannounced.

For four days there was no word. Eventually his wife received a call. Oliverio confirmed that he was a prisoner of the Adonai Ardila Pinilla Front of the ELN guerrilla force. Six days later, without warning, he was released. According to press reports, no ransom had been paid. An ELN commander, alias Oswaldo, denied his organization's involvement.

Rincón was seized on 21 January 2000, a Friday. Lucho Herrera was travelling abroad at the time. Intuiting that the abduction might not be the last from the community of former cyclists, he prolonged his trip. When he finally returned home, events proved him right.

Esther Herrera, seventy-eight, was pouring coffee when they came. 'I'd just offered my son a cup. As I turned, he was closing the door. They wore black hoods, with pistols and rifles.' Esther cried out and lunged for the telephone; one of the kidnappers tore away the receiver and severed the line. Herrera was abducted on the morning of Saturday 4 March. With no telephone it took Esther half an hour to inform the police, and the police a further half an hour to issue descriptions and man roadblocks. It was far longer than the bandits needed. In the nearby mountains to the south a whole army could disappear.

The evening was spent scrambling across wooded slopes at gunpoint. 'They blindfolded me and made me spin around until I was disorientated,' Herrera was to recall. 'Then we walked, six or eight hours, deep into the night. They interrogated me as we went: they wanted to know about my money and investments. A military helicopter flew overhead, and they began to get tense. I was in fear of my life.'

Yet after less than twenty hours in captivity, Lucho was free. At

8.30 a.m. on Sunday 5 March his brother Álvaro collected him from the roadside. Police sources claimed that their actions had prevented the criminals from leaving the area and led to Herrera's early liberation. Lucho insisted no ransom had been paid. And although the hills around Herrera's hometown of Fusagasugá belong to the FARC's 42nd Front, Lucho claims he never found out who his abductors were or what they wanted.

The incidents seemed inexplicable. True, the guerrilla armies had never pandered to public opinion. But to threaten figures bound to Colombia's most religious sense of self was to risk visceral alienation. However, new developments were leaving the armies of subversion in disarray. Even as Lucho Herrera made his way home, Vice-President Gustavo Bell Lemus was preparing to leave for Washington to discuss the details of an aid package that would threaten to push Colombia into civil war.

President Andrés Pastrana had been elected on 22 June 1998 on a platform for peace. The son of Misael Pastrana, president in 1970, Andrés was a former television journalist who had reported on Colombia's cyclists in Europe: he had interviewed Lucho Herrera after his Tour of Spain win in 1987. His Plan Colombia, explicitly modelled on the Marshall Plan, through which the US had contributed to the reconstruction of Europe after the war, was designed to energize the peace process, fight poverty and develop alternative income sources for families dependant on coca and poppy cultivation. It depended on massive international finance. However, since 1996 Washington had chosen to identify subversion with cocaine and heroin production, and in October 1999 CIA director George Tenet claimed that the FARC had become a cartel and represented the main obstacle to the drugs war in Colombia.

Informed observers disagreed. In 1999 researcher Ricardo Vargas Meza was saying that the guerrillas were primarily focussed on the taxation of illicit crops, and that they had called for a development plan and sustainable alternatives which would allow coca eradication. Early in 2000 Klaus Nyholm, director of the UN Drug Control Programme, insisted curtly, 'The guerrillas are something different from the traffickers.' If they were the same, Washington would see no place for dialogue, amnesties, demobilization or pardons. The peace process, in short, would be unthinkable.

US drug czar General Barry McCaffrey and Under-Secretary of State Thomas Pickering had visited Colombia in July and August 1999, and made it clear that American support would be more forthcoming if the military campaign against the drugs industry were intensified. Pastrana redrafted his proposals accordingly, yet the text presented to the Committee for Foreign Relations of the US Congress in October 1999 still contained substantial non-military elements. Its alternative development budget was US$570.8 million, including US$86 million for conservation projects and US$42.3 million for indigenous communities.

But election years have dangerous tides, and 2000 was the wrong year to seek Washington's largesse. The plan was sucked into the maelstrom and ripped apart, emerging far downstream of Colombia's needs. When American helicopter manufacturers began splashing campaign money around, Blackhawk and Huey helicopters climbed the list of Colombia's primary necessities. The US petroleum companies active in Colombia appeared as witnesses before Congress to support the hawks. As part of that indispensable electoral ritual, drug war posturing, clauses on crop destruction were inserted, and the plan was recast as a military aid package worth US$1.3 billion. By the time of Oliverio's kidnapping in January 2000, Plan Colombia envisaged a major military offensive in the south of Colombia and the creation of three new anti-drugs battalions.

The measures flew in the face of a study sponsored by the US

Army and the Office of National Drug Control Policy. It concluded that funds spent on domestic drug treatment within the US were twenty-three times more effective than source country control like Plan Colombia, eleven times as effective as prohibition, and seven times as effective as domestic law enforcement. Indeed, when President Nixon had declared a drug war in 1971, two-thirds of the funding had gone on treatment. Record numbers of addicts were helped, and the number of drug-related arrests and federal prison inmates dropped sharply. That, of course, was long before Hollywood voted Colombia world public enemy number one, with a stream of demonizing storylines: *Scarface*, *Delta Force 2*, *Imminent Danger*, *Let's Get Harry*, *Marked for Death*, *McBain*, *Carlito's Way*, James Bond in *Licence to Kill*, *Drug Wars*, *The Specialist*, *Proof of Life*, *Collateral Damage*.

Since 1980 the war on drugs has increasingly shifted to punishing offenders, border surveillance, and fighting production at the source countries. When Plan Colombia was being formulated, near unanimous opposition greeted a proposal to channel US$100 million from the US$1.3 billion then planned for Colombia into treatment for US addicts. The suggestion was dropped.

Colombia's drugs trade was being removed from the domain of the police and handed over to the military. The proposals undermined tentative peace talks initiated in 1998, and the guerrillas, recognizing that the new weapons would be trained on them, began to prepare a war chest, announcing that any Colombian with assets of more than US$1 million would be subject to a 'revolutionary tax' or face the threat of kidnapping. Colombia's athletes were no exception, and the million-dollar threshold was a matter of interpretation.

Oliverio Rincón was snatched for the second time at the end of March 2000, by the FARC this time. Again, masked gunmen seized him in front of his children. His wife Gilma was held until the following morning; Oliverio was released twenty-four hours later. That day the Chamber of Representatives in Washington approved Plan Colombia and passed it on to Congress. The Pastrana administration had paid millions of dollars to a prestigious American PR company to lobby on its behalf. In July 2000, George W. Bush now having acceded to the White House, Congress authorized the Plan.

But instead of the original US$570.8 million alternative development budget, Colombia received sixty helicopters: eighteen Sikorsky Blackhawk and forty-two Huey. Of the US$860.3 million finally approved, just US$68.5 million was destined for development, plus another US$10 million to cushion the effects of the crop-destruction offensive in the south of the country. The new Plan allowed the US to send military advisors to Colombia: a maximum of 500 military and 300 civilian. The civilians, retired US soldiers or former CIA agents – mercenaries by any other name, working for firms like Military Professional Resources and DynCorp – instructed the military in guerrilla warfare and operational planning. Contracted to the State and Defence Departments, they could take part in anti-subversive activities without implicating the US government. Side-stepping Congressional control and public outrage in case of casualties, they were effectively George W. Bush's private army.

By comparison, Oliverio's kidnapping by three masked men with handguns was not a major operation. But that was all it took to consign the mystical relationship between Colombia and its cyclists to the past. The message to Colombia's cyclists was that they should leave the country if they were financially successful. Once they had crossed demarcation lines and no-go areas like ghosts through castle walls. Now the threat of violence and extortion hung over them too, and all for the drug war, a clownish pose powered by the sound-bite culture of politics.

As the cyclists of the past faced up to the new reality, another vacuous posture, this time on the part of cycling's world governing body, the UCI, threatened to destroy the career of Colombia's finest active rider.

On 4 September 1999, hours before the start of the three-week Tour of Spain, Santiago Botero, who six years earlier had survived the double bomb-blast near his home, was rushed through the basement of a Córdoba hotel and smuggled out of the staff door, covered with a blanket like a sex offender. Thirty-five days later the Colombian Cycling Federation announced Botero's suspension for six months and a fine of 2000 Swiss francs: he had been found guilty of doping. His results obtained between February and March 1999 – second and a stage win in the Tour of Andalucía, fifth in the Tour of Valencia, third and a stage win in the Paris-Nice, seventh in Catalan Week – would be airbrushed out of history. Jorge Tenjo, the President of the Colombian Cycling Federation, appeared before the Colombian press and announced, 'I continue to believe that Santiago is innocent.'

Botero was a new type of rider in Colombia. The son of a small businessman, he graduated in Business Administration and was discovered competing in weekend mountain bike trials by a Medellín sports scientist. An inadvertent athlete, he went from weekend mountain biking in the hills around Medellín to professional road-racing in Europe in a matter of months.

Botero, tall, blond and blue-eyed – like Honorio Rúa four decades before him – seems anything but Colombian. Indeed, his build hindered his early career, as Dr Juan Darío Uribe Uribe, his first sports doctor and former manager, recalls: 'Santiago's physique is remarkable, but it isn't typical for a Colombian cyclist. The success of Lucho Herrera in the 1980s created a dictatorship of the tiny, 55kg body; everyone had forgotten Cochise. Santiago has Cochise's build: tall, muscular, powerful. Before his performance at the 2000 Tour de

France, Santiago was never even considered a good climber in Colombia. I wanted him to serve his apprenticeship in Europe, not Colombia, because his qualities suited European, not Colombian, racing. In Colombia you have to be a pure climber, which Santiago isn't. Someone compared that to going to university when you'd never been to primary school. But if I had a son and I could send him to the University of Antioquia, which is excellent, or to Oxford, which is better, I'd send him to Oxford.'

Santiago signed for Kelme in 1996 and went to Europe. At home in Medellín he told me, 'I had to learn things so basic that no one explains them, like how to grab my musette or ride in echelons.' In 1998 after two seasons learning his trade, Botero was able to prepare systematically for the first time. Aiming for the Giro d'Italia in May, he rode a series of modest events rated category five by the UCI. At the three-stage GP Mitsubishi Internacional in Portugal he won a stage and finished second overall; at the Vuelta a La Rioja in Spain he lost by just six seconds. Then he travelled to Switzerland for a more prestigious event.

The six-day Tour de Romandie is rated *hors catégorie* by the UCI: one level below a three-week tour. Leading his Kelme team, Botero finished fourth behind some big names – Laurent Dufaux and Alex Zülle, Swiss riders on home territory, and the Italian Francesco Casagrande. 'I was still completely unknown, climbing with these giants, and all the rest. It was a landmark in my career.'

The race was also a landmark in pharmacological malpractice, which would never have come to light had a major doping scandal not broken during July's Tour de France. From the subsequent investigations, the 1998 Tour de Romandie emerged as one of the most chemically charged events in sports history. The winner had taken illegal cortisone supplements; he and the second-placed rider, both on the notorious Festina team, had been systematically using synthetic erythropoietin, known in sports slang as EPO, to boost its riders' red blood cell count and enhance their performance. Another rider fell ill during the race with a condition connected to abuse of perfluorocarbon (PFC), a substance whose side-effects are said to be so severe that it was withdrawn from clinical trials. The third-placed rider, Francesco Casagrande, had tested positive for testosterone at the previous week's Tour of Trentino in Italy, and did so again at Romandie. Also positive for testosterone was Santiago Botero.

The event proved that the UCI anti-doping programme was pure farce. Neither Dufaux nor Zülle – who later confessed their guilt – had failed any doping test, while no categorical proof could be offered that the two riders who did, Casagrande and Botero, had used any illegal substance. For the approved testosterone test is incapable of distinguishing endogenous testosterone, produced naturally in the body, from exogenous testosterone, synthesized in a laboratory. Testers merely compare the presence of testosterone with the presence of a related hormone, epitestosterone, expelled in the urine. An abnormally high ratio suggests, but does no more than suggest, the absorption of exogenous testosterone. However, the judge of the Tour de France doping trial concluded in December 2000 that 'it is impossible to define a hormonal "norm" [because] hormone rates vary from individual to individual and, in the same individual, from one period of time to the next'. And given that it was Botero's first European doping test, the testers can have had no idea of his natural hormone balance.

At the end of 1998 Botero underwent exhaustive tests first in Madrid, then in Switzerland, confirming that his testosterone levels were naturally high and allowing him to ride. In spring 1999 after a series of excellent performances, Botero took more doping tests, which repeated the earlier findings. 'In August Kelme selected me for the Vuelta a España,' Botero remembers. 'At the race start in Córdoba I was in the best form of my life.' He telephoned his former doctor Uribe. 'The overwhelming favourite to win the Vuelta was the brilliant German, Jan Ullrich. Santiago said to me, full of enthusiasm, "I'm riding as well as Ullrich,"' Uribe remembers. 'Ullrich won the race: Santiago didn't even start.' Ten hours before the start of the Vuelta a España, Kelme's directors were contacted by the UCI. Hints were dropped that other teams would not think highly of Botero's high testosterone levels. Some sort of threat may have been implied. Botero was withdrawn.

The UCI instructed the Colombian Cycling Federation to sanction the rider. The Kelme team doctor, Dr Eufemiano Fuentes, travelled to Colombia to appear before the investigating committee and argued that the UCI was lagging behind current understanding. 'Ten years ago they said six was the maximum natural limit. Today they say twelve. Santiago Botero tested at fourteen. Perhaps in ten years time they will accept that natural ratios may reach fifteen or eighteen. Santiago is exceptional. He has a remarkable metabolism.'

After the hearing, the Colombian Federation absolved the athlete, dispatching a four-page scientific dossier to the UCI explaining their decision. The UCI's reply, in short, was that if the Federation didn't sanction Botero, the UCI could come down on them hard.

'So the Federation was forced to impose the minimum permissible penalty, a six-month ban. I thought of suing the UCI by using human rights law,' says Dr Uribe, 'demonstrating that Santiago had been denied the right to work. But it was dangerous. In any case, Santiago didn't want to do it, Kelme was afraid, and his father was afraid because it could prejudice his career.'

CYCLING'S WORLD GOVERNING body, it is pertinent to add, has long approached the subject of doping with a degree of complacency. The French judge who heard the Festina trial after the 1998 Tour de

France concluded that 'the institution in charge of spearheading the international struggle [against doping] had taken a deliberate and long-term decision to restrict its action to *excessive* [use of doping products], and therefore, shown quasi-tolerance [of doping]'. And the attitude of UCI President Hein Verbruggen to doping in sport is a matter of record. 'The International Olympic Committee (IOC) makes me laugh with its calls not to cheat, when all the pressure on athletes are evident,' he observed in 1989, as Chairman of the International Federation of Professional Cycling (FICP), adding, 'If there are $3 million at the end of the track, I'll take a pill to win. And 90 per cent of human beings will do the same as me... Thankfully, the FICP does not belong to the IOC.' Within a year the FICP merged with its amateur counterpart within the UCI. Verbruggen, the UCI's first president, was soon elected to the very International Olympic Committee whose anti-doping rhetoric he had so recently found contemptible. Today Verbruggen chairs the IOC committee, which visits and monitors cities bidding to host the Olympic Games. One day he could be President of the International Olympic Committee.

And even now, years after the Festina affair came close to destroying cycling's credibility, the regime allows riders who have demonstrably abused doping products to serve brief suspensions before resuming their careers, qualify for UCI coaching certificates, hold UCI posts and attend its most prestigious events as guests of honour. Those who break cycling's law of silence and reveal details of its endemic doping practices, by contrast, are also suspended – even in the absence of a positive doping test result or, indeed, any prior suspicion of their guilt – and ostracized. The former was the case with France's 1996 world mountain-bike champion Jérôme Chiotti, suspended for three months with three further months suspended, and dropped from the French national team at the 2000 World Championships, when he was French national champion, after he confessed in April 1999 to a French mountain-bike magazine that he had won his national and world titles with the help of the illegal hormone EPO and other doping products. All of the UCI anti-doping tests he had taken, needless to say, found him clean.

By contrast, where grounds exist for believing that a positive doping test result is false – as in Santiago Botero's case – a young athlete's reputation and, potentially, career can be, quite simply, destroyed. The alternative, given to the highly politicized reality of modern-day cycling, would be for the governing body to show signs of humility, even if this weakened its power within the bureaucracy of world sport.

BOTERO, HOWEVER, REFUSED to give up. During his six-month suspension, fuelled by anger, he trained hard, and began the 2000 Tour de France riding for Kelme's two Spanish leaders, Fernando Escartín and Roberto Heras. 'On stage ten, the first mountain stage, I attacked and attacked and finally managed to escape with Francisco Mancebo [who eventually won the prize for Best Young Rider]. [Five-times Tour de France King of the Mountains] Richard Virenque crossed to us, and the three of us were going well until I was ordered to wait for Roberto and Fernando. I rode about 30 kilometres flat out to gain time on Armstrong and Ullrich, and by the final climb I was burnt out.' Botero lost eleven minutes fifty-eight seconds to race favourite Lance Armstrong on the stage. Yet from that day on, consistent high placings, including second the following day, fifth the day after, and first in the hardest stage of the Tour through the southern French Alpes from Draguignon to Briançon, proved that Botero was Kelme's strongest rider. He finished the race in seventh place overall, with one stage win and the mountains title, fourteen minutes eighteen seconds behind Armstrong. It invited comparison with

Herrera's finest performances: seventh in 1985 with two stage wins, fifth and sixth with none in 1987 and 1988. Herrera, an undisputed leader with a team working for him, had thrilled a nation: but in a country devoted to a new sport – motor racing – and a new hero – Juan Pablo Montoya – Botero, handicapped by starting as a *domestique*, and stigmatized by his doping suspension, was a mere footnote in the day's news.

Cycling had, nonetheless, continued to give Colombia poignant memories. The 1997 Under-21 Tour of Colombia champion Victor Hugo Peña made his name in international cycling by winning against the clock on stage eleven of the 2000 Giro d'Italia over a mirror-flat route from Lignano Sabbiadoro to Bibione in Italy's north-east. It was another chapter in the history of Colombian time trialling, building on the success of a thick-set giant from Medellín named Duván Ramírez, who had finished fourth in the world time trial championship behind Miguel Indurain, at Duitama in 1995.

And after Botero's Tour de France stage win and mountains title, Félix Cárdenas, his Kelme colleague, won a mountains stage in the Tour of Spain. It was the first time Colombians had won stages in each of the major three-week Tours; in 2001, with Carlos Contreras in the Giro d'Italia, Cárdenas in the Tour de France and Botero (three times) in the Vuelta a España, they did so again.

In October 2001 Botero travelled to the World Championships in Lisbon. There he won Colombia's first professional World Championship medal by finishing third in the time trial. He had indisputably become one of the finest riders of his generation. Even in the absence of a major national team, Colombia was as successful as it had ever been.

But Formula One, with its massive budgets, global reach and aggressive marketing, offered what Colombia now most desired: not a mirror or lens, but an unattainable vision, something glamorous and irrelevant. An escape. And with the advent of cable television, the Formula One Grand Prix in any part of the world, in which Montoya was certain to be a protagonist, was as accessible as any local spectacle, and more attractive than a bike race of 200 competitors, one or two per cent of whom are Colombian.

Under attack from rival sports with global appeal, Colombia now fell victim to the globalization of cycling itself. The UCI ranking system means that teams rise or fall in the UCI rankings according to the total number of points won by their riders. Riders earn points according to their placings in UCI-ranked events. The mountains category, incidentally, even in a major stage race, is rewarded with no UCI points.

A number of factors contribute to a race's UCI category, including photo-finish facilities, the presence of international race commissaires, the participation of international teams and the variety of anti-doping tests employed (which, besides being farcically ineffective, can also be extremely expensive). In a developing nation these are neither affordable nor easy to find. Consequently, only four Colombian races have UCI rankings: the Vuelta a Colombia and the RCN, and the national road and time trial championships. In no other Colombian event can local teams and riders improve their position in the world lists. The sixteen-stage Tour of Colombia is a category five event. Accordingly, the winner of each stage wins four UCI points, the race leader at the end of each day two points, and the overall victor twenty-five points. In global terms it's a pathetic haul: stage one of the five-day Tour of Luxembourg, not a celebrated date on the international cycling calendar, takes twenty points for the stage and another six for the race lead. The rider who finishes thirty-first in the three-week Tour of Spain, for instance, wins twenty-five points. And to match the seventy points on offer for a stage in the Tour de France, a Colombian national rider would have to win eleven stages of his national Tour, and the overall title. If Cochise had competed according to the present rules, he would never have accumulated enough UCI points to interest a professional European team.

But the maths is not the point. What matters is the message it conveys, which is this: riders and teams based beyond the confines of Western Europe are not invited to the party. With so few UCI points at stake, Colombian events could only appeal to professional European or North American teams as altitude training. Yet the terrain and the opposition is too demanding. Because bringing overseas competition to Colombia is unfeasible, the alternative is to take Colombian teams to Europe and earn UCI points there. But such trips are irregular and brief, for the costs are prohibitive. To the cycling nations beyond the European core, therefore – Colombia, Venezuela, and Argentina, but also Ukraine, Kazakhstan and Hungary – the UCI offers few incentives. Even countries that are new to the sport have better opportunities. For the economically stable among them like Australia and Malaysia, or even the wealthy like USA or Qatar, events use fine weather, luxury accommodation and handsome prizes to tempt overseas teams, and wealthy markets to attract their sponsors. Colombia offers no such options.

The 2001 Vuelta a Colombia had no sponsor until hours before it was due to depart. Cochise made the provocative suggestion that Plan Colombia should fund it. After all, every year the Vuelta fortifies the psyche, even of those whose interest in cycling is minimal, by demonstrating that the national infrastructure is functioning normally and that the infinite needs of the riders and their entourage can be met wherever the Vuelta passes. It also brings the succour of national solidarity to its lost regions. So when in January 1999 a series of powerful tremors hit the town of Armenia, leaving 750 dead, the route of May's Vuelta a Colombia was instantly re-designed, and the race began in the earthquake zone.

In the event the 2001 national tour was saved by the largest national telephone company, Telecom – which then saw the team sponsored by its greatest commercial rival, Orbitel, steal the limelight. Telecom are unlikely to repeat their altruism. No sponsor could be found for the RCN Classic; the race went ahead for the sake of its venerable tradition, but on a shoestring.

Given the financial crisis of the nation's two most prestigious events, there is little prospect of the smaller, regional events gaining UCI status. Without a change in UCI policy, it is unlikely that a Colombian team supporting a Colombian leader will ever again compete in the great European events. And as the athletes competing abroad gain greater material rewards, the risks they run by remaining in their homeland increase. Unless guarantees are given, this outstanding pool of athletic talent will be forced to emulate Ethiopia's distance runners and many of Russia's best athletes by fleeing their homeland to live abroad.

However, not even a sporting event as evocative and self-consciously campaigning as the Tour of Colombia can turn the tide of a country's collective misfortunes. In the last four years an estimated 2 per cent of the Colombian populace has abandoned the country. Some depart for Miami, New York or Toronto. Others seek a new life in Costa Rica or Spain. Countless professionals are trained to high standards in Colombian universities, only to grow weary of the crises, corruption and violence. With every skilled professional that leaves, transferring intellectual resources acquired at their homeland's expense to wealthier nations for free, Colombia's prospects deteriorate. The fate of the nation's most successful athletes, repelled from Colombia by the threat of violence and attracted by their greater earning power abroad, provides a model for the young that bodes ill for the future.

BUT STILL THE cycling endures. In 1994 a charismatic young rider named Marlon Pérez, already the holder of ten national track and road titles, won the world junior points title on the track. Pérez had grown up in the Antioquian village of Támesis, training on its unmade roads. Once a month he would load his bike on a bus and ride down to La Pintada to train on the Alto de Minas. He was Colombia's second world champion, twenty-three years after Cochise's 1971 pursuit win in Italy.

Támesis celebrated with a huge festival. Weeks later Pérez won the Under-18 national tour, and in 1998 the Under-23 version. With the help of Giovanny Jiménez, a Colombian who had married a German girl and moved to Belgium, where he had a successful career riding criteriums (circuit races around town centres), Pérez came to Europe and became one of the stars of Belgian national cycling. Talks with US Postal were in their early stages when a British team sponsored by the Linda McCartney vegetarian foods brand offered Pérez a contract. He signed, and in January 2000 flew to Madrid to meet his colleagues, only to be told that there was no sponsorship money after all – the team had ceased to exist. Pérez returned to Colombia and signed for the best national team, 05 Orbitel. There he dominated the domestic season. In the 2001 Vuelta a Colombia he won the prologue at a remarkable record speed of 59.259 kilometres per hour, then won the first four stages, before being defeated in the mountains by Hernán Buenahora. Pérez was still improving as a defensive climber.

But Pérez discovered a special plenitude riding in his homeland. For the first time in decades, a rider of international standing chose to remain in Colombia. This, along with the advent of extreme sports and an international taste for unique sporting events across extraordinary landscapes, potentially opens new perspectives for Colombian cycling. And, paradoxically, the age of cable television, bringing new audiences and new sponsors to an increasingly differentiated sporting calendar, could allow the Vuelta a Colombia to rediscover itself – not as a parody of European cycling or a peripheral gloss to a text written elsewhere, but as one of the great, punishing challenges in world sport, with a meaning and value of its own.

For, as Emile Durkheim wrote, 'There can be no society that does not feel the need to preserve and renew, at regular intervals, the collective feelings and ideas that constitute its unity and personality.' The Vuelta a Colombia is one of those ritual events. Yet the feats of the Indomitable Zipa, Ramón Hoyos or Honorio Rúa are almost forgotten by Colombia's youth. But without the sport that they established in this cruel land, without the connections it describes, the continuities; without its celebration of the landscape and of youth, its example of self-imposed suffering for uncertain rewards; without its spirituality, its organic commixture of past and present, its sense of place; without its *arepa* and *aguapanela*, its *bocadillo*, its Sacred Heart and Fallen Man and Virgin of Morcá, its Poporo Quimbaya; its Cochise and Lucho Herrera; its pain, sweat and blood, mangled limbs and buckled wheels, those old wooden rims and splintered fingers, the Indomitable Zipa ascending impossible heights... Without all that cycling has been here, its Colombian-ness, what future will the young have? What country will remain to them? What is Colombia, or any of the world's poorer nations, deprived of their organic sense of self, but a longing to be Switzerland or California, or something out of Disney, or anything but that which they are: lowly figures on the global table of relative wealth?

At the turn of the Millennium I visited the town of Bucaramanga to interview two of Colombia's finest riders, Hernán Buenahora and Victor Hugo Peña. It was Christmas, and they invited me to join them on a gentle training ride with some local riders. We chatted quietly as the group assembled, then took the main road east out of town. Over the previous weeks I had been training hard: now I found I could hang on the professionals' wheels, breathing hard as they chatted effortlessly. After forty minutes, the group divided. I stayed with

Buenahora and Peña, and we turned into a sudden, vertiginous ascent. The temperature dropped noticeably as we climbed. We rose out of the valley like condors on the morning thermals. The city peeped above the hills in the distance to our right. With it, dozens of smaller homesteads appeared, populating the land as far as the white horizon. We gazed over them, as though we were gods of altitude. Still the climb continued, until, daydreaming of vertigo, I found myself leaning away from the gathering precipice. The start of the climb had long receded now, and the city had been enveloped in haze. Each successive brow revealed a new ascent, and the very idea of an ending to the climb seemed increasingly remote. As each corner approached, I began to hope that the gradient would relent. I comforted myself with the thought that this was incontrovertibly the essence of Colombian cycling. The ends of the road were mere abstractions; all that remained was the present segment of an infinite line, journeying up to Heaven in one direction, falling in the other. We, the cyclists, were locked between the extremes in a pure process of becoming, holding the pain of the ascent before us like a mirage or rainbow, blanching as the sweat ran into our eyes, nestling warily against the threshold of endurance. My body was beginning to demand more oxygen than my breathing could supply: I was going into serious oxygen debt.

I snapped out of my daydream with a shock. I was being asphyxiated. Unable to breathe in the oxygen I needed to stay alive, I tore my glasses away from my face, trying desperately to inhale through my eyeballs. It was an automatic, involuntary response. The pores in the skin on my calves were trying, like gills, to absorb oxygen from the thin air. I was losing the feeling in my extremities. Although the air pressure was lighter than at sea-level, I felt that it was crushing me. My pulse was racing: 190, maybe 200 beats per minute. A true athlete would have been able to withstand this degree of discomfort. I had to slow down to crawling pace. I had approached the col with ridiculous optimism, turning the pedals with vigour, arrogantly believing that I could unravel Colombia's mystery, its silences and fears, its joy and pain. I had imagined that I was looking with the eyes of the gods. Now I was struggling to survive. I fought for air, and by dropping suddenly off the pace, I raised my heart rate still higher. The pounding was terrifying: I thought I was having a heart attack. Looking a fool was the least of my worries. My vigour was a sham. I was nothing but a faker, and the riders knew it now. We had been climbing for an hour and a half without reaching the end of the ascent. The task was obviously far too arduous for my journalist's physique, comfortably enhanced by city gyms and spinning machines, to my own pathetic limits.

Yet it wasn't the climb that disheartened me. I'd finish it eventually, at my own pace. It was something else, in which I had perhaps been destined to fail from the start. How to capture a nation's essence, with its subdivisions and contradictions, its refusal to conform, its resistance to words? And, once captured, how to use that elixir to heal it? It was an impossible ambition, as beyond me as this turning, relentless road of dreams at such an unforgiving gradient. I needed lungs like my climbing companions, lungs and legs, unfathomable, unyielding, to whom the sensations I had absurdly thought were killing me were utterly, comically, alien. At their lazy pace they had long disappeared ahead of me. Perhaps, somewhere above me in the mountains, their most natural element, they could succeed where I had so signally failed.

14. Cathedrals in the Sky

BETWEEN THE EMERALD mines and the coalfields of the department of Boyacá stands the town of Sogamoso. Built into the sky at 2,740 metres, Sogamoso meant 'Temple of the Sun' to the Muisca people who lived here before the conquistadors. Here more than anywhere else cycling, Colombia and Catholicism come together.

This is the hometown of José Jaime González Pico, 'Chepe' González. Chepe won the Tour of Colombia in 1994 and 1995, and in 1996 started a revival of Colombian cycling by winning a stage on his first Tour de France. He was my first interviewee in Colombia, and my first Colombian friend. His dark eyes emit an intense energy, the fire that powered his ambition. We first met in Bogotá, and he invited me to spend the weekend in his hometown. 'You could go up the Virgin of Morcá,' he teased. 'Who's that?' I asked. 'The patron saint of cycling.'

It was some time before I could take up his invitation. We eventually travelled on the day England beat Colombia at the 1998 World Cup in the USA. When David Beckham's free kick gave England the game, I offered words of sympathy. There was no need: Boyacá is cycling country. Anyway, Chepe replied, when the national soccer team is winning, the finance seeps out of cycling.

Sogamoso is defended by a line of lime kilns and cement works, breached only by a constant stream of heavy traffic. Through the dust and fumes the parish church of Morcá, a neighbouring village on a mountainside at the top of a steep climb, shines brightly in the cold sunlight. Nearby, a tiny shrine marks the place where the Virgin Mary appeared on a hillside 300 years ago. On the first Saturday of each month a pilgrimage of townsfolk ascends to her sanctuary. Some are aspiring cyclists seeking the Virgin's help. Others are professional athletes come to receive her blessing before travelling to the Tour de France and the other monuments of international cycling. For this is a Mecca of Colombian cycling: the town that produced Raphael Acevedo, Edgar Corredor, Henry Cárdenas and Álvaro Sierra – four of Lucho Herrera's great mountain lieutenants, and countless other fine professionals. All of those I spoke to had the same story: 'At the start of each stage of the Tour de France we would receive her blessing and commend ourselves to her. The Virgin grants us many miracles.'

But this is also home to an extended family that formed a dynasty in Colombian cycling. One of them was Chepe's uncle, Epimenio. Epimenio has Chepe's brilliant, back-lit eyes, although in place of Chepe's fire, his kindliness shines through. Epimenio peaked at the 1970 Under-21 Tour of Colombia: coming second in the King of the Mountains competition and third overall behind Raphael Antonio Niño. At the Vuelta in May a series of inopportune punctures and the absence of a Boyacá team car left him out of touch with the leaders, and his poor finish starved him of future sponsorship. Today Epimenio – in keeping with Sogamoso's hard traditions – keeps fighting cocks. When Chepe competes in Europe, villagers ask him, half-smiling, half-hoping, to bring back one of those prized black cocks from Valencia, Spain.

Among Epimenio's scalps at the 1968 departmental championships were those of his cousins Ezekiel Pinto González and Humberto Parra González. Ezekiel Pinto was the first townsman of Sogamoso to compete in the Vuelta a Colombia. The following year he was joined by his brother-in-law, Humberto Parra, who finished third in the new riders table. 'The athletic capacities shown by Humberto Parra mark him out as a rider of true talent, with an excellent physique,' commented *El Tiempo*. 'He could be competing for a place on the podium at the next Vuelta a Colombia.' During my stay in Sogamoso I met Humberto each day to drink camomile tea in the café opposite his bike shop. Cheerful but also intense, given neither to drink nor late nights, Humberto, in his sixties, could still top the climbs around Sogamoso faster than all but the professional cyclists in town. But when he had been at his peak there had been no money, and he had had a family to support.

He had, however, taught his sons an athlete's discipline, and produced three professional cyclists. It was Fabio Parra, his eldest son, who had stood on the podium of the Tours of Spain and France in the late 1980s. The second brother, also called Humberto, was a good national level rider. The youngest, Iván, was sixteen when his elder brother won his last Tour of Colombia, but he was seemingly lost to road-racing, climbing instead through the national mountain-bike categories. Iván was a national MTB champion in 1994, and represented his country internationally.

Now, though, he had become a fine professional road racer, who first went to Europe in 1999, and finished ninth in his first European stage race, the Tour of Spain. Like his father and brothers, he wears a scapular of the Virgin during every race. With his winnings he was contributing bricks and mortar for the Virgin of Morcá basilica's reconstruction. 'She's helped me achieve everything I've asked of her,' he told me. 'When I was a small child my father taught me to have faith in Her, and I thank her before and after races, no matter where I finish. I thank her because she gives me good health and the opportunity to express God's will through cycling. We often finish our training rides on the climb up to Morcá, and then we pray.'

Back in London I pursued my obsession and finally obtained a derisory budget from Channel Four to fund a documentary about the patron saint of cycling. I returned to Sogamoso with a digital video camera to record interviews with its finest cyclists. One morning I filmed Chepe, Iván, Bolivarian champion Jairo Pérez, and Chepe's cousin Javier González – Epimenio's son and the latest in the Parra-González dynasty – on a training ride finishing on the climb up to Morcá.

From the roadside down in Sogamoso, the basilica at Morcá had seemed clear. But from that point slope had risen against slope, turn against turn, lips and hollows had been hidden; and as the road snaked higher, mud and puddles reflected the sky and made the spaces seem bigger. Perception itself was problematic as the altitude gathered.

I had ridden this climb at humbler speeds. But these professional athletes attacked the gradient with such impetus that their dance and circulation suddenly seemed to generate an independent gravitational force. With carefully modulated physical stress, they pushed themselves into a near-animal state, struggling upward with crude beauty.

As a child my father had explained to me that when a bag of sugar falls from a shelf, both Earth and bag move towards each other, even if the Earth moves only a tiny distance. I had found wonder in the notion. Now, as the ascent to Morcá began and the air thinned, a huge silence swooped down to meet us from the mountains. With my miniature camera I reduced these creatures of gravity to a digital swirl rising towards the sky. Absorbed in their own meditation, they oscillated between the digital opposites of oneness and nothingness. They danced higher and higher; I clung to the roof of an old Toyota.

As the mass poured out of them it was as though a harmonic was sounding across the landscape. They were pure objects of gravity, mid-way between Earth and Heaven, climbing in a knot of movement, bodies tumbling in slow motion towards some idealized limit.

This is a land where gravity pulls too strongly. Colombia seems unable to rise above its violence. The invisible network of lines its cyclists trace over the nation sometimes seem the only force holding it together, weaving past and future, carrying the cross of their homeland into the mountains, and there, through voluntary acts of suffering, paying penance for Colombia's sins.

When the gradient steepens, the hidden moorings that anchor humanity to this earth are released, and the riders are drawn irresistibly towards the heavens. Angels dancing not on pinheads but on the air's indistinct turbulence, the folds of imperceptible updraughts, gliding between stillness and motion, they dissolve into a pure form of rhythm, a subliminal pattern where past and future meet, gravity collapses and the universe sucks them into space.

AT MORCÁ WE sat on the steps of the Basilica. Then the cyclists went inside to pray. Iván told me, 'Now let's do what we came here for.' I wasn't sure if by 'here' he meant Morcá or Planet Earth.

The camera lens was the least of the filters that separated us. Divided by culture, mother tongue, social class and education, we were odd acquaintances. Inside the basilica I meditated on angels.

Afterwards, when I tried to imagine these young men ascending on the climb, I could no longer see the friends I had mixed with far below. Either the enormous tragedy in Colombia's bent shoulders, or the Promethean transgression of their pact with gravity, had caused them to metamorphose. A single face staring down from the mountains, rapt in partial horror, belonged to a beautiful, terrifying creature.

Perhaps it was an angel of history that these beautiful athletes brought to mind, the angel which the German philosopher Walter Benjamin had imagined in his *Theses on the Philosophy of History* – reading matter from my university days, far removed from this rude, enchanted reality.

'Where we perceive a chain of events,' Benjamin wrote, '[the Angel] sees a single catastrophe which piles wreckage on wreckage and hurls it before his feet. The angel would like to stay, awaken the dead, and make whole what has been destroyed. But a storm is blowing from Paradise; it has got caught in his wings with such violence that the angel can no longer close them. This storm irresistibly propels him into the future to which his back is turned, while the pile of debris before him grows skyward.'

Benjamin finished his thesis with a redemptive clause: 'This storm is what we call progress.' Colombia has no such cause for optimism. In December 1999 one of Sogamoso's old cyclists and a contemporary of Humberto Parra and Chepe's Uncle Epimenio, Joselín Peña, was murdered. Over the next year a number of Sogamoso shopkeepers were abducted, and a mayoral candidate kidnapped and murdered. The Parra family left Sogamoso, and Henry Cárdenas began to spend more time in Bogotá.

But if the goddess of cycling smiles on anyone, I thought, she surely smiles on Chepe. Only later did I learn that he now rode unshackled from the old saints and martyrs. 'The Catholic Church tells us to reach God through the saints,' he told me. 'But I don't believe in the Virgin.' I was astounded. To the eternal question, why? the Virgin of Morcá had supplied with a very Colombian answer.

Her absence seemed to threaten this world of enchantment, abandoning me among the familiar uncertainties. What, after all, is sport about? Empty ritual? Hard cash? Or is it just a freak show? Did Chepe's lack of belief herald the end of something – another Colombian death?

But Chepe was merely warming to his theme. When he resumed, it was with a profession of faith as profound as any I had yet encountered. 'I believe in God who sent the commandments,' he confessed. 'I have no need of intermediaries. I offer my prayers and victories to Him, not to some saint. My faith helps me live. Human beings need something to plead to. I suffer most when the road is flat and the wind blows: that's when I pray for God's help.' If I had thought of him, however briefly, as somehow less Colombian, the error was mine, not his. Colombia, it seems, is incapable of seeing cycling as anything but a form of devotion – if not to the old beliefs, to new ones, and in Sogamoso the religion rises up from the landscape. And although he spent the cycling season abroad, leaving Colombia permanently was unthinkable. 'Europe is wonderful,' he reflected. 'It has none of Colombia's problems. But this is my home. I was born here and grew up here, and I'll probably die here too.'

Sogamoso has seen droves of residents leave for the capital, dismayed by the arrival of the violence. But Raphael Acevedo remains, with his albums full of fading photographs. So too does Chepe, proud of his home and his horses, and burning inside with that tenacious, stubborn pride.

Acknowledgements

Over five years I made six lengthy trips to Colombia seeking information. This I found, and much besides, for friendship is in generous supply there. Marco Tulio Ipuerto of Caracol Radio first sent my imagination reeling with stories of Colombian cycling. Alberto Galvis, sports writer and historian, cemented my interest. Germán Castro Caycedo, a truly important journalist (and now novelist), gave me his friendship and his interpretation of cycling in Colombia.

Héctor Urrego of *Mundo Ciclístico* magazine and RCN Radio invited me to join the RCN truck at a regional race in 1997. Before I could object, he had thrust a microphone into my hand and incorporated me into the commentary team. Ever since, I've been an informal RCN correspondent. Héctor is special. More than most European journalists, he has witnessed at first hand every twist of his nation's cycling history since the late 1960s

Two retired cycling correspondents, Rafael Mendoza, formerly of *El Espectador*, and Oscar Salazar (*El Colombiano*), allowed me to draw on their memories. So too did the statistician Tobías Carvajal. Of current journalists, Pablo Arbeláez of *El Colombiano* provided encouragement, friendship, and welcomed me to his newspaper as another informal correspondent. Pilar Montoya of *El Espacio* also helped.

Colombia's first great cyclist, Efraín Forero Triviño, and one of its most recent, the wonderful climber José Jaime 'Chepe' González Pico, invited me into their lives and homes. So too did Victor Hugo Peña – Lance Armstrong's team-mate – and his father Hugo. All shared their knowledge with typical kindness.

Many present and past cyclists kindly agreed to be interviewed, and made this book possible. In Bogotá: Samuel Cabrera, José Duarte, José Patrocinio Jiménez, Rafael Antonio Niño, Álvaro Pachón, Padre Efraín Roso and Miguel Samacá. In Bucaramanga: Severo Hernández, Clímaco Guzmán, José del Carmen Valdivieso and Hernán Buenahora. In Duitama: Oliverio Rincón and Alberto Camargo. In Facatativá: Pablo Wilches. In Fusagasugá: Luis Herrera. In Medellín: Santiago Botero and family, Roberto Escobar, Gabriel Halaixt Buitrago, Ramón Hoyos, Marlon Pérez, the incomparable Martín Emilio 'Cochise' Rodríguez, Honorio Rúa, my dear friend and *padrino*, Javier 'el Ñato' Suárez, and Mario Vanegas. In Sogamoso: Rafael Acevedo, Henry Cárdenas, Edgar Corredor, Epimenio González and his son Javier, Humberto Parra and his sons Fabio and Iván

Parra, and my close friend Álvaro Sierra.

Cycling coaches, officials and administrators who told their side of this story include the following: Gonzalo Agudelo, Miguel Ángel Bermúdez, Andrés Botero, Omar Buitrago, Hugo Carreño, Marcos Cortéz, Giancarlo Ferretti, Alfredo Guevara, Raúl Mesa, Donald Raskin, Roberto Sánchez, Gianni Savio, Jorge Tenjo, Dr Juan Darío Uribe and Pedro Pablo Valdivieso. Arturo Ospina was especially generous.

Fabio Castillo of *El Espectador* provided expert advice on the topic of the cocaine trade. José Alejandro Castaño of *El Colombiano* helped me secure an interview with Roberto Escobar. At the Gold Museum in Bogotá, María Alicia Uribe provided me with archaeological documents relating to the Poporo Quimbaya. Pilar Velilla of the Museum of Antioquia provided invaluable help and put me in touch with the artist Fernando Botero, who kindly agreed to be interviewed.

A number of international cyclists who rode in Colombia or with Colombians in Europe and the USA provided me with their memories. They are: Lance Armstrong, Felice Gimondi, Giovanni Battaglin, Luigi Casola, Julio Jiménez, Ettore Milano, Andrei Tchmil, Romans Vainsteins and Fred Rodriguez.

Long conversations with Consuelo Onofre and her father Leonel helped my arguments take shape. Additional memories, comments and suggestions were contributed by Marlen Toro.

My literary agent John Pawsey approached me with the suggestion that I write a book, and allowed himself to be convinced that this was the book I should write. My publisher Graham Coster at Aurum Press accepted the risk, which he lessened by allowing me the full benefit of his boundless energy, attention to detail, and writing know-how. When I try to conceive of a finer editor, my imagination fails me.

I read successive versions of chapters to my mother. My father scoured the text for infelicities, contradictions and typos.

This book, and the documentary film that preceded it – *Kings of the Mountains* (Id World Productions Ltd/Channel Four, 2000) – could not have been completed without the hospitality of Chepe and Marlen González, Consuelo Onofre, Dr Roberto Amaya and family, David Amaya and Nancy Moreno. The friendship and example of Gary Imlach and Ken McGill sustained me throughout. As if Colombia had not already given me more than my fair share of friendship and inspiration, it then gave me my wife Viviana – by no means an avid cycling fan, and therefore a model reader for this book.